SCHOONER
PASSAGE

SCHOONER PASSAGE

Sailing Ships and the Lake Michigan Frontier

Theodore J. Karamanski

Wayne State University Press • Detroit

In association with the
Chicago Maritime Society

Great Lakes Books

*A complete listing of the books in this series can be found at
the back of this volume.*

Philip P. Mason, Editor
Department of History, Wayne State University

Dr. Charles K. Hyde, Associate Editor
Department of History, Wayne State University

04 03 02 01 00   5 4 3 2 1

Library of Congress Cataloging-in-Publication Data

Karamanski, Theodore J., 1953–
Schooner passage : sailing ships and the Lake Michigan frontier /
Theodore J. Karamanski.
p.   cm. — (Great Lakes books)
Includes bibliographical references and index.
ISBN 0-8143-2911-X (alk. paper)
1. Shipping—Michigan, Lake—History. 2. Schooners—Michigan,
Lake—History. 3. Michigan, Lake, Region—History. I. Title. II.
Series.
HE630.M5 K37   2000
386'.54'09774—dc21
00-010684

*To the captains and crews
of the inland seas,
and to the women and men
who preserve their history.*

Contents

List of Illustrations   9

Acknowledgments   11

Foreword   15

Introduction   17

1.

The Evolution of the Lake Michigan Schooner   25

2.

The Maritime Frontier:
Schooners and Urban Development on the Lake Michigan Shore   43

3.

Before the Mast and at the Helm:
Captains and Crews on Lake Michigan Schooners   77

4.

Schooner City:
The Life and Times of the Chicago River Port   127

5.

Lost on Lake Michigan:
Wrecks, Rescues, and Navigational Aids   173

Epilogue: Schooner Twilight   209

Works Cited   241

Index   255

Illustrations

Lake Michigan's maritime frontier, 18
Lucia A. Simpson, 1929, 21
Two-masted clipper, 26
Scow schooner, 30
Canaller schooner, 33
Lucia A. Simpson in the Milwaukee River, 35
David Dows, 37
Bertha Barnes, 39
Champion shorn of her topmasts, 41
City of Grand Haven, the "Grand Haven rig," 42
Old Fort Dearborn, 44
Isolda Bock of Benton Harbor, 46
Map of the mouth of the Chicago River, 52
Shipment of grain from Chicago, 61
Three-masted schooners tied up at a Chicago grain elevator, 64
Schooner *Day Spring,* 66
Tug and lumber schooner, Charlevoix, 68
Rouse Simmons off Beaver Island, 70
Lumber being loaded at South Haven, 71
Chicago Lumber Company yard, 74
Hans Simonsen of the *Lucia A. Simpson,* 76
Crew of the *Joses,* 84
The *Lyman Davis* under way, 90
Typical lake schooner, 94
Entrance to forecastle, *Lucia A. Simpson,* 96
Making sail on the *Lyman Davis,* 97
Crew of the *City of Grand Haven,* 98
Sailing a schooner, 100
Two schooner masters, 112
The *Lucia A. Simpson* in Chicago River, 118
Schooner *Granger,* 124
Mouth of the Chicago River, 1893, 128
Chicago River from the Clark Street Bridge, 129
Conquest and *Helen Pratt* in Chicago River, 130

9

"Bridged" in Chicago, 132
Chicago River bridges, 134
Tug *S. P. Hall*, 138
A tug and schooner enter Chicago, 139
Steam barge and schooner in Chicago River, 142
Wolf Point, 144
Lumbershovers at work, 149
Schooners after the Great Fire, 151
Christmas tree ship, 161
Schooner *Mishicott* idled for the winter, 162
Miller Brothers shipyard, 165
Bertha Barnes with raffe sail, 175
J. J. Case in dry dock, 178
Miller Brothers shipyard, north branch of the Chicago River, 181
Ice on an overloaded schooner, 188
Chicago's first lighthouse, 191
Crew of the Jackson Park Lifesaving Station, 194
Tug in heavy surf, 200
Augusta's fatal collision, 203
Deck of a typical schooner, 207
The old and the new, 211
Lakeshoring schooner, 212
Last crew of the *City of Grand Haven*, 216
End of the *City of Grand Haven*, 217
Alvin Clark rises again, 220

Acknowledgments

As captain of this volume, I am responsible for any and all of the mistakes encountered by readers on their journey through the text. That this volume set sail at all is in no small measure due to the assistance of an extensive shore-based establishment. Deane Tank, former president of the Chicago Maritime Society, is as good a vessel owner as any master could wish. In 1996 he conceived the Chicago Schooner Project with the goal of gathering images and eyewitness accounts of Chicago schooners to create exhibits and public programs for a Chicago maritime museum. This book is an attempt to bring the results of that project to the public until such time as the Chicago Maritime Society can have a museum space that will allow us to add the drama of artifacts and photo murals to the presentation. Deane Tank's vision, financial support, and maritime expertise were invaluable to this endeavor.

Ariel Orlov served as the very able researcher for the Chicago Schooner Project. Her work assembling the published books and articles on the subject saved hours of research. Her U.S. Census research on the ethnic background of Chicago schoonermen made a considerable contribution to the volume, as did her work locating schooner photographs. Brian Coffey and Jennifer Bridge of the Loyola University Public History Program helped to complete the census research. I appreciate the help of copy editor Jonathan Lawrence, and Kristin Harpster, project editor at Wayne State University Press.

As in the past, it was a pleasure to work with Thomas Willcockson on this book. His keen interest and commitment to the subject of the age of sail on the Great Lakes is amply demonstrated in the fine line drawings he contributed to the volume.

The Chicago Schooner Project had many participants and friends within the Chicago Maritime Society, including Trig Waller, Rita and Ralph Freese, and Kris and Tom Kastle. I am further indebted to the Kastles, whose music has done so much to revive public interest in Lake Michigan maritime history. Carl Neal did a wonderful job preparing the photographic images from the society's collection. Philip Elmes, president emeritus of the society, deserves special acknowledg-

11

ment for exciting my interest in maritime history and for his long work to try and bring that history to the public.

This book would also not have been possible without the commitment of able volunteers and professionals in numerous Lake Michigan museums and libraries. In particular, I would like to thank Kenneth Pott of the Michigan Maritime Museum; Suzette J. Lopez of the Marine Collection, Milwaukee Public Library; Isacco Valli at the Wisconsin Maritime Museum; Archie Motley and Russell Lewis at the Chicago Historical Society; and Harry Miller at the State Historical Society of Wisconsin, as well as the reference staffs at the Newberry Library and the Bentley Historical Library, University of Michigan. Lorna Newman at Loyola University's Cudahy Library was a great help with interlibrary loan requests. A bit further afield, I wish to thank Frank Cartelas of the Program in Maritime History and Nautical Archaeology at East Carolina University for helping to keep me abreast of recent fieldwork on Lake Michigan.

Several fellow historians' cooperation in sharing their research was much appreciated. Without Betsy Mendelsohn I never would have known of the marvelous letters of sailor Leonard Withington Noyes in the Peabody Essex Museum or the George W. Wilbur Papers at Yale University. Sandra J. Zipperer at the Wisconsin Maritime Museum shared her work on the career of Captain Thomas Kelley. Like others working on the sailing era on the Great Lakes, I also benefited enormously from the numerous published articles and the unpublished dissertation of Jay C. Martin, also of the Wisconsin Maritime Museum. His study "Sailing the Freshwater Seas" remains the best single social history treatment of a Great Lakes maritime topic. Randall Rohe of the University of Wisconsin, Waukesha, generously shared his research on Wisconsin lumber ghost towns. Laura Quakenbush and Steve Harold of the Maritime Heritage Alliance read a draft of the text and provided many valuable comments.

Special acknowledgment is also due to the late Theodore S. Charrney, a former merchant seaman who in his latter years turned to the subject of maritime history. Charrney was a fine writer and an assiduous researcher committed to telling the story of the *Rouse Simmons,* the last of the Christmas tree ships. His handful of published articles and papers given at regional history symposia are genuine contributions to Chicago and Lake Michigan history. His massive (but unpublished) manuscript "The Christmas Tree Ship: The Saga of the *Rouse*

Simmons"* is the most complete study every done of a Great Lakes vessel. The opportunity to read this manuscript in the collection of the Chicago Maritime Society greatly enriched my understanding of the lumber trade. I am grateful for Charrney's pioneering work on Lake Michigan sailing ships.

Personal acknowledgments begin at Loyola University of Chicago, where a great group of colleagues helped to keep this ship on course, particularly Robert Bucholz and Patricia Mooney-Melvin. Department chairs Cheryl Johnson-Odim and Anthony Cardoza graciously offered me a teaching schedule that allowed for research and writing. Former Loyolans John McManamon, S.J., and David J. Keene shared their research and enthusiasm for maritime preservation and archaeology. Rich Lackner and his sloop *Kitti* provided a memorable sail around Green Bay. My sisters, as they know, were a source of inspiration.

For me this voyage ends where it began, at home. Writing entails few of the dangers of sailing the inland seas, yet both writing and sailing require considerable time apart from wife and children. Time spent on ships, real or historic, is time away from the responsibilities of home. For giving me that opportunity I thank my wife, Eileen. Her embrace, and the joy of our sons, Teddy and Joey, are my safe harbor.

Foreword

If we were to view the Chicago River from the docks of the late nineteenth century, the most apparent and most prominent sight would be the lake schooners. Their huge hulls and tall masts dominated their surrounds. These ships visually commanded the harbor in the same way they dominated the commerce, not just of Chicago, but of all the towns and cities along the shores of the Great Lakes. If every ton of grain, lumber, coal, and other freight carried by these schooners could be reassembled in one place, we would see a mountain towering over the skyscrapers of the modern city, surpassing even the peaks of the mighty Rockies.

From such prominence, how did these great carriers become first rare and then extinct? With the exception of wrecks discovered on the lake bottom, gone are even the rotting hulks and skeletal remains of these vessels that were once an integral part of Chicago's maritime past and so essential to the growth of the city.

Chicago's advantage was as a nautical connector of the Great Lakes to the great continental interior—primarily the Mississippi watershed. Yes, there were steam-powered vessels contributing to the settlement and development of the Lake Michigan region, but it was the schooner's ability to harness the lake breezes that made it economically feasible to distribute the bounty of the heartland to the rest of the country.

Add to this sense of their utility a special Great Lakes nautical romance. Accounts of schooners ghosting along on a quiet summer's night, or struggling to shorten sail in anticipation of a sudden Lake Michigan squall, remind us that the sailing experience—or even the sighting of a schooner—embodies a sense of nostalgia and adventure.

Today, physical evidence of their past is scarce. No lake schooner remains, and only a few replicas exist. Luckily, we have accounts, photographs, artifacts, and other materials . . . but these are widely scattered among the historical, commemorative institutions and some private collections. In order for the Chicago Maritime Society to present this story to the public through exhibits and programs, there was an obvious need first to compile these materials and then to create a historical account of the role and significance of the lake schooners.

Just such a task was begun in 1995. Professor Ted Karamanski of Loyola University; Ariel Orlov, a public history graduate student; and myself, then president of the Chicago Maritime Society and a student of Chicago's nautical history, implored the Chicago Maritime Society to support a project to compile all available information on Chicago's lake schooners. We began with the Chicago Maritime Society's considerable collection of images, articles, and artifacts, then expanded the search to a wide variety of regional historical institutions. With our collection nearly complete, Professor Karamanski constructed this historical narrative using his experience and knowledge of regional history—particularly its nautical history. The project team identified an extensive collection of photographs. Many of these photographs and much of the source material gathered during the project are part of a special project collection at the Chicago Maritime Society and will be used to assemble an exhibit on the schooner era.

As the book emerged, it was obvious that Professor Karamanski succeeded in portraying for the first time the sailing ship era in its full historical context. I hope readers will share our satisfaction and enjoyment in this account of Lake Michigan's age of sail.

Today, freight is carried by truck and train. Their predecessors are the lake schooners, which brought Chicago from little more than an initial strategic position to the status of one of the world's great port cities. Although there is little left to remind the public of their importance, we are happy to be able to contribute this volume to preserve the schooner tradition.

So pull your chair closer to the fire, make yourself comfortable, and enjoy this history of Lake Michigan's schooner days.

Deane Tank, Ph.D.
Chair, Chicago Schooner Project
Chicago Maritime Society

Introduction

O nly a handful of old sailors saw the sorry end of the *Mary A. Gregory*. Since her last voyage two years before, the two-masted schooner had rapidly deteriorated into a rotted hulk. In the spring of 1926 a steam tug pulled the old lady out of her berth on the North Branch of the Chicago River, and for the last time she headed for the open waters of Lake Michigan. Fifty-one years before, the *Mary A. Gregory* had made that same journey as a newly commissioned commercial vessel, fresh out of the shipyard of John Gregory. At the time of her launching in 1875 she was only one of 20,900 sailing vessels to annually clear the port of Chicago. A half century later the vast schooner fleet was gone and the *Mary A. Gregory*, the last commercial sailing vessel in Chicago, was towed out to deep water for a Viking funeral. Unmourned by the skyscraper-crowned city behind her, the *Mary A. Gregory* was torched, sunk, and forgotten.[1]

The *Mary A. Gregory*'s end was typical of the demise of the old sailing ships on the Great Lakes. For the better part of a generation, from 1890 to 1920, the surviving sailing ships were scrapped, burned, or, more tragically, lost in storms their battered boards were incapable of resisting. With each one went a living link to the early history of the American heartland and a tangible connection to the unique maritime culture that flourished there.

Romance has shrouded the maritime history of the Great Lakes. Images of white-winged sailing ships dancing across pristine waters or of proud vessels battered by a November gale are the stuff of high adventure. Perhaps that is why books on shipwrecks outnumber all other histories of the inland seas. What is lost in histories of

17

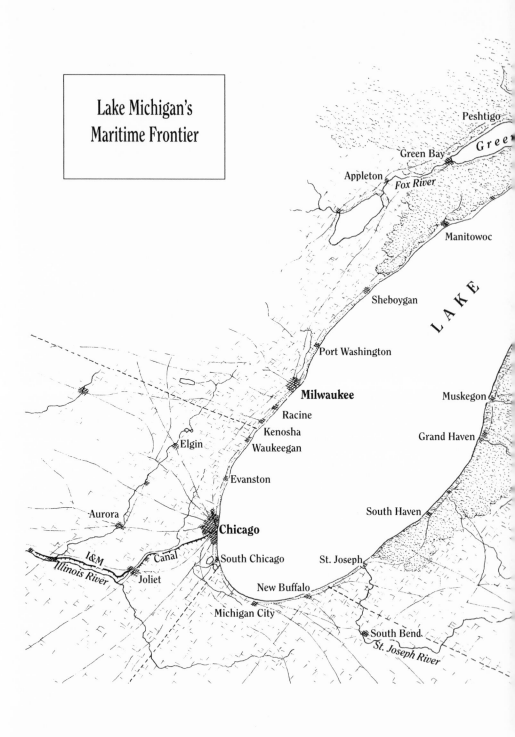

Lake Michigan's
Maritime Frontier

Peshtigo

Green Bay

Gree

Appleton
Fox River

Manitowoc

Sheboygan

LAKE

Port Washington

Milwaukee

Muskegon

Racine

Kenosha
Waukeegan

Grand Haven

Elgin

Evanston

Aurora

South Haven

Chicago

I&M
Illinois River

Canal

Joliet

South Chicago

St. Joseph

New Buffalo

Michigan City

South Bend
St. Joseph River

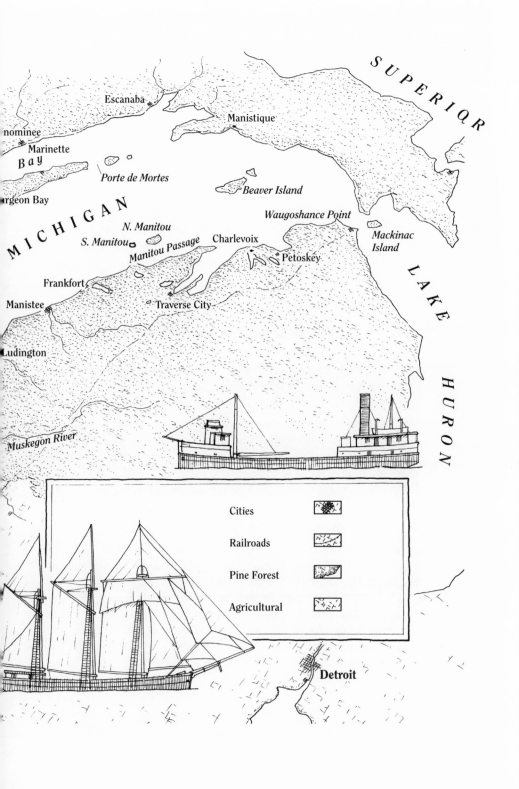

SUPERIOR

Escanaba

Manistique

nominee

Marinette

B a y

Porte de Mortes

Beaver Island

rgeon Bay

MICHIGAN

Waugoshance Point

N. Manitou

Mackinac
Island

S. Manitou

Charlevoix

Manitou Passage

Petoskey

LAKE

Frankfort

Traverse City

Manistee

Ludington

HURON

Muskegon River

Cities

Railroads

Pine Forest

Agricultural

Detroit

shipwrecks and in the technical discussions of tonnage, displacement, and rigging is a clear sense of the role of the schooner in the pioneer life of the Great Lakes states. In the last several years, however, scholars working from the perspectives of geography, archeology, literature, and history have done much to flesh out a more fulsome picture of Midwestern maritime history. It is the goal of this volume to share with the reader the newly emerging story of the men and women who crewed the sailing ships of the Great Lakes, to explore the role of the schooner in the market revolution that transformed the Lake Michigan basin, and to see the sailing ships as both expressions of a regional maritime culture and a valuable technology of urban development—without forgetting to add a story or two about shipwrecks.[2]

The focus of this book is on Lake Michigan schooners. Schooners were not the first or the only type of sailing ship on the Great Lakes, but they were the most numerous, and as such they will occupy the center of our story. Lake Michigan is one of the five Great Lakes of North America. Through navigational improvements of the nineteenth century, these inland seas were linked to form one continuous navigable waterway. Lake Michigan ports were frequented by ships from the lower lakes and, indeed, from as far away as Europe. Cargoes loaded in Milwaukee or Chicago made their way throughout the Great Lakes and beyond. Since most ships journeyed to other lakes during their careers, it might seem impractical to focus strictly on Lake Michigan schooners. Yet Lake Michigan can serve as an effective microcosm for understanding the role of sailing ships in the entire region. The lake basin is both large and discrete; though connected to the other lakes, it is also a cul-de-sac. Lake Michigan is the only one of the inland seas to be wholly within the territory of the United States. Its long basin,

---

One of the last old schooners, the *Lucia A. Simpson,* is towed out of Milwaukee harbor in 1929. Built in 1875 at Manitowoc, Wisconsin, and employed largely in the lumber trade, the *Simpson* worked steadily on Lake Michigan until a disabling storm off Algoma in 1929. Yachtsmen in Chicago hoped to refit the vessel to serve as a clubhouse, but after several years no repairs were made. A last-minute attempt by the city of Manitowoc to buy the *Simpson* and convert her to a floating museum came to naught when a fire destroyed the hulk on December 3, 1935. From the Great Lakes Marine Collection of the Milwaukee Public Library/Wisconsin Marine Historical Society.

unlike the other Great Lakes, is oriented on a north-south axis, enclosing 22,400 square miles of water and forming the coastlines of four states. Because the lake extends 307 miles from north to south, it cuts across environmental zones—from the corn belt to the boreal forest—thereby placing vastly different economies within a single geographic system. Lake Michigan provides a wonderful opportunity to explore the role of the schooner in integrating a diverse range of shoreline communities into a coherent region.[3]

Historians of the frontier have highlighted the role of technologies such as barbed wire on the treeless Great Plains and windmills and irrigation for the settlement of land west of the hundredth meridian. But on the Great Lakes frontier, with water and wood in abundance, the technology critical in developing the region was maritime. Schooners were an indispensable tool in shaping the Midwest's relationship with the rest of the country. Historians have long recognized the importance of steam power in tapping the potential of inland rivers to link the heartland to coastal markets, but they have been slow to see the persistently more important role of the older sail technology. Steam power appeared on the upper Great Lakes in 1818 with the *Walk-in-the-Water*. As early as 1833 there were eleven steamboats on the upper lakes carrying more than sixty thousand people per season. Steam power succeeded in driving non-steam vessels, save for the lumber raft, from inland rivers during the period before 1850, but on the lakes non-steam vessels dominated commerce. At the opening of navigation on the Great Lakes in 1860 there were 535 steam-powered vessels and 1,122 sailing ships. In fact, the number of sailing ships on the Great Lakes continued to grow throughout the era of both steamboat and railroad expansion in the Midwest, and it was not until 1868 that the number of sailing vessels peaked on the Great Lakes, at 1,855. Schooners continued to be built on Lake Michigan through the 1880s and remained a critical part of lake commerce through the end of the nineteenth century. It was schooners that brought the market revolution to the Lake Michigan country. It was schooners, exploiting the Erie and Welland Canals, that opened an inland and isolated region to the possibilities of national—even world—markets. The determining role played by the Great Lakes states in the crisis of the Civil War was made possible by that region's nationalism, a perspective fostered in the heartland through integrative schooner trade. The thousands of windjammers that cleared each year from Chicago to Buffalo or

22

Oswego to Milwaukee linked Lake Michigan to New York in an inter-state commerce and a national culture.[4]

Schooners shrank the distance between the Old Northwest and the Northeast. Sailing ships and canals brought the towns along the shore of Lake Michigan into easier communication with New York City than most landlocked eastern communities. The towns that developed within the basin were also knitted into their own integrated economic network by vessels of steam and sail. State boundaries were meaning-less to the burgeoning ports of Michigan, Wisconsin, Indiana, and Illinois. Schooners were the practical, adaptable technology that initi-ated an interregional movement of people, demonstrated the need (through the campaign for navigational improvements) for govern-ment intervention in the economy, and provided a vehicle for the Lake Michigan basin's rapid environmental transformation. Grain schoo-ners facilitated the plowing up of the prairies, while lumber hookers were integral to the logging of the northern forests. Because of the critical role of sailing ships in pioneering the region, the Lake Michi-gan frontier was, for good and for ill, from its infancy fully engaged in the market economy. Subsistence farming and premodern economic aspirations were largely foreign on the shores of Lake Michigan's blue-water frontier.

Schooners were an expression of the distinctiveness of the Great Lakes frontier experience. Lake Michigan was a medium of circulation for commodities, ideas, and people. Unlike the railroad, it could not be controlled and manipulated by a powerful few. Willa Cather, a daughter of the plains, grasped the difference between the lake's open-ness and that of the land. "But the great fact in life, the always possible escape from dullness, was the lake," she wrote in *The Professor's House*. "The sun rose out of it, the day began there; it was like an open door that nobody could shut. The land and all its dreariness could never close in on you. You had only to look at the lake, and you knew you would soon be free." The type of "hydraulic society" de-scribed by Donald Worster and other historians of the arid West, a society dominated by a capitalist and technical elite whose control of water led to their domination of society, was inconceivable in a region of abundance.[5]

Omitting the schooner from the history of the Great Lakes frontier is like trying to understand the development of the trans-Mississippi West without talking about covered wagons or railroads. What the latter meant for an arid region with few navigable rivers, the schooner meant for a region distinctive for its abundance of water. The schooner's formative role on the Great Lakes frontier was made possible by the conjunction of the right maritime technology, the promise of a vast lacustrine region, and the antebellum surge in North American population. Perhaps political geography has caused historians to neglect the significance of the maritime frontier. The Great Lakes are divided between two countries and eight states. States like Illinois, Ohio, Indiana, Wisconsin, and Minnesota have also been greatly shaped by inland rivers such as the Ohio or the Mississippi. By looking at the basin of Lake Michigan, the regional significance of the sailing vessels of the inland seas becomes apparent.

People who were caught up in the rapid transformation of the region did not make the job of future historians very easy. Schooners were taken for granted by nineteenth-century Midwesterners, noted with as much attention to detail as a modern motorist bestows on a tractor-trailer chugging in the right lane of an interstate highway. It is true that, like the operators of the big rigs of today, the men who skippered or sailed before the mast on schooners knew well their ships' quirks and characteristics. Regrettably, few of them—and few of those who traveled as their passengers—have left letters or diaries. The story of these old ships has to be painstakingly assembled from the newspapers of the era, brief recollections preserved in local historical societies, and occasional government documents. It is hoped that from the chapters that follow, the reader will appreciate the importance of the schooner era, like a three-master emerging from a morning fog, slowly coming into clear view, topsails set, rigging taut, westward bound.

1
The Evolution of the Lake Michigan Schooner

While far-ranging, tall-masted clipper ships and whalers have been immortalized in story and film, the much smaller, humbler schooner was by far the most important sailing ship in American history. As carriers of grain, lumber, produce, manufactured goods, and even slaves, schooners were crucial elements in the Atlantic community's eighteenth- and nineteenth-century market revolution.[1]

It is the arrangement of a ship's sails that determines if it is a brig, a bark, or a schooner. Although there is some debate on this point, to qualify as a schooner a ship needs to have two or more masts with its sails set side to side, or what mariners call fore-and-aft rigging. This sail arrangement was born on salt water and was particularly popular for coastal trading vessels because, as most yachtsmen today know, a fore-and-aft rig allows for sailing closer to the wind and easy maneuvering, and requires a crew of minimal skill. Although schooners made their first appearance on the Great Lakes in the early eighteenth century, they did not become the dominant sailing ship on the inland seas for almost 150 years.[2]

The first ship to sail Lake Michigan, the ill-fated *Griffon* of René-Robert Cavelier de La Salle, was modeled on the Dutch trading vessels known as galliots. La Salle's selection of this shallow-draft, round-

25

bottom design was clearly an attempt to adapt to the requirements of navigation on the unexplored Great Lakes. That principle—modifying saltwater designs to suit freshwater needs—marked the development of ships on the lakes. Square-rigged vessels, smaller versions of those used for oceanic voyages, dominated early shipping on the Great Lakes. They boasted large sails set from wooden spars hung perpendicularly from the mast. Setting or furling these sails was very time-consuming, requiring crewmen to scramble aloft to set or secure the canvas sheets. In return the square sails offered exceptional speed, at least when the ship was blessed with a wind at her back. To cope with the more variable wind conditions found on the Great Lakes and to make for greater maneuverability, ship designers experimented with combining square and fore-and-aft sails. These modifications, known as barks or brigantines, dominated commercial sailing on the lakes until the Civil War.[3]

A trim two-masted clipper heads for the open lake ca. 1880. Michigan Maritime Museum.

The First Lake Michigan Sailing Ships

The fur trade provided the first cargoes for Lake Michigan sailing ships. In 1679 the *Griffon* was lost on the return leg of her maiden voyage, taking with her a fortune in furs traded in Green Bay. Nearly a century would pass before a commercial vessel would again enter the lake. The *Archange* was the first recorded schooner on Lake Michigan. In 1778, British fur trader John Askin sent *Archange* from Mackinac to Milwaukee and Green Bay. Askin was an important supplier for the Canadian fur traders who were following the canoe routes west of the Great Lakes and into the Rocky Mountains. He relied upon Native American farmers in Michigan and Wisconsin to grow the corn that fed the far-ranging voyageurs. A year later the forty-five-ton sloop *Felicity* was sent on a similar mission. The two-week voyage of Captain Samuel Robertson and his crew of eight reveals the hazards of pioneer navigators on Lake Michigan. They endured stormy autumn weather that made even reaching the trading posts and Native American villages highly problematic. Attempts to enter the Kalamazoo River and the St. Joseph River had to be abandoned because "the wind did not abate." When *Felicity* approached "litel fort," the modern city of Waukegan, Robertson ordered his men to haul down the mainsail and "lay too" in order to guarantee that the sloop did not sail past Milwaukee during the night. Later in the voyage the prudent captain also laid up in the lee of the Manitou Islands on a dark, brisk night rather than chance what even then were known to be dangerous waters.[4]

Little ships such as the *Archange* and *Felicity* gave fur traders the means to transport large cargoes more quickly and less expensively than the traditional birchbark canoe or the bateau. Nonetheless, canoes and bateaux only slowly yielded their dominant role in the fur trade. By 1793 the Northwest Company, the strongest of the Canadian-based fur traders, had two sloops on Lake Superior and two more sharing duty on Lakes Erie, Huron, and Michigan. Independent traders who could not afford sailing ships continued to use canoes. The smaller craft were also needed to reach the interior trading posts. For short journeys, from Mackinac to the mouth of the Grand River or even to Green Bay, the versatility of canoes, which were able to access all water, mandated their continued use well into the nineteenth century. It was in bringing supplies from the lower lakes or transporting furs to market that sailing ships proved their worth.[5]

Sailing ships were also an important means of projecting political and military power quickly and deeply into the region. After Pontiac's Rebellion of 1763–66, the British government operated a shipyard at Detroit to build and maintain lake vessels. *Felicity* slid from its stocks in 1773. While her main purpose was to carry people and cargo, *Felicity*, like most early lake ships, was also an effective gun platform equipped with at least four swivel pieces. During the American Revolution and the War of 1812, Lake Michigan sailing vessels were a major British asset. The little armed sloops strengthened garrisons, supplied loyal Native Americans, and evacuated vulnerable troops. The successful establishment of American forts at Chicago and Mackinac between 1796 and 1812 was carried out by the formidable 150-ton brig *Adams* and the sloop *Tracy*, the first American naval vessels to sail Lake Michigan. When the second war with England began, the *Adams* was captured in its Detroit dry dock. The fall of that city and ship doomed Forts Dearborn and Mackinac. At the conclusion of both the Revolution and the War of 1812, the Americans found themselves driven from the shores of Lake Michigan by the British and their Native American allies.[6]

The Origins of the Lake Schooner

British naval power made itself felt even more acutely on the Atlantic coast. Aside from a few spectacular single-ship victories by the USS *Constitution* and the other American heavy frigates, it was the Royal Navy that dominated American waters during the War of 1812. The only ships capable of regularly piercing the British blockade were swift-winged schooners. The most important of the schooner designs was the "Virginia-built" boat, better known by its later name, the Baltimore clipper. This two-masted, fore-and-aft-rigged vessel with a sharp-lined hull evolved slowly from the 1740s through the beginning of the nineteenth century in the Chesapeake Bay region. So successful were these vessels in eluding patrolling British warships that by 1814 it was estimated that Baltimore clipper schooners carried nine-tenths of all American foreign trade.[7]

The Baltimore clipper design appears to have been the inspiration for most of the early Great Lakes schooners. However, as sailing ships proliferated on the inland seas the saltwater designs were modified by local builders. The most important of these Great Lakes designers was William Bates of Manitowoc, Wisconsin. In 1851 Bates had on the stocks of his shipyard a new variation of the Baltimore clipper: a shoal-draft, almost flat-bottomed, clipper schooner with sharp ends. These changes improved the ship's cargo capacity without creating a vessel that drew more water, something that would not do with all the sand-bars blocking Lake Michigan harbors. To give the ship greater stability under full sail, Bates added a retractable centerboard to the keel. Bates's new-style schooner was launched in 1852 and christened the *Challenge*. Doubters were quickly silenced by the *Challenge*'s speed, which was regularly thirteen knots, as well as her reliability. A year latter Bates launched *Clipper City*, which, along with *Challenge*, became the model for Lake Michigan clipper schooners.[8]

The use of a centerboard to give a shallow-draft ship greater stability had a long history on the Great Lakes. The first experiments with a retractable keel were made by Captain John Schank of the Royal Navy on the eve of the American Revolution. Schank conducted his original experiments in Boston harbor, but he was latter transferred to the Great Lakes, which may be the explanation for the gradual adoption of the drop keel concept on inland waters. There are reports of drop keel vessels on the lakes as early as the late eighteenth and early nineteenth century. The innovation was reportedly used in 1813 at Lake Erie's Put-in-Bay shipyard, and by the 1830s they appear to have been regarded as common on the Great Lakes. In 1837, Gabriel Franchere told an agent of the American Fur Company that he "decided upon building three slip keel Boats for our fisheries." Two of these were destined for Lake Superior, while the other was intended for use at the head of Lakes Michigan and Huron. The flexibility a centerboard or slip keel offered to lake sailors, giving stability in the open lake and allowing passage into shallow, sand-choked harbors, made them a standard component on all lake sailing vessels.[9]

Another important variation on the schooner type that was adapted for use on the Great Lakes was the scow schooner. While the hull of a

The scow schooner *X-10-U-8*. Built at South Haven, Michigan, in 1888, the uniquely named vessel awaits its cargo in the slip of a well-stocked sawmill. Captain Charles Allers took the name, pronounced "extenuate," from a grog shop he favored on the south side of Chicago. Based at Beaver Island, *X-10-U-8* was a lakeshoring schooner. Michigan Maritime Museum.

clipper was built for speed, a scow was designed to maximize cargo capacity. Scows tended to have an even shallower draft than other schooners, and are easily distinguished in historical photographs by their boxy appearance. Lacking the sleek V-shaped lines of clipper schooners, the scows were not regarded as good sailors, particularly in rough weather. Scow schooners tended to be small ships, under 100 tons (although the largest was over 250 tons), and generally were two-masted. Captains of tall-masted barks or sleek clippers would sometimes dismiss the ubiquitous scow schooners that scudded from port to port as the "mosquito fleet." Yet if they were mocked and dismissed in Chicago harbor as mere "mason's mud boxes," to frontier towns in Wisconsin or Michigan making their first foray into the regional marketplace they were symbols of a vital new metropolitan link.[10]

The first scow schooner was the *Bolivar*, built at Erie, Pennsylvania, in 1825. In 1836 the American Fur Company built a scow schooner at Sault Ste. Marie for use on Lake Superior. The popularity of ships of this type was due both to the ease with which they could be built by shipwrights with minimal skill and to their ability to efficiently carry heavy bulk cargoes. There is, however, an erroneous tendency among historians to dismiss all scow schooners as crude and unsophisticated. Some were slapped together during the winter, their sides consisting of rough planks spiked into place, and intended for no more than a season or two of summer use. Others, however, were built with traditional internal frames, their hulls braced by oak members, decks planked, and fully rigged. Scows, like all Great Lakes schooners, were built in a wide variety of settings and circumstances. Those that were not given the fore-and-aft rig of the schooner were afforded the even simpler rig of a sloop. The flat bottoms of the scows are reputed to have had another advantage: if the ship became grounded it was easier to refloat than a sleek-hulled ship. Despite their uncomely appearance and uninspiring name, scow schooners were a successful adaptation of marine technology to the requirements of the Great Lakes.[11]

Schooners were a classic "frontier" technology in the sense that they were adapted to a peripheral region's need to send raw materials and other unimproved products to eastern production and distribution centers. They were like the flatboats and keelboats of the Ohio valley during the period before 1830, whose *raison d'être* was to carry heartland agricultural surplus to the Gulf. The principal flow of commodities on the Great Lakes was from west to east. Coal and occasionally manufactured products went up the lakes on schooners. While that was a profitable bonus, it was on the schooners' downbound journeys, laden with grain or lumber, that they performed their indispensable service. When the economy of the Lake Michigan basin matured, when Chicago and Milwaukee themselves became production centers utilizing their central location to meet a national market, many old grain schooners were able to extend their life by making short hauls within the Lake Michigan basin. In their heyday, however, schooners tied Lake Michigan to New York the same way Chicago later used the railroad to bind the plains to its manufacturers.

Another variation on the lake schooner was the canaller. These stubby schooners were built to accommodate the Welland Canal, which opened a ship passage around Niagara Falls and, together with the St. Lawrence River locks, made direct shipping from the Atlantic

31

to the upper Great Lakes possible. After 1846, when the Welland Canal was enlarged, canallers could be no longer than 150 feet (including the bowsprit) and no wider than 26 feet. The ship's stunted appearance was the result of its small bowsprit and the snubbed taper of the stern. Like the scow schooner, a canaller had an almost flat bottom. Without its drop centerboard the ship would have been almost unseaworthy. As it was, canallers were less than endearing to their crews due to their cramped quarters and their maddening slippage across the wind. Canallers were much more common on the lower lakes, near the Canadian canals, than on Lake Michigan.[12]

Canallers were a maritime response to the duel between New York City and Montreal for control of the Great Lakes trade. With the building of the Erie Canal in 1825, the state of New York had snared the bulk of the agricultural produce of the heartland. The building of the Welland and Lachine Canals by the British was an attempt to divert the golden stream of grain to the natural outlet of the Great Lakes, the St. Lawrence River. Montreal never succeeded in its bid for an American commercial hinterland, but the canals did open up Lake Ontario and the Atlantic Ocean to Lake Michigan schooners. Free trade between the United States and the Canadian colonies between 1855 and 1865 was a considerable success and caused a boom in the use of canallers. Ironically, the Welland Canal was also used to send Canadian grain to Buffalo and Canadian lumber to Chicago.[13]

The first canaller was the *St. Clair,* built in 1824 by Samuel Ward in the Belle River of Michigan. Ward's ship, a schooner of twenty-eight tons burden, was described as "modeled like a canal boat, having full ends, her rudder hanging over the stern." Ward was under the impression that the first ship through the newly built Erie Canal would receive a special "bounty." Yet as the *St. Clair* made her way through the farms and fields of upstate New York, laden with a cargo of Lake Michigan forest products, Ward discovered that the only financial prize awaiting him was a large toll bill! Ward realized a whopping $6,000 profit from the voyage, but it was a journey he never repeated.[14]

A canaller schooner under sail on Lake Michigan. The stubby bowsprit and "boxy" look of the flat-bottomed canaller were adaptations to the limitations of the Welland Canal that connected Lake Erie with Lake Ontario. Canaller schooners became notorious as bad heavy-weather ships. Collection of the Chicago Maritime Society.

Transatlantic Trade

U nlike the Erie Canal, which was largely meant for canal boats, Canada's Welland Canal was a true ship canal. Merchants from St. Joseph, Michigan, hazarded the first direct voyage to Europe in 1854–55 with the brig *Scott.* In 1856 a group of Chicago and Montreal merchants experimented with shipping grain directly from Lake Michigan to Europe. The inaugural venture was well capitalized. A brand-new schooner, the *Dean Richmond,* was built in Cleveland. The 140-foot-long vessel, described as "a trim looking flush deck schooner with a rather flat sheer, high bulwarks, two tall masts and a long bowsprit," set sail from Chicago on July 14 amid speeches and celebrations. Such was the civic pride engendered by the voyage that when underwriters refused to assume the risk for the voyage, members of the Chicago Board of Trade pledged their personal guarantees. It took the *Dean Richmond* forty-one days to sail the 1,401 miles to Quebec and an additional thirty-six to cross the Atlantic to Liverpool. The cargo of Chicago and Milwaukee grain fetched a healthy profit, and then the ship herself was sold for $27,000.[15]

A year to the day after the *Dean Richmond* set sail for Europe, the Old World returned the favor when the *Madeira Pet,* eighty days out of Liverpool, docked at the north pier near the mouth of the Chicago River. The ship's arrival set off two days of celebration. The ship brought a mixed cargo of glassware, china, and paint, hardly materials that would revolutionize life in Chicago. Despite the hundred-gun salute and the band playing "God Save the Queen," the fact was the *Madeira Pet* was a mere ninety-seven feet long and her visit, like her cargo, was of marginal economic significance. Throughout the remainder of the nineteenth century, Lake Michigan ports engaged in occasional direct commercial connections to Europe. Probably the most significant European ships to visit Lake Michigan were the immigrant ships that brought Scandinavian settlers to the region. From 1862 to 1865 Chicago received an annual immigrant ship from Bergen, Norway. When 107 passengers disembarked from the first such ship, the *Sleipner,* the *Chicago Times* optimistically noted that "only four [people] have died on the passage," and that loss was partially offset by the birth of a child on Lake Erie.[16]

Lucia A. Simpson in the Milwaukee River displays her half an acre of canvas. From the Great Lakes Marine Collection of the Milwaukee Public Library/ Wisconsin Marine Historical Society.

The Persistence of Schooners

A remarkable feature of the schooner era on Lake Michigan was that it took place in the face of growing numbers of steamships on the inland seas. Although the use of steam increased tremendously on the lakes from its beginning in 1818 to the Civil War, the new technology did not directly replace the use of sailing vessels.

Rather, the innovation complemented rather than competed with sail. For trade that required speed and predictable schedules, such as passengers, mail, and packages, steamships forged to the forefront. For bulk cargoes, however, steamships could not compete with the cost-effectiveness of the sailing ships. While sailing ships might seem to have been an outdated technology by the mid-nineteenth century, numerous small improvements were made which, together with the enduring utility of their basic design, allowed these ships to effectively serve out the century. To the master of a steel steamship, looking down from his quarterdeck, the wooden schooners he surged past in the harbor might have appeared a quaint relic of a bygone era. Yet he would have done well to remember that nineteenth-century sailing ships, while the last of their kind, stood at the peak of two thousand years of continuous adaptation and improvement. They were not primitive tools to be rapidly discarded, but highly complex vessels capable of adaptation and continued evolution within their form to adjust to a changing market. They would not sail meekly into the night of history.

The apogee of the age of sail on the Great Lakes was reached in 1868. In that year, 1,855 sailing ships were registered on the inland seas. While the number of sailing ships steadily declined thereafter, the actual total tonnage of sailing ships increased on the lakes, rising from 294,000 tons in 1868 to 298,000 in 1873. The building of larger clipper schooners accounted for this increase in tonnage. Beginning in the 1860s, new three-masted vessels boasting 300 to 500 tons burden dominated the Lake Michigan grain trade. While some of these were rigged with a square sail from the foremast, more common was the use of another distinctive Great Lakes design: the raffe. This was a triangular sail set from the foremast that had nearly the pulling power of a square sail, but was not as difficult for a small crew to set. These vessels differed from their saltwater cousins because of their slightly longer hulls and taller masts. The mainmast of a Lake Michigan schooner frequently topped one hundred feet, and with all sails set these ships offered half an acre of canvas to the wind. Some of the finest and fastest sailing vessels to sail Lake Michigan, like the *Lake Forest, Invincible,* and *Moonlight,* were three-masted schooners. Some critics have disparaged the three-masted rigs because the main or middle mast interfered with unloading bulk cargo and allegedly blanketed the other sails when running before the wind. What could not be denied, however, was that the smaller sails used on three-masters made for lighter spars and fewer crew members—an important factor in sustaining the economic viability of schooners.[17]

Experiments to make schooners larger and larger continued into the 1880s. The *James Crouch,* launched in 1871, was 221 feet long and 1,000 tons burden, the largest sailing ship on the lakes, yet it was dwarfed by the *David Dows,* a 275-foot, five-masted schooner launched at Toledo, Ohio, in 1881. The Bailey Brothers shipyard, which utilized one hundred craftsmen to produce the ship, was proud that the *David Dows* was the largest schooner in the world, although purists noted that because the foremast was rigged with square sails the *Dows* was technically a barkentine. For all the attention lavished on her, however, the *Dows* was from the beginning a "crank." Just months after her launching she ran down and sank the three-masted schooner *Charles K. Nims.* After a second such incident, in which four men were killed, the *Dows* was declared a menace and removed from the ranks of first-class merchant ships, reduced to the role of being a mere tow barge. In that humble capacity the *Dows* met her end in November 1889: after springing a leak off South Chicago, she sank in thirty to forty feet of water.[18]

The *David Dows* passing through the locks of the Sault Ste. Marie canal in the early 1880s. The *Dows* was the only five- masted vessel to sail Lake Michigan. Her 275 feet dwarfed many other sailing ships, but she could not match the steam-powered bulk carriers being built in the late 1880s. After a brief career she was lost off South Chicago in November 1889. Collection of the Chicago Maritime Society.

The building of larger schooners in the twenty years following the Civil War reflected both the growing importance of Great Lakes navigation and the gradual improvement of the region's harbors. Schooners held their niche in Great Lakes commerce, in part because of their ability to handle the shallow river mouths and harbors of Lake Michigan. As more and more harbors received the benefit of civil engineering, larger vessels became increasingly effective. The twilight of sailing ships on Lake Michigan came not simply because steam and steel ships were technologically superior, but because the conditions for which schooners had been adapted changed. Unfortunately, as the sad history of the *David Dows* indicated, there were limits to the ability of wooden sailing vessels, within the confines of the inland seas, to respond to the demand for larger ships. The sinking of the *Dows* in the degraded capacity of a tow barge presaged the final stage in the evolution of the Lake Michigan schooner.

From the perspective of the old windjammer sailors, the schooner barge was the subordinating of old sailing ships to steam technology. But schooner barges were also an example of the continued adaptation of sailing ships to steam, the coexistence of old and new. The inspiration for schooner barges came from a Buffalo lumber merchant who in 1861 used dismasted sailing ships as barges. Most commonly the schooners were stripped of their topsails—and sometimes even their decks—in order to increase their cargo capacity, then towed by a tug or a steam barge from destination to destination. The schooners were allowed to keep their masts in order to reduce the burden on the tug during favorable winds.

The first use of schooner barges on Lake Michigan took place in 1868 when two tugs and six barges transported lumber from Peshtigo to Chicago. The moving force behind this innovation was Isaac Stephenson, a sometime lake mariner who had made his fortune in the lumber business. Previous to Stephenson it was believed that the open waters of Lake Michigan were too rough for a tug or steam barge to long maintain several vessels in tow. Stephenson later improved on this scheme by having specially designed steam barges pull the schooner barges. The steam barges were loaded with four-foot slabs of wood and could carry enough fuel for round trips between Marinette and Chicago. Eventually the Marinette Barge Company had three fleets in constant motion during the navigation season. While one would be loading in Marinette, a second was being unloaded in Chicago and a

The *Bertha Barnes,* a top-sailed, three-masted schooner, under sail. Note the steam donkey engine just left of the foremast. By the 1880s it was common for the larger schooners to reduce operating costs by using steam power to hoist sails, thereby reducing the size of the crew. The *Bertha Barnes* was a 330-ton schooner built in Sheboygan, Wisconsin, in 1872. Ivan H. Walton Collection, Bentley Historical Library, University of Michigan.

third was in transit on Lake Michigan. The company acquired one of these fleets in 1872 from the Manistee lumber firm of Tyson & Robinson. Rather than use old clipper or scow schooners as barges, Tyson & Robinson actually had three schooner barges built to deliver their product to the Chicago market. When fire terminated Tyson & Robinson's mill, their schooner barges were sold across Lake Michigan to the Marinette Barge Company.

Captain James Norris of St. Catherines, Ontario, also claimed the honor of having innovated the tow barge system on the lakes. In 1869 the tug *Samson* pulled three schooners to Chicago and back to Ontario, just beating the winter freeze. Regardless of who tried to first tow schooners during the 1880s and 1890s, most of the old veterans of the lake fleet underwent conversion to barges. So successful was this policy that it was also adopted on salt water. During the opening years of the twentieth century, old clipper schooners from Maine to Chesapeake Bay ended their days tethered to a towline.[19]

The last variation on the schooner design before the age of commercial sail was completely eclipsed was the "Grand Haven rig." This two-masted rig was probably borrowed from schooner barges, which were found to sail tolerably well even after being shorn of their mainmast and topsails. A popular legend on the lakes claims that the rig was discovered by a miserly Grand Haven skipper who cut down his rotted mainmast and, rather than pay to have a new mast installed, extended two triangular sails—one from the foremast, another from the mizzen—to catch the wind at midships. These staysails could be easily removed to load or unload cargo, which made for cheaper harbor costs. One less mast also made for easier handling under way, which often meant a smaller and cheaper crew. In the parlance of salt water, a two-masted, fore-and-aft-rigged ship with the masts set so far apart was called a ketch. This design was very popular in Scandinavia, a fact that may explain the origin of the rig, since so many lake mariners were of Norwegian or Swedish origin. A Grand Haven–rigged vessel presented an awkward profile on the horizon, with the large open area at midships creating the impression that something was missing. But despite its homely appearance, the Grand Haven rig helped schooners that otherwise would have been uneconomical extend the twilight years of the age of sail on Lake Michigan.[20]

The schooner *Champion*, shorn of her topmasts and laden with a deck cargo of lumber. Schooners without their topsails could be more easily sailed by smaller and inexperienced crews. The *Champion* was built by the renowned shipbuilders Quayle & Martin of Cleveland, Ohio. Ivan H. Walton Collection, Bentley Historical Library, University of Michigan.

Conclusion

*L*ake Michigan schooners represent an important, if not original, chapter in American maritime history. The sailing ships that scudded the inland seas were a variation on the type of sailing ships that dominated the coastal trade along the Atlantic and Gulf

41

The *City of Grand Haven* and her crew. The mainmast has been removed to ease sailing and the loading of cargo. This arrangement was called the "Grand Haven rig," or as its detractors referred to it, the "jackass rig." Michigan Maritime Museum.

seaboards. The evolution from two-masted schooners, to the prevalence of three-masters, to the experimentation with larger schooners of five or more masts, to the final, inglorious triumph of the tow barge occurred both on the lakes and along the ocean. The significance of the Lake Michigan schooner was less a matter of their design than of the role they played in the social and economic history of their region.

There is something about all sailing ships that even today inspires affection. To men and women of the nineteenth century, the sight of a sailing ship had an even more powerful impact. A ship under sail was to them a symbol of nature harnessed in the cause of personal freedom and economic advancement. When the Norwegian schooner-brig *Sleipner,* in the midst of the Civil War, journeyed to Lake Michigan, the *Chicago Times* editorialized, "Let the cities of the seaboard look to their laurels, for whether in peace or war, in fighting, buying or selling, we are bound to go ahead, though all the world should stand still." For people in towns large and small along the Lake Michigan shore, the white sails of the schooner were the wings of a dream: a means to move products, people, and aspirations.[21]

2
The Maritime Frontier: Schooners and Urban Development on the Lake Michigan Shore

The official seal of the city of Chicago has four related symbols: a Native American, representing the city's earliest inhabitants; a sheaf of wheat, a nod to the bounty of the prairie; a fully rigged sailing ship; and a baby, rising metaphorically from a seashell. The seal is recognition that Chicago, like Milwaukee, Green Bay, and scores of other Lake Michigan cities, is the spawn of the lake. Because Lake Michigan was the single most important feature in the development of these cities, schooners played a crucial if underappreciated role in the urban development of the region. As the principal means by which the Great Lakes states were economically linked to the Northeast during the frontier era, schooners were the thread that bound together critical sections of the country. They were the key technology by which fur-trading posts or speculators' plats could be transformed into cities. What covered wagons were for Denver and Salt Lake City, what steamboats were for St. Louis and New Orleans, schooners were for the metropolises and towns of the Lake Michigan basin.[1]

Lake Michigan was a blue-water frontier for Michigan, Wisconsin, Indiana, and Illinois. The fish, lumber, and mineral and agricultural resources of the lake basin were among the richest in the world, yet their value was greatly enhanced because of their proximity to the shipping lanes of the Great Lakes. There was a democratic character to lake transportation. The lake waited open and available to all at the doorstep of scores of communities, a resource too big, empty, and free to be dominated, as were the railroads, by corporate interests. During the nineteenth century, sailing craft on the lake—particularly the schooners, but also the more humble mackinaw boats—were simple, relatively inexpensive, and potentially lucrative means by which ordinary citizens could profit from the abundance of the region. Even in mill towns dominated by a handful of lumber barons, the lake was a door open to the outside world—a means of escape as well as an avenue for the arrival of immigrants from the East and beyond the ocean. The story of the schooner is the story of the means by which the opportunities of the lake and the aspirations of the people on its margins were joined and, in many cases, realized.

While Chicago, Green Bay, Muskegon, St. Joseph, and many other Lake Michigan towns trace their beginnings to fur-trading posts supplied by brigades of French-Canadian canoemen, it was the arrival of sailing ships that signaled the beginning of their growth as urban cen-

The original Fort Dearborn, at the site of Chicago, was supplied by regular visits from the brig *Adams* and the sloop *Tracy*, the first United States military vessels on Lake Michigan. Reprinted from Alfred T. Andreas, *History of Chicago* (Chicago: A. T. Andreas, 1884–86). Collection of the Chicago Maritime Society.

ters. The sloop *Tracy* brought the Fort Dearborn garrison to Chicago. Before Chicago was incorporated as a village, it had a lighthouse, and before it had its first newspaper, Congress appropriated funds to improve its harbor. Chicago was a port before it was anything more than, in the words of an army engineer, "a few huts, inhabited by a miserable race of men scarcely equal to the Indians from whom they are descended. Their log and bark houses are low, filthy and disgusting." At a time when only sixty people resided in the village, sailing ships would travel over a thousand miles to anchor off the Chicago River.[2]

Not only in Chicago, but all along the Lake Michigan shore, schooners were at the cutting edge of the frontier. The arduous character of travel over the wet prairies of Illinois and the forest and marshlands of Indiana and Michigan was a powerful inducement for early settlers to risk the hazards of lake navigation. Solomon Juneau, Milwaukee's founder, inaugurated the commerce of that city in 1823 when he chartered the schooner *Chicago Packet* to bring his trade goods and carry away his furs. In August 1835 a schooner bearing settlers for Kenosha arrived off that nascent settlement. Shoals made it impossible for the ship to approach the shore, while heavy seas prevented small boats from tying up to the side. Adults had to time their leap from the schooner with the roll of the surf, while children were tossed from the deck into the waiting arms of their parents. That first winter the settlers suffered through a desperate food shortage, ended only in May by the arrival of the *Van Buren* laden with supplies. Manistee, Michigan, was similarly saved from starvation in 1848 through the dangerous November passage by the schooner *Mary G. Boneystiel*, which resupplied the lumber town just before the arrival of winter. In 1836, A. G. Knight, one of the first settlers of Racine, Wisconsin, arrived at the site of that future city. The only way families could disembark from the sailing ship was for the men to wade out to the vessel and take their wives and mothers ashore on their shoulders. The schooner *Supply* brought Grand Haven, Michigan, its first permanent settlers, Rev. William M. Ferry, his family, and sixteen other homesteaders, in November 1834. Two years later the schooner *St. Joseph* arrived from Buffalo with another load of families. The *St. Joseph* then inaugurated regular passenger and cargo traffic between Grand Haven and Chicago. Ludington, Michigan, was settled more than a decade later when the schooner *Eagle* brought Burr Caswell's family of six to the mouth of the Pere Marquette River. The family came ashore in the captain's yawl, but their oxen, cows, and swine were pushed overboard and forced to swim ashore.[3]

The founding stories of these cities reveal that the lake was each settlement's doorway to the outside world. The lake brought pioneering families and life-sustaining supplies, and it was the avenue for expanding commercial horizons. The schooners that made these pioneer voyages were small (fifty to sixty feet long) two-masted vessels. Their captains referred to the general cargo and passenger trade as "lakeshoring."

The schooner *Isolda Bock* of Benton Harbor, Michigan, waits out the winter. Michigan Maritime Museum.

Lakeshoring Schooners

The logbook of Captain Justice Bailey, an early practitioner of the lakeshoring trade, provides some insight into how schooners operated on the frontier. Bailey was born in New York state, and after being "bound out" to a farm family in childhood he went off to the Great Lakes to work as a shipwright and sailor. By 1838 he was master of the *Gazelle,* a sixty-seven-foot, seventy-five-ton, two-masted schooner. From April to July the *Gazelle* carried cargoes between Lake Michigan and Lake Erie, with stops at Port Huron, Thunder Bay, Death's Door, Two Rivers, and Mackinac. Manufactured goods such as steam boilers and agricultural produce (beans, butter, and flour) were sent north. Other cargoes reflecting the needs of a frontier region included nails for building houses, furniture shipped to immigrant families, and salt needed by the pioneer fisheries. At the isolated settlements the *Gazelle* took on barrels of fish, loads of lumber or bark, and passengers. Captain Bailey's wife, Lucinda, accompanied him on the *Gazelle* until the children became "too numerous and active." Baileys Harbor, Wisconsin, which was first visited by the *Gazelle* in 1838, is named after Captain Bailey. The *Gazelle,* after getting a major rebuild in 1850, continued in service on Lake Michigan until 1867, when she was driven ashore by a southwester at Little Point Sable.[4]

The logbooks of the *Hero* and *Mary Elizabeth,* both schooners in the lakeshoring trade during the 1840s, reveal how the quest for cargoes and the lack of charts made for long, slow journeys. Henry B. Ketcham, another New York–born shipwright turned master, was the skipper of both schooners. His log for the *Hero* in October 1846 includes the following entries:

Oct. 5   Left Big Sturgeon Bay wind South East
   6th   wind S.E. worked up to Baileys Harbor
   7th   Ran down to Washington harbor
   8th   Ran over to Poverty & Summer Is
   9th   Lay there with the winds S.S.E. gale
  10th got under way with wind S.S.E. carried away
         forward sail

11th Left Big Summer Island wind west—light in morning
continued so all day at night blew a gale at W.S.W.
13th Put in to Big Beaver harbor wind to N.W. and Blew a
gale with rain.

The *Hero* undertook a week's worth of sailing and probably covered
less than two hundred miles, all for the sake of a couple of loads of
fish, which were most likely not worth the cost of the canvas lost in
the gale, let alone the wages and food consumed by the crew.[5]

In 1991 the remains of an 1840s lakeshoring schooner that failed
to find safe anchorage were found buried at a beach near Naubinway,
Michigan. Archaeologists discovered the vessel's cargo intact. Tea
from China was found still wrapped in its original paper. The hold also
contained barrels of salted fish, meant for urban markets, and the
barrels of salt from New York, meant for Lake Michigan fishermen.
The Naubinway ship seems to have been blown aground in a gale and
abandoned on a wilderness shore. The fate of this unnamed ship is
testament to the difficulties faced by pioneer mariners as they sought
to harness a resource which, in its natural state, was at best unimproved for commerce and at worst deadly dangerous.

Both commercially and from the standpoint of personal safety,
early schooner voyages on Lake Michigan were highly risky. In the fall
of 1816 a young Métis girl, Elizabeth Therese Baird, journeyed with
her mother to Chicago from Detroit by sailing ship. They arrived at
Mackinac, the halfway point of their journey, in October and discovered to their distress that there would be no further ships to Chicago
that year as "no vessel would brave the autumnal storms." Fortunately, a traveling companion had a relative on the island and they
spent the winter in crowded but comfortable quarters. Not until mid-
June was a vessel prepared to journey to the end of the lake. The
schooner was loaded with pork, flour, and butter—products Chicago
would in later years export to the world but which now were in desperate demand by the soldiers and fur traders at Fort Dearborn. After
about a ten-day voyage—unbroken by any other landings, as "there
were no ports on the west side of Lake Michigan, at which to stop"—
the schooner reached the Chicago River. Young Baird played in the
river and on the surrounding sand hills with the children of fur trader
John Kinzie while her mother visited with friends. "We remained in
Chicago for some time," she later recalled, "the vessel master seeking

48

for a cargo which was not secured. It was too early for furs, so finally the vessel had to take on a ballast of gravel and sand." With three other passengers, Baird and her mother began their schooner trip home. "Pursuing our journey northward, we coasted along the east side of the lake, stopping where we could, to secure if possible a cargo." At no point could the vessel master obtain a cargo. This was no doubt maddening to the master, who wanted to make the voyage pay, but the young girl was delighted to have a cargo hold full of sand in which to play and hunt for shells. An African American sailor was "uncommonly kind to me," Baird recalled. He would "take me down, and while I played, sit by and mend his clothes, talking all the while to me, and I not understanding a word, as he spoke English, and I only French." As the ship neared Mackinac a violent storm beset the schooner, the wind ripping the sails and stripping much of the rigging. At one point the little ship was thrown up on a rocky reef. This very well might have meant the end for the ship and its passengers, but in a "providential" manner the schooner worked itself free and was able to limp the next day to Mackinac Island. The passengers and their friends were "overwhelmed with joy" at their safe return. With no cargo and a ravaged vessel, the schooner captain must have been more restrained in his reaction.[6]

Baird's child's-eye view of passenger travel on a schooner left out the discomfort of cramped, wet voyages on small wooden ships. In 1815 Jacob B. Varnum, manager of the government fur-trading post at Chicago, "took passage on a miserable apology for a schooner." The majority of his trade goods were ruined by water, while he himself was soaked through most of the voyage owing to a cabin "so near the bottom of the vessel that in a rough sea our shallow little schooner would roll up the bilge water and spurt it into my berth." Mary Per Lee, journeying from New York to Grand Haven in 1844, found the passenger accommodations and food on the schooner *St. Joseph* miserable. Yet, she consoled herself, "we had sheets and pillow cases on our beds," unlike the canal boat on which she had begun her journey. Lee's journey nearly ended tragically when the *St. Joseph* became grounded on a sandbar, but thanks to the "excellent management of our captain" the ship was floated free before a storm came up and she safely reached her new frontier home.[7]

The near wreck of Baird's schooner and the grounding of Lee's, however, reflected an unfortunate reality for early Lake Michigan

49

sailing ships. There was little in the way of navigational improvements and no charts available during the first half of the nineteenth century. Early settlers had to wade ashore or be transferred to small boats because there were so few harbors or even piers on Lake Michigan. The want of a safe harbor on a contained body of water given to sudden and violent storms was a dangerous combination. English traveler Charles Latrobe, who visited Chicago in 1833, complained: "The total absence of harbors round this southern extremity of the lake has caused the wreck of many a vessel, as the action of the storm from the northward upon such a wide expanse of fresh water is tremendous; and from the great height and violence of the surf, which then thunders in upon the base of the sand hills, and the utter solitude of this coast, lives are seldom if ever saved." The weathered ribs of the schooner *Hercules,* a U.S. Army supply ship lost with all hands in 1818 near what is now Michigan City, Indiana, for years stood as a warning to all mariners of the dangers of the dune-rimmed southern shore of the lake.[8]

The Struggle for Harbors

A critical phase in the development of the maritime frontier was the engineering of harbor facilities to allow for the easy transfer of cargoes and to provide safe anchorage. There are very few natural harbors on Lake Michigan, save for the shelter provided by the numerous rivers that flow into it. Unfortunately, the river mouths tended to be blocked by sandbars. The bar at the mouth of the Chicago River, for example, was generally only about two feet under the surface of the water. At Chicago and other Lake Michigan towns, frustrated townspeople would sometimes fasten the towline of a small schooner to several yoke of oxen and pull a ship over the bar. Such an expediency, however, could not substitute for a harbor. What was needed at most rivers was to excavate a channel through the bar and to build a series of cribs and piers to retard the sand from returning, thereby providing a protected entrance to the river-harbor. Such a project required the skills of a civil engineer and a considerable amount of money, both of which were in extremely short supply on the frontier. Therefore, as towns were established along the Great Lakes, they appealed to the federal government for technical and financial support. In a manner that would embarrass today's proponents of frontier self-sufficiency, the would-be ports of the lakes, beginning as a few forlorn voices in the 1820s and swelling to a chorus in the 1840s, called for Congress to build their harbors.[9]

The first Lake Michigan city to gain the attention of Washington was St. Joseph, Michigan. In 1826 federal funds helped to divert the main channel of the St. Joseph River, thereby washing away the sandbar and opening a clear-flowing channel to the lake. While St. Joseph, one of the oldest settlements on Lake Michigan, received federal assistance, Chicago languished. Major William H. Keating, dubious of Chicago's prospects, warned that "the extent of the sand banks, which are formed on the eastern and southern shore, by the prevailing north and northwesterly winds, will . . . prevent any important works from being undertaken to improve the port of Chicago." Besides, Keating observed in 1823, "the whole annual amount of trade on the lake did not exceed the cargo of five or six schooners." Milwaukee also had to endure the slings and arrows of eastern doubters. In 1837 a New York newspaper complained that Milwaukee had a "peculiar location . . . the greater part of the ground upon which the city had been laid out was under water." The correspondent concluded by observing that the people of the settlement were "dissatisfied; many are leaving and moving further west . . . there is little hope that Milwaukee shall ever reach a modest mediocrity."[10]

Ignored by Congress, some citizens made an independent effort to build a harbor. One such person was Brevet Major J. Fowle, commander of Fort Dearborn. In 1828, disgusted with the time and effort his men wasted transferring the cargoes of supply ships to small boats, Fowle ordered the troops to cut a direct channel through the sandbar at a meandering bend of the Chicago River. The high water of early spring gave the normally sluggish river a strong current so that after only several hours of digging the water surged into the cut, creating a fifteen-foot-deep passage into the Chicago River. Fowle's cut was a momentary improvement, since without piers and cribs the sides of the cut soon collapsed and sand and gravel choked off the channel. These types of ad hoc efforts were not infrequent along the shores of Lake Michigan. When water levels were favorable, shipowners and merchants were not shy about improvising a harbor. One spring during the 1860s a schooner captain noted that the water in the Manitowoc

River was higher than the level of the lake. He landed his schooner alongside the bar and with a shovel cut a drain through the sand. The river did the rest and opened up a temporary channel through which to bring his ship. Another technique particularly adapted to scow schooners in sandy-bottomed waters was for the ship to drop its anchor in deep water and then by means of a line have the ship hauled over a bar or shoal. When the vessel was loaded the crew would then haul the boat back over the sand shoal using the windlass and anchor.[11]

On March 2, 1833, Congress appropriated $25,000 to clear a channel into the Chicago River. The schooner *Austerlitz* brought the supplies and skilled workmen necessary for the task in July, and work was

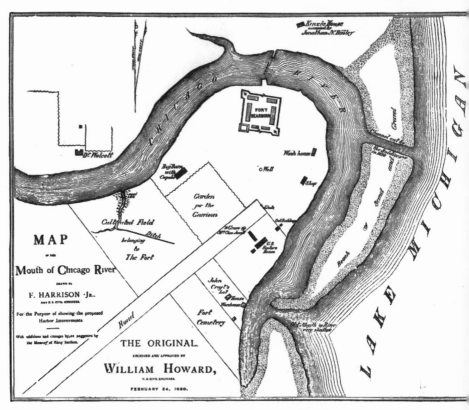

Map of the mouth of the Chicago River showing the cut made by the Fort Dearborn garrison in 1828 to create a temporary passage through the sandbar blocking the harbor. Reprinted from Alfred T. Andreas, *History of Chicago* (Chicago: A. T. Andreas, 1884–86). Collection of the Chicago Maritime Society.

begun shortly after. The task, however, proved to be a major undertaking. An additional $38,801 was appropriated for the project in 1834, as well as further funds during the next four years. Ships were able to use the new channel long before the project was completed, however. The first ship to enter through the new channel was the schooner *Illinois,* a stubby little canaller. Her arrival was an occasion for considerable celebration. As she passed between the piers being constructed out onto the lake, enthusiastic Chicagoans jumped onto the schooner while others packed Fort Dearborn's wharf to greet her. Forty-eight bottles of champagne were cracked open for the *Illinois*'s crew and the celebrating throng. When the champagne bottles were emptied, the captain of the *Illinois* raised sail and took the crowded vessel up the river, past the town's first drawbridge, and to the forks of the river, finally landing "her Merry Crew" in front of the taverns at Wolf Point. One of the taverns was occupied by the city fathers trying to hold a justice of the peace election. "The evidence of the Champagne was now raised to its highest pitch," one observer noted, and not for the last time the sober business of government gave way to a good old-fashioned blowout.[12]

The *Illinois* was only one of 180 ships to call at Chicago during the town's first year as a port. "Every day," a resident reported that summer, "you may see vessels and steam-boats put in here from the lake crowded with families who came to settle in Chicago." Immigrants with means came by steamboat, but plenty of settlers disembarked seasick and wobbly-legged from schooners. In May 1834 the *Illinois* had taken 104 newcomers from Buffalo to Chicago. That many passengers, jammed with their baggage, supplies, and even a wagon, taxed the capacity of the small schooner. Thanks to good weather the *Illinois* made it to Chicago with her deck crowded with eager immigrants and with wagon wheels tied to the rigging.[13]

The early development of a harbor at Chicago funneled settlers from New England and New York into the Illinois prairie. Chicago's rise as a port restarted the construction of the Illinois and Michigan Canal, which had faltered after the Panic of 1837. The port also enabled Chicago to develop at an early date as the rail center of the West. Schooners entering the river-harbor brought the first steam locomotives to Illinois. Chicago was a rail town before it had its first rail link to the East because it was a port capable of receiving the new steam technology. Throughout the 1850s, when the Illinois Central was becoming the longest railroad in the world, it was schooners that brought the rails, spikes, and ties that allowed the construction to go forward. Railroad equipment accounted for the highest-valued goods annually received by schooner in Chicago.[14]

In 1839, with the construction of the harbor at Chicago complete, the army engineers could look back in pride over what they had helped to accomplish. Captain T. J. Cram, head of harbor improvements on Lake Michigan, did not hesitate to claim credit, nor was he shy about making predictions for Chicago: "After only six years it numbers from five to six thousand inhabitants . . . [yet] the present Chicago is but a nucleus about which there will grow up, at no remote period, one of the most important commercial towns upon the lakes." Cram's problem was that what the federal government had done at great cost for Chicago was soon demanded by all of the nascent communities along the shores of Lake Michigan. Thomas Jefferson Cram, an 1822 graduate of West Point, established his headquarters at Racine and tried to respond to the demands for aid. The engineers surveyed harbors for Kenosha, Calumet, Milwaukee, Racine, Manitowoc, Sheboygan, and Kewanee, but the congressional will that committed over $100,000 to improve Chicago's harbor no longer existed. At the very point when demand for navigational improvements on the lake was reaching a peak and the engineering expertise was in place, federal funding began to evaporate.[15]

The completion of the Erie Canal in 1825 had made the Great Lakes suddenly very accessible to the people of New England, the Mid-Atlantic states, and immigrants from Europe. The ports of Lake Erie, such as Buffalo and Cleveland, were the first to benefit from the influx of new settlers. It took until 1832 and the conclusion of the Black Hawk War for the tide of immigration to burst into the Lake Michigan basin. The Panic of 1837, which resulted in a nationwide depression, hit the western states particularly hard. The real estate bubble burst in Chicago and several other lake towns, but it was only a temporary setback. In the decade of the 1830s, Michigan's population grew from 31,000 to 212,000, and the Wisconsin Territory did even better, swelling from 30,000 to 300,000. Against the demand for navigational aids by these new citizens was arrayed the Democratic Party—committed to placing strict limits on the actions of the federal government and beholden to catchpenny southern politicians.[16]

Resentment of Washington ran high along the shores of the lake. So-called indignation meetings were frequently held in would-be ports. Although the commercial value of a harbor to a frontier town dominated the drive for harbors, participants at these meetings emphasized to Congress the dangerous condition of lakes navigation. In the seven years following the opening of the port of Chicago, 118 lives were lost on Lake Michigan, and the total financial loss was over $1 million. When fatalities resulted from the upset of a boat trying to enter the Milwaukee River, the local newspaper proclaimed: "Two more citizens have found premature graves in consequence of the cruel justice of Congress in not making appropriations for our harbor." Isaac Stephenson, an immigrant from New Brunswick who tried his hand at lake sailing, claimed that the Democratic Party's frequent veto of harbor appropriations meant "every sailor on the lakes became a Whig and afterwards a Republican." Many lake mariners believed that the lack of safe harbors, lighthouses, and reliable charts had less to do with a strict interpretation of the Constitution than with a lack of appreciation for the enormity and power of the Great Lakes. "The idea that the lakes were little more than a 'goose pond' prevailed in Congress for some years," Stephenson claimed. Many mariners agreed with the captain who expressed the "fervent hope, when he had a United States Senator aboard as a passenger, that he might run into a gale to convince the unsuspecting legislator of the hazards of inland navigation." Boosters of the region found vexing the fact that by the 1850s Lake Michigan ports like Milwaukee and Chicago were returning hundreds of thousands of dollars annually to the federal government in customs duties, yet they still had to beg for appropriations.[17]

Between 1839 and 1861, national political divisions restricted the development of the Lake Michigan basin. Harbor construction and maintenance became a matter of local initiative mixed with an occasional influx of federal support. Desperate for a port, Milwaukee tried in 1840 to raise the necessary funds by private subscription. Enthusiasm, however, ran deeper than the frontier town's pockets. Two years later, the *Milwaukee Sentinel* tried to shame the government (and win subscribers) by offering to loan federal authorities the money to begin harbor work. Finally, in 1843 Wisconsin's territorial representative was able to win passage of a $30,000 appropriation, and within a year a passage was cut through the sandbar. Federal funds were also awarded to Racine and Southport (Kenosha).[18]

The congressional appropriation, however, neither fully satisfied the citizens of those towns nor fully provided for the needed harbor facilities. Milwaukee's business community went from celebrating their appropriation to immediately wrangling with the army engineer, who was described as "not over friendly to Milwaukee," over how the funds should be spent. Even more heated clashes between the engineers and the citizenry took place at Kenosha. There were two rival settlements in the Kenosha area: Southport, at the mouth of Pike Creek, and Pike River. When Captain Cram's initial survey of Wisconsin's southeastern shore seemed to indicate that neither of the Kenosha locations was as favorable for a harbor as Racine, located ten miles to the north, the citizens of the rival Kenosha settlements banded together and accused Cram of having "conspired against the interests of both Pike River and Southport." Cram's report was condemned as unfair, "mischievous," and the result of the fact that he owned property in Racine. The unified front of the Kenosha property owners vanished in 1844 when a $12,500 appropriation was granted. Then both Kenosha-area communities tried to ingratiate themselves to the army engineers. When it appeared that Pike River was going to be chosen for the harbor, property values plummeted in Southport and the citizens, in dread of the future, stopped all improvements. Then, at the last moment, Southport was chosen for the harbor works and rival Pike River sank into obscurity.[19]

While funds for harbor improvements were long in coming and short on substance, the federal government did a better job establishing lighthouses on the shores of Lake Michigan. These navigational beacons were a critical element in the safety of mariners, particularly on the Great Lakes where most ships were guided by dead reckoning. The first lighthouses on the lake, at Chicago and St. Joseph, were both completed in 1832, and by 1840 there were eleven lighthouse on the lake. As ship traffic grew on the lake, so did the number of lighthouses, and by 1852 there were twenty-seven beacons on Lake Michigan, the most of any of the Great Lakes.[20]

Internal Improvements and Urban Rivalries

Although in retrospect Chicago's rise to its status as the greatest city on Lake Michigan seems the preordained result of its favorable position astride a continental divide separating the Great

Lakes from the Mississippi valley, politics played a large role in the city's emergence over rivals such as Milwaukee and Green Bay. Originally Chicago was in the Wisconsin Territory. It was only when Illinois was ready to enter the Union as a new state in 1818 that its boundary was pushed north, at the Wisconsin Territory's expense, to include the lower end of Lake Michigan. Congress went along with the land grab because Illinois, as a new state, had political clout, while Wisconsin, still a territory, was locked in a subservient status. The boundary shift made it possible for the entire length of a canal uniting the Great Lakes and Mississippi River basin to be in the state of Illinois. The building of that waterway, the Illinois and Michigan Canal, between 1836 and 1848 played a large role in Chicago's development as the lake's dominant port. By the time Michigan became a state in 1837 and Wisconsin in 1848, Chicago had already benefited from the state of Illinois's extensive internal improvement program, and its port had secured the bulk of harbor funds expended on Lake Michigan.

In the 1820s it seemed that Green Bay was more likely to emerge as the major port on Lake Michigan. It was the oldest permanent settlement on the west shore of Lake Michigan, and like Chicago, it had the benefit of a major federal military installation, Fort Howard, which attracted population and commerce to the area. Also like Chicago, Green Bay was positioned astride a natural link between the Great Lakes and Mississippi waterways. Only a short portage was required to follow the Fox and Wisconsin Rivers to the Mississippi valley. In 1822 Green Bay loaded lake schooners with lead from the Fever River mining district of western Wisconsin and Illinois. With no waterway connection to this fast-growing part of the frontier, Chicago benefited little from the mining boom, while the Fox River waterway gave Green Bay a thriving connection to the developing interior. Green Bay had another natural advantage: unlike all the other river-harbors on Lake Michigan, the mouth of the Fox River was deep enough for sailing ships to enter. When the Erie Canal opened in 1825 it was a shipment of Green Bay lumber, potash, and furs that constituted the first Lake Michigan cargo to reach New York City. Captain Samuel Ward's little schooner, *St. Clair,* made the entire journey—under sail from Green Bay to Buffalo, then relieved of her sails and rigging under tow to Albany, and then once more under sail down the Hudson River to the Empire City. Not surprisingly, one of the first sailing ships built on

Lake Michigan, the *Wisconsin,* was launched at Green Bay in 1832, three years before shipbuilding was inaugurated in Chicago.[21]

Business leaders in both Green Bay and Milwaukee understood the importance of enhancing their hinterland communications. In the summer of 1836, when the state of Illinois began building the Illinois and Michigan Canal, Green Bay's newspaper, the *Wisconsin Democrat,* agitated for the territorial legislature to take up the improvement of the Fox-Wisconsin waterway. But other communities derided the plan as the "Green Bay Hobby." The town of Milwaukee had its own rival scheme for encouraging commercial development. The "Milwaukee Hobby," as it was called, was to build a canal between that city and the Rock River. Torn between rival proposals and limited by the capabilities of a frontier territorial government, Wisconsin's leading lake ports could not match Chicago's transportation infrastructure.[22]

There was a measure of bootstrapping as well as boosterism in the development of Lake Michigan ports. Although they fought vigorously for federal aid, most towns never would have developed as ports without the civic will to fund some of the costs themselves. Chicago and Milwaukee frequently undertook independent harbor improvements. In 1854, sand accumulation at the mouth of the Chicago River all but blocked the harbor. Four ships sank trying to cross the bar, and seven lives were lost. Army engineers had neither the funds nor the authority to respond to the emergency. The Chicago Board of Trade petitioned Secretary of War Jefferson Davis to allow Chicago to borrow the army's steam dredge, with the promise to return it in good condition. When Davis refused, disgusted Chicagoans seized control of the machinery and cleared the bar themselves. In 1851 Congress approved $15,000 for work at Milwaukee, while the city raised an additional $50,000 to see that the work was done right. Racine went even further in its determination to build a maritime future and purchased its own steam dredge. Through taxes, the sale of town lands, and even private donations, this town of only six thousand, was able to spend $43,000 on harbor improvements between 1843 and 1851. Kenosha also went into debt to maintain its harbor, and in 1851 citizens voted a $10,000 tax levy. All along the lake, local merchants, unwilling to wait for federal action, invested in piers that would at least allow vessels to load and unload in fair weather.[23]

Schooners retained their niche in Lake Michigan commerce due, in part, to the improvised nature of most harbors and the great number of commercial piers reaching out from the sandy shores. Because of the inconsistent appropriations, Lake Michigan mariners during the period before the Civil War never had an assurance of the depth of any harbor. Schooners were the vessels that tied up most frequently at commercial piers. At places like Sheboygan, Port Washington, Two Rivers, and Manitowoc—all of which would eventually receive federal aid for genuine harbors—commercial piers were a temporary means to accommodate schooner traffic. Unlike harbors, however, the piers were not open to the use of all comers. Paid for by individual investors and run as a profit-making business, commercial piers often charged exorbitant use fees. The use of Sheboygan as a port by local farmers was discouraged by the high rates charged by owners of the town's two main commercial piers. At a time when the cost to transport wheat from Wisconsin to Buffalo by schooner was four cents per bushel, the piers levied a matching rate just to use their facilities. Commercial piers offered their customers use of warehouse facilities at the foot of the pier and the ability to drive heavy wagons alongside the waiting schooners. Piers were also built at locations that never had the potential to be developed as commercial harbors. Plumerville, Michigan, near Saugatuck, was one such place. Its pier was built by a joint stock company composed of the owners of a sawmill and a tannery located at the mouth of a creek. The two companies were the principal users of the pier, which was too weak to support horsecarts and barely extended out enough to allow scow schooners to dock. Such rickety piers were common. During the 1850s and 1860s there were five piers built for farmers to ship their cordwood to Chicago along the forty miles of shore between Saugatuck and South Haven.[24]

The Golden Stream:
The Lake Michigan Grain Trade

The schooners and steamers that brought settlers to the unimproved ports of Chicago, St. Joseph, Racine, and Milwaukee during the 1820s and 1830s planted the seeds from which sprang, in the early 1840s, the Lake Michigan grain trade. The days when schooners returned from Chicago with holds ballasted by sand ended when prairie farmers began to arrive in the city with wagons of surplus grain. The wagons trickled in during the 1830s. Between 1834 and 1841 Chicago's total grain export was only 13,756 bushels. Then, in the fall of 1841, something remarkable happened. Chicago was flooded with grain wagons: "Clouds of dust on every avenue by which the city can be approached," the *Chicago Daily American* reported, "and extending as far as the eye can reach, announce the advent of our industrious yeomanry with trains of wagons over flowing with grain and often fifteen or sixteen in number." Although the writer feared that "we absolutely have not vessels enough to carry it away," Chicago sent 40,000 bushels of grain east by schooner that year. By 1845 the city was sending more than a million bushels to Buffalo per year, which climbed to more than 2 million in 1847. Milwaukee attained the million-bushel threshold in 1853 and within a year doubled that number. The rush of golden grain had begun.[25]

The slow pace of harbor development left only two locations, Chicago and Milwaukee, prepared to compete for dominance in the grain trade. Green Bay, a destination for sailing ships on Lake Michigan since the time of La Salle, squandered its early prominence in lake shipping. With aggressive urban leadership, Green Bay might have easily eclipsed Milwaukee and challenged Chicago's preeminent position in the grain trade. Milwaukee outhustled Green Bay for harbor funds and in railroad development. It was not until 1866 that Green Bay received funds to improve its naturally attractive harbor, and by that time history had determined it would never be a major city. The prize Milwaukee won was dominance over Wisconsin's prodigious wheat harvests. As the demand for wheat accelerated worldwide in the 1850s, Wisconsin farmers increased the amount of improved land in the state by 260 percent. Wisconsin accounted for 15 percent of the total increase in American wheat production during the 1850s. Wheat made fortunes in Milwaukee. In 1846, Daniel Newell had to borrow $300 to get involved in the grain trade. Ten years later he owned a fleet of twenty grain ships. By 1862, Milwaukee even surpassed Chicago as the greatest wheat market in the world.[26]

Racine, Kenosha, and to a lesser extent Sheboygan also competed for the grain trade. Because they had to bootstrap their own harbor improvements, these cities were not fully prepared when the grain rush began. Grain brought to Racine in the early 1840s had to be carried out to the schooners in small boats known as lighters. The

In 1839 the mercantile firm of Newberry and Dole loaded 3,678 bushels of grain on the *Osceola*. Rigged as a brig, the *Osceola* has been given credit for shipping the first grain from Chicago. Actually, a small amount had been shipped a year before. Reprinted from Alfred T. Andreas, *History of Chicago* (Chicago: A. T. Andreas, 1884–86). Collection of the Chicago Maritime Society.

loading of the lighters and the reloading of the grain onto the schooners was backbreaking work. "There were large hoppers built on the docks opposite the warehouse with spouts in them, with a bag nailed over each spout," one former stevedore recalled. A boy standing on the dock held a bag on the spout, which when filled would be taken away onto the scow; a smart boy could 'hold spout' for at least eight men offbearing the grain." To load a single schooner, three lighters or scows would be used: one loading at the dock, one unloading on the schooner, and one moving to or from the schooner. Piers reaching out to deep water greatly simplified the process but could not compete with the giant grain elevators of Chicago and Milwaukee.[27]

Grain elevators saved on labor costs and could store corn and wheat for weeks or months. Even after Racine and Kenosha fully developed their ports they could not offer the flexibility of the Chicago elevators, which by 1857 had the capacity to store over 4 million bushels of grain. Grain elevators were essentially vertical warehouses that stored grain in bulk through the use of bins. Storage in bulk meant that elevator operators did not have to bother with laboriously loading and unloading sacks of grain, since the elevators could handle cargoes by mechanized means. The Illinois Central Railroad elevator in Chicago could unload twelve railroad cars and load two ships with 24,000 bushels in the course of one hour. Cities like Racine, Kenosha, Port Washington, and Sheboygan, which had earlier lost out in the quest for harbor aid, found that the economies of scale in the grain trade further strengthened the dominance of Chicago and Milwaukee.[28]

So prodigious, however, was the grain harvest of the Great Lakes region that substantial streams of the gold escaped the giant maws of Chicago and Milwaukee. Racine boasted a fleet of grain ships, and five or six ships from Racine would annually join the rush of Lake Michigan vessels vying for the honor of being the first to Buffalo. Between 1836 and 1914 it is estimated that more than three hundred ships were based in Racine. Kenosha and Sheboygan also competed for the grain trade. In 1858, Kenosha was Wisconsin's third most important grain port with the export of 238,817 bushels. Sheboygan did not receive its first harbor appropriation until 1852, yet within two years there were as many as fourteen sailing ships moored in the harbor at the same time.[29]

Schooners were the backbone of the grain fleet. In 1845 some 270 schooners were involved in the Chicago-to-Buffalo trade. The grain trade commanded the service of the largest and fastest schooners. The journey from the ports of southern Lake Michigan to the grain elevators of Buffalo was the long haul of Great Lakes commerce, nineteen hundred miles. On average, a fast schooner could make the trip in five to seven days, although bad weather or difficulty with negotiating a tow through Lake St. Clair could result in a voyage twice as long. In September 1880 the *Lake Forest,* a renowned clipper, made the trip from Ford River, Michigan, to Buffalo in three days. Perhaps the fastest passage for the wheat fleet was recorded by the bark *Canada,* which made the trip from Chicago to Buffalo in three days, eight hours in 1854. Rivalries between vessels developed over who would make the fastest passage, and owners or friends onshore often made wagers. The greatest interest was stirred by the first voyage of the season. By April 1 every vessel would be fitted out and ready to sail, held back only by fear that the Straits of Mackinac were still blocked by ice. "No one," Captain Timothy Kelley later recalled, "would permit another an advantage he could prevent." When one captain decided the time had come and slipped his mooring lines, the news shot through the port. "Away he would go out of Chicago to Buffalo and like a flock of pigeons the rest would be right after him." A drop in the temperature could leave icebound a fleet of fifty or more schooners, though, and Captain Kelley was once caught in the ice floes for twelve days because of a premature departure.[30]

In the fall of 1882 the Chicago marine community organized a race between four of the largest and fastest ships in the grain trade. The ships—the *Annie M. Peterson, Pensaukee, Porter,* and *Wells Burt*— were filled with corn and wheat and set sail on November 3. Brisk winds from the northeast slowed the ships' pace and made the race a real test of seamanship. The ships reached Mackinac in two days, by which time the *Annie M. Peterson* had a two-hour lead. In spite of southeasterlies blowing at thirty-six miles per hour that forced the ships to lie up for a time, the *Annie M. Peterson* held her lead all the way to Buffalo, which she reached on the morning of November 11. The *Wells Burt* finished last, although her owners had the consolation that she delivered the most grain, 53,000 bushels.[31]

When the grain trade began in the 1840s, ships were the only way to get the harvest to the eastern markets, but as early as the 1850s railroads became rivals for at least some of the golden harvest. To meet the challenge, mariners strove for greater efficiencies in order to offer rates that would be not only competitive with rail during the shipping season but also low enough to induce storage of the harvest during the winter, when the ships were laid up. Smaller crews and larger ships were part of this strategy. In the 1850s, big ships involved in the grain trade, like the *Monteith* and the *Helfenstein,* could bring over 11,000 bushels of wheat to Buffalo, while the ships of the 1860s, such as the *Chicago Board of Trade,* would bring about 28,000 bushels to the elevator. The launching of the *David Dows* in 1881 was the last step in this evolution toward larger and larger sailing ships for the grain trade. The *Dows* was built with a capacity of 150,000 bushels of grain, but she could carry only 119,000 bushels because most of the harbors were too shallow to allow her to pass fully loaded. The ship's poor sailing performance and competition from larger, more efficient

Several three-masted schooners tied up at a grain elevator adjacent to a Chicago River slip, ca. 1870. In a single hour a grain schooner could be loaded with 300,000 bushels of corn. Railroad tracks on the dock were used to bring trains of grain from the prairie to the elevator. Photograph by Gates, n.d. Negative no. ICHi 21601, Chicago Historical Society.

steam vessels meant that after the *Dows* few large schooners would be built for the grain trade.[32]

Grain was the most important product shipped from west to east on the Great Lakes. The length of the voyage from Lake Michigan to Buffalo and the large number of ships involved in the trade made it imperative for the schoonermen to find an appropriate cargo to carry on the homeward leg of their journey. With the rise of industrial production on Lake Michigan during the era of the Civil War, coal emerged as the preferred return cargo. It had the benefit of being a bulk cargo, like grain, readily available on Lake Erie, and in demand at Lake Michigan ports.

Wooden Hulls and Timber Cargoes: The Lake Michigan Lumber Trade

While grain had the distinction of being the most important product exported from Chicago, lumber was the most important product carried by ship to the city. More than even the grain trade, lumber was the backbone of Lake Michigan shipping. It was the trade that occupied the majority of Lake Michigan schooners in their heyday of the 1870s, and it was the product that allowed the ships to retain a niche in lake commerce into the twentieth century. The grain trade built Racine, Kenosha, and Sheboygan, as well as Chicago and Milwaukee—cities along the southern portion of the lake with access to the grain belt. The lumber trade was just as critical to Chicago, and it brought into existence another class of Lake Michigan ports—north of the fertile agricultural zone, on the fringe of a land of thin soils and giant trees. Cities such as Muskegon, Manistee, Ludington, Peshtigo, Marinette, Menominee, and Manistique were born in sawdust and nursed on the trade of Lake Michigan schooners.

The Lake Michigan lumber trade began in the mid-1830s. It is likely that the first lumber was shipped to Chicago in 1833, a schooner-load of whitewood from St. Joseph, Michigan. By 1835 the first cargo of white pine, the lightweight but durable wood that would become the backbone of the trade, arrived in Chicago. These and other early shipments came to Chicago because it was a growing lakeside town with a need for building materials. What made Chicago the great market, first on Lake Michigan and eventually in the entire world, was its fortunate geographic position. Bordering the lake and backing onto the vast tree-poor prairie, Chicago was poised on the border between supply and demand for lumber. Transportation improvements—particularly the

Illinois and Michigan Canal, which opened in 1848, and railroads, which began a year later—gave Chicago an unrivaled ability to move lumber economically to the west, south, or east. The booming grain market of the 1850s, which lured more and more farmers to the prairies, worked to stimulate Chicago's lumber trade as canal boats or railcars sent east to Chicago with wheat or corn returned with pine for houses, barns, and fences. Canals and railroads bound the farmers of the interior to the Chicago market the same way Lake Michigan schooners indentured the northern mill towns to the city. Chicago emerged by 1860 as both the world's greatest grain market and the world's greatest lumber market, since schooners exporting the grain and importing the lumber had also made Chicago the world's busiest port.[33]

While Chicago was able to use its lumber market to establish economic control over the vast hinterland of the western prairie, the trade

The schooner *Day Spring* docked at a lumberyard. Michigan Maritime Museum.

had a more problematic impact on the sawdust cities of Wisconsin and Michigan. The lumber business, particularly as it was structured in the nineteenth century, was a purely extractive industry. The logging and milling of old-growth forests could only produce a brief economic boom. The ties between the port and the hinterland created by the grain trade, unless broken by railroad competition, could be sustained over time, but the ties between the upriver pinelands and the sawmill ports were cut when the trees were removed. The logging frontier produced a much wider array of ports of call on Lake Michigan than any other industry, but like the white pine, these towns were rooted in thin soil.

Because the lumber industry was essentially extractive, there was a temporary, improvised atmosphere about those ports. Lumbermen generally tried to get by with minimal investments and improvements, even for something as crucial to profitability as a port from which to ship their product. The twin cities of Marinette, Wisconsin, and Menominee, Michigan, were the site of some of the largest and most profitable lumber operations on the entire Great Lakes, yet the lumber companies made no expenditures on harbor improvements. The timber barons endured the cost of lightering lumber out to schooners and hoisting it into their holds, even though it ran between ten and forty dollars per vessel. In stark contrast to Racine's bootstrap approach, they waited until one of their own was elected to Congress, secured a seat on the House Rivers and Harbors Committee, and dispatched the U.S. Army Corps of Engineers's dredge to the mouth of the Menominee River at public expense. This bottom-line thinking presaged the lumber companies' hasty abandonment of Marinette when its hinterland was cut over. Other lumbermen were a more dynamic element in the development of their communities. In 1860, Charles Mears, one of the most important lumbermen in western Michigan, was disgusted with the delays "heavy seas" caused to his shipping. Without so much as a by-your-leave from other settlers at the mouth of the Pere Marquette River, Mears set off with a group of shovel-toting mill hands and closed off the natural mouth of the river. He then ordered his men to dig a new channel strait through a narrow river bend, creating the current entrance to Ludington harbor. Before he retired to Chicago in his old age, Mears had funded the construction of five crude harbors on the Lake Michigan shore.[34]

Charles Hackley of Muskegon consciously tried to build a city as well as his lumber business. He had arrived on the west shore of

About 1892 a tug pulls a heavily loaded lumber schooner out of Charlevoix, Michigan. Michigan Maritime Museum.

Michigan in 1856 with only seven dollars in his pocket, money he had managed to save by working for his passage on the schooner that brought him. By noon that first day he found a job and the first wrung of the ladder. As a logger he earned a dollar a day, yet it introduced him to the industry in which he would eventually, on his best day, earn $365,000. Hackley, like other Muskegon lumbermen, saw to it that all the wealth of the forest did not flow directly to the Chicago market. As early as the 1870s he worked to establish in the city a diversified manufacturing base. Initially this meant experimenting with wood-related businesses such as furniture manufacturing, but later he supported the creation of chemical and metal fabrication plants in Muskegon. He also donated money for parks, libraries, schools, and a hospital. Charles Hackley and the lumbermen of Muskegon were proof that lumber could, when properly managed, be an effective foundation for building a lakefront city.[35]

Like many other owners of large lumber companies in Wisconsin and Michigan, Hackley operated his own fleet of lumber ships. The schooners of the Hackley fleet were among the finest vessels engaged in the lumber trade. One of these was the *Rouse Simmons,* a famous lumber schooner whose story is in many ways the story of all the numerous and durable Lake Michigan lumber schooners. Built in 1868 by the Milwaukee shipbuilding firm of Allan, McClelland and Company, the *Rouse Simmons* was a three-masted, 220-ton schooner, 127 feet long with a twenty-seven-foot beam and a hold eight feet deep. Her size and design were unexceptional, except for her double centerboard. Most schooners did just fine with one movable keel. Her first cargo was lumber, and that was what she carried for most of her career. The *Rouse Simmons* was a little too small for participating in the grain trade and took only one journey from Chicago to the head of Lake Erie, in October 1868. She could only handle a cargo of 14,000 bushels at a time when the leading members of the grain fleet could handle twice as much. The *Rouse Simmons* was what lake mariners called a "lumber hooker," a ship that engaged in repeated short-haul voyages, taking lumber from mill to market. Almost her entire career was spent on Lake Michigan. Over a thousand times she would enter Chicago harbor with a load of lumber, usually from the western Michigan towns of Muskegon or Manistee. Theodore Charrney, the most devoted student of the ship's storied career, estimated that during her lifetime spent serving the Chicago market the *Rouse Simmons* piled up a veritable mountain of lumber dockside, 200 million board feet.[36]

The focus of the *Rouse Simmons*'s career on Chicago was by no means an aberration. The city was arguably the busiest port in the world during the 1870s, and that was largely due to the lumber schooner. In 1872 over 12,000 vessels arrived at Chicago, and better than 9,000 of those came with cargoes of lumber. A total of 740 ships were based in Chicago that year, and a large majority of them were lumber schooners. Historian James Parton, who visited the city in 1867, was impressed by the scale of the city's lumber market. "Miles of timber yards extend along one of the forks of the river," he wrote. "The harbor is choked with arriving timber vessels; timber trains snort over the prairie in every direction." At the lakeshore Parton was greeted by an even more impressive sight, a horizon white with the canvas of arriving schooners. As he watched, "a favorable wind blew into port two hundred and eighteen vessels loaded with timber."[37]

After Chicago, the most frequently visited lumber port for schooners like the *Rouse Simmons* was Muskegon. At the mouth of

The schooner *Rouse Simmons* loads a cargo of bark, possibly off Beaver Island, ca. 1890. Note the raft stacked high with bark used as a lighter to bring the cargo from shore. Schooners' ability to service the unimproved harbors of the numerous and often temporary lumber towns along the shore of Lake Michigan allowed them to maintain their niche in the lumber trade long after they were replaced by steam vessels in the grain and iron trade. Ivan H. Walton Collection, Bentley Historical Library, University of Michigan.

Michigan's longest river, Muskegon was the destination for logs driven on spring freshets from as far away as three hundred miles in the interior. Lumber mills ringed Lake Muskegon, littering its shores with sawdust and clouding the horizon with billows of steam. Between 1850 and 1900 no Lake Michigan port exported more board feet. The town claimed 40 percent of all commerce on the lake's eastern shore, and the Chicago market devoured more than its fair share of this wealth. In 1879, one of the peak years for Muskegon's lumber boom, Chicago received 86 percent of all shipments. Green Bay was Muskegon's rival as the lake's leading lumber exporting port, yet as with the grain trade, Green Bay's relative success with lumber was cheapened by very real images of what it might have achieved. The failure to transform the Fox and Wisconsin Rivers into a usable commercial connection between Lake Michigan and the Mississippi River cost Green Bay its chance to dominate the lumber trade. As it was, Green Bay captured the considerable harvest of the Wolf River and was the leading shingle producer on the lake.[38]

While schooners like the *Rouse Simmons* made Chicago the world's greatest lumber market, they were also an important link be-

Lumber cargoes being loaded at South Haven, Michigan. Michigan Maritime Museum.

tween sawdust towns and the outside world. After unloading their cargoes of boards, schooners were often then loaded with the equipment and supplies needed to sustain the lumber operation. The harvest of the treeless prairie was forwarded from Chicago as cargoes of hay, bags of flour, sides of beef, and barrels of salt pork. In that sense the schooners were a lifeline for the often isolated settlements. In 1846 the schooner *Gallinipper* brought some of the first lumberjacks to Escanaba, a circumstance repeated at most lumber settlements. Facing a strike in 1867, Charles Mears wrote to his Chicago office, "All our Captains should endeavor to bring over as many good hands as they can." Schooners and steamers made the mill towns of Lake Michigan suburbs of Chicago.[39]

The *Rouse Simmons* was part of the elite Hackley fleet from 1873 until 1898. During a good season she would make between thirty and forty trips between Muskegon and Chicago, while during slack or depressed years she made only half as many voyages. The *Rouse Simmons* could transport in her hold between 180,000 and 210,000 feet of dimension lumber such as two-by-fours and planks as well as a deck cargo of lath or shingles. The tendency was to overload the schooners during the fair-sailing months of summer and then reduce the cargoes as the autumn storms descended on the lakes. By 1898, when Hackley sold the *Rouse Simmons,* Muskegon was beginning its transition away from the lumber industry as its hinterland was logged off. The ship, however, continued in the lumber trade. Her ports of call increasingly were along Michigan's Upper Peninsula—the last frontier of logging on Lake Michigan. During the peak of the logging boom, schooners would often be in constant motion during the season, stopping only for as long as it took to load or unload a ship. As the century drew to a close the *Rouse Simmons* often waited several days, even weeks, for a cargo. By the early twentieth century there were no more cargoes of pine lumber to be had, although the ship's diligent owners did find a way to reap a profit by hauling loads of cedar posts, telephone poles, or cordwood. As a tramp schooner, she frequented the most remote lumber settlements on the lake, towns like Garden, Thompson, Cedar River, Nahma, and Epoufette. Anywhere the cargoes were small and the waters shallow, the schooner still found a niche. The *Rouse Simmons* ended her days under the ownership of Herman Schuenemann, a veteran lumber skipper renowned as the preferred purveyor of Christmas trees to the city of Chicago.[40]

Like many other lumber schooners, the *Rouse Simmons* had her share of rough sailing during her forty-four-year career. Collisions with bridges, breakwaters, and other ships had all been endured, as well as waterspouts, white squalls, and gales. Storms had dismasted her, and once, in 1903, she actually sank while docked at a Torch Lake, Michigan, pier. The *Rouse Simmons* met her end on November 23, 1912. Laden with goodwill and Christmas trees, she succumbed to ice and heavy seas.[41]

Being lost on the lake with all hands like the *Rouse Simmons* was not the end most lumber schooners met, yet the twilight years of this ship reveal some hard truths about the lumber trade. A large, well-run company like Hackley-Hume could afford to keep its vessels in good trim, yet a large portion of the lumber fleet was made up of tramp schooners, owned and managed from behind the wheel by their captains. Even as late as 1907, more than half of the lumber transported by water was carried by small owner-operators. Ships no longer capable of serving as grain or ore carriers were sold cheap and put in the lumber traffic. The short hauls and buoyant cargoes of the lumber trade encouraged captains to overload vessels and delay long-term maintenance. Rather than have a ship dry-docked and caulked, lumber captains often tolerated a leak, since the crew could man the pumps during the one- or two-day voyage up the lake. A ship hauling grain could not afford a leaky hull, though, since water in the hold would ruin the cargo. In the 1860s and 1870s there were fine new ships tailor-built for the lumber trade, like the *Rouse Simmons* and the *C. H. Hackley,* but a portion of the fleet was always made up of ships too worn out for any other use. As the years went on, more and more of the lumber brought to the Chicago market came by rail. In 1860 only 3 percent of Chicago's lumber came by rail, but by 1897 rail shipments had climbed to 44 percent. By the turn of the century many of the remaining lumber companies in the Great Lakes region were experimenting with bypassing the Chicago middlemen and using the region's expanding rail network to market their lumber directly to merchants across the country. Hence the decline of the Chicago market went hand in hand with the decline of the Lake Michigan lumber trade. The result of these trends was a distinct unwillingness on the part of investors and owner-operators to sink money into schooners. As the lumber trade slowly declined in the 1890s, so too did the quality of sailing vessels engaged in the trade.[42]

After 1890, when money was invested in bottoms for the lumber trade it went to purchase propeller-powered steam barges. With their top masts cut off, the schooners were increasingly utilized as mere tow barges. Schooner barges were often regarded as expendable. In the interest of speed and profit, lumbermen would often arrange dangerously long tows, sometimes as much as a mile long, composed of six or seven schooners. If violent weather was encountered, the captain of a steam barge had orders to cut the schooners free. Ill-rigged and with reduced crews, the schooners were poorly positioned to survive, while the cargoes of schooner barges that ran aground or foundered could generally be easily salvaged. It was in such reduced circumstances that schooners served out their time in the Lake Michigan lumber fleet.[43]

Persion of
c. Lumber yard
manistique

The Chicago Lumber Company's lumberyard, Manistique, Michigan. Typical of the giant lumber companies that flourished on the shores of the lake in the 1880s, the Chicago Lumber Company owned 160,000 acres of pinelands, employed about fifteen hundred men, and operated three mills, nine logging camps, and a fleet of steam barges and schooners. The lumberyard was annually filled with 80 million board feet of lumber. Michigan Maritime Museum.

Conclusion

Grain and lumber were the two giants of Lake Michigan schooner traffic, but the commerce of the lake during the nineteenth century was widely regarded as the most diverse of all the Great Lakes. This diversity fostered the emergence of a wide range of ports along the lake. Iron ore, salt, fish, and fruit played an important role in sustaining local port-to-port traffic. Iron ore was a cargo that grew steadily in significance after the Civil War. Escanaba, Michigan, at the head of Green Bay, became the leading ore port on the lake. Beginning in 1864, Escanaba, which had been a fairly large lumber port, sent ore to Milwaukee, Chicago, and other nascent iron and steel centers. Schooners initially were the preferred means to move the ore, but the tediousness of loading and unloading iron ore and the need to clean the hold of the fine red dust made it an unpopular cargo with schooner sailors. Eventually, steel producers felt the same way about schooners, and the schooners' inability to adapt to automated unloading equipment drove them from the ore trade. Fish were an important commercial product at every Lake Michigan port during the age of sail, and initially schooners carried the bulk of the fish harvest to market. Coasting vessels would drop anchor off of the numerous small fishing stations, and kegs of salted fish would then be rowed out for loading. The dependence of sailing ships on favorable weather conditions made them less important when the market began to move toward fresh fish. During the last years of the nineteenth century, fruit became an important export for the southwestern Michigan ports of Grand Haven and St. Joseph. Package steamers, which also operated as excursion boats for tourists, captured much of this trade, although schooners were often used for the less perishable fruits such as apples and pears. "Lots of fruit moved by schooner in those days," recalled Frank Carland, who grew up at the mouth of the Chicago River.[44]

While most Lake Michigan schooners were based in Chicago or Milwaukee, almost every town along the shore had one or two sailing ships to call its own. Many of these ships were locally built. Yet even if the new vessel was merely a scow, its launching was an occasion for celebration and an affirmation of community progress. In July 1867 the first schooner built in Algoma, Wisconsin (then known as Ahnapee), a small town on the shore of Green Bay, was launched. A crowd of two hundred cheered as the scow schooner *Ahnapee* slid sideways into the Wolf River. Barrels of liquor and tables of food were laid out for a party on the vessel's new deck, and a fiddler led the townspeople in a celebratory dance long into the night. Three days later, on the Fourth of July, a second schooner, the *Irene,* was launched. The festive scene was repeated with even greater gusto, since this launching coincided with nation's benchmark of progress. Unlike the *Ahnapee,* which was financed and designed by Chicagoans, the *Irene* was purely the product of local interests. Her launching was, in the words of one local booster, a "declaration of independence" for the backwoods port.[45]

Schooners were an inexpensive, flexible means of transforming the blue-water frontier of Lake Michigan into a commercial waterway. Through schooner traffic, isolated lakeshore settlements developed into cities and Lake Michigan emerged as a economically integrated regional system.

Hans Simonsen on the ratlines of the lumber schooner *Lucia A. Simpson*. Note the work clothes, typical of a lake sailor in the early twentieth century. Courtesy of the Wisconsin Maritime Museum.

3

Before the Mast and at the Helm:
Captains and Crews on
Lake Michigan Schooners

While the two visitors were amiable and welcome, it was also clear that they were liars. Not that the sailors regard the obvious falsehoods as in any way malicious; rather, the two Great Lake mariners who had bummed aboard their ship for a friendly "jaw" were merely exercising their seaman's right to "spin yarns." For the crew of the *Petrel*, newly arrived in New York harbor, listening to such yarns was a pleasant way to meet some American sailors and pass a spring evening. The lakemen, as was usual for sailors' yarns, spoke of sensual pleasures, but did not mention tropical maids. They "told us what good things they had to eat on the lake vessels," recalled William Callaway, a young Bristol mariner. "They said they had ham and eggs for breakfast, two kinds of meat and pie or pudding for dinner, and hot biscuits and cake for supper. They also said that when they want a drink, all they had to do was to drop a bucket overboard and draw it up full of fresh, cold water." Callaway thought the men "were awful liars," but as with most good yarns, there was something intriguing about what they had said. The wormy food and stale water he had known sailing the world on British bottoms was uninspiring and monotonous. In 1857, a year after hearing those first stories about the

Great Lakes, Callaway shipped on his initial inland seas passage. To his delight, he discovered the men had been telling the truth. Callaway was a lake mariner for the rest of his life.[1]

As William Callaway discovered, sailing the Great Lakes, both for the men before the mast and the captains at the helm, was a unique maritime experience. Smaller crews and shorter voyages made for laxer discipline and better food than was to be found on the high seas. With over a thousand schooners on the Great Lakes, there were abundant opportunities for ordinary seamen to rise to officer rank. The flexible, dynamic frontier economy of the region offered vessel captains the opportunity to own their own ship. Saltwater sailors, immigrants, and new settlers from the East all signed on Great Lakes schooners. For some it was merely seasonal employment, while others cast their lot with the schooner trade and trusted the promise of Lake Michigan's blue frontier.

The Migration of the "Salts"

The first Great Lakes sailors were saltwater men. The pilot of the *Griffon,* a man named Luke who was described as a "malcontent," was the first saltwater man to misjudge the power of Lake Michigan. The Recollet missionary Louis Hennepin reports that Native Americans warned Luke to remain anchored in a sheltered bay because there was "a great storm in the middle of the lake." The pilot raised sail anyway, and the ship was last seen "tossing in an extraordinary manner, unable to resist the tempest." This first account of a Great Lakes shipwreck reveals a consistent theme in the maritime literature of the region: the unwillingness of saltwater sailors to truly respect the inland seas.[2]

Several of the skippers of the first United States vessels on the Great Lakes were also former saltwater men. The master of the schooner *Porcupine* in 1815 was a Lieutenant Packer, who had served under Oliver Hazard Perry on Lake Erie.[3] Jacob Varnum, the government factor at Chicago, described him as "a Virginian as well by overbearing hauteur as by birth and with all a perfect tyrant." As the little ship neared Mackinac, Packer gave a demonstration of the type of discipline which, while common on the oceans, would not be long tolerated on Great Lakes ships. He felt the helmsman was not doing a good job holding the ship on its course in the face of the contrary winds and currents of the straits. This "raised the ire of Packer against the helmsman. He ordered a fresh hand to the wheel and the former man to receive a dozen lashes. Scarcely a minute elapsed when she went to the opposite tack and then he made another change at the wheel and gave another dozen or so [and] on successively until every seaman on board took his turn at the wheel and received his quota of lashes." Packer was a military man on a military vessel, yet Varnum and the other passengers were shocked by his harsh discipline, which they found out of place on the lakes and "unworthy" of an American.[4]

During the frontier period, while the lakes' own maritime culture was taking root, the Great Lakes territories needed men with seagoing experience, even if all of the traditions of the sea, such as brutal punishment, were not appropriate. James Fenimore Cooper's novel *The Pathfinder*, which is set on Lake Ontario, contrasts the arrogant and potentially dangerous actions of a saltwater mariner with the intuitive talents of the young hero, born and raised on the shores of the inland sea. "Just as I expected," blustered the sailor upon seeing the lake for the first time. "A pond in dimensions, and a scuttlebutt in taste. . . . This bit of a pool looks like an ocean!" In *Moby Dick*, Herman Melville, who had personal experience with Lake Michigan, tried to put this prejudice to rest. Through the character of Steelkilt, a Great Lakes sailor, Melville had a chance to warn that the inland seas were "swept by Borean and dismasting blasts as direful as any that lash the salted wave; they know what shipwrecks are, for out of the sight of land, however inland, they have drowned full many a midnight ship with all its shrieking crew." A lakeman, Melville concluded, was "as much an audacious mariner as any."[5]

On Lake Michigan it was the saltwater men who had to make adjustments or risk becoming the object of scorn. Lakemen were particular about terminology. A trip from Chicago to Buffalo was not referred to, as a saltwater man might, as a voyage, but rather as a "run." Nor was time kept on a Great Lakes vessel as it would have been on an ocean ship, by "bells." A saltwater man had to learn to say that his watch ended at twelve o'clock, not eight bells. Nor did many lake skippers know or care to learn the mariner's method of calculating a vessel's speed in knots, since speed was calculated in terms that made sense to ships sailing near shore—in miles per hour. A saltwater man who was foolish enough to make fun of such landlocked language would quickly win the enmity of his mates. Captain Daniel Buie claimed that "a trip or two generally took the conceit out of them."[6]

John Kenlon, a saltwater master assigned to his first Lake Michigan ship, tried to disguise his unfamiliarity with the ways of the lakemen. "Unconsciously, however,I gave myself away by one of those small natural actions which a man will perform when somewhat off his guard," he later recalled. He was alarmed to find the vessel's water casks empty and asked the cook where she was getting the water to prepare the meals. She drew herself up "majestically" and eyed him over. Then, in a voice that could be heard by much of the crew, she exclaimed, "By the Heavens, fresh from salt water." Kenlon found it difficult to "keep my dignity under the circumstances, but I solemnly helped myself to a drink from the lake and after the first taste was pleasantly surprised to find the water cold and sweet." As Kenlon walked aft he "could literally 'feel' the silent laughter of the crew as they followed me with their eyes."

Kenlon's unfamiliarity with the freshwater conditions later almost led to the loss of the *Resumption,* the three-master placed in his charge. Ice formed on the masts and decks of the schooner. As the wind began to blow a gale, Kenlon ordered the fully set sails to be lowered, only to discover that they were frozen in place. The ice accumulation on the deck soon became severe enough to cause the vessel to list. While the captain fretted that the schooner would either capsize or lose her masts, the mate acquainted him with a " 'wrinkle' of Great Lakes seamanship." With not a moment to spare, the mate set the crew to spreading salt over the deck and working it into the blocks so that the sails could be lowered. The ice gradually broke away, and the vessel righted itself. While immensely relieved, the ocean mariner observed, "Of course, such tactics would have been of no avail except on fresh water."[7]

Not infrequently, lake sailors were prejudiced against saltwater men who advanced too rapidly on the inland seas. Leonard Withington Noyes was a twenty-two-year-old Newburyport Yankee who immigrated to the Lake Michigan frontier in 1841. After serving only a year before the mast, he proudly wrote home that he had been made a master. Back home, he complained that there was little opportunity for a young man without means. "Show me the Man in Newburryport that would give me a vessel to saile, they have Sones enough for all their vessels there." He admitted that the schooner was "a homley Craft" but quickly added that "I have the promise of a better one next Spring." Young Captain Noyes's rapid ascent, however, was not universally appreciated. He complained that "the Old Captains and Sailors on these Lakes" were "very jealous of me." Noyes's experience revealed the tension between the lakemen and the saltwater sailors:

> They think I am getting along too fast for a boy, and consiquently [sic] reported all sorts of Stories about me last season (such as he is no Sailor but a Sailmaker; Knows nothing of the Lake. nothing but a green Yankee Boy, and even Reported me Drunk to the Owners several times). . . . I weathered it out in spite of them. Made two more trips than aney vessel in the same trade and weathered out gales that some men lost in. I found one friend among them Capt. Peterson of the Sch St Joseph he is the finest man in Grand River fleet, and a sailor too more than I could say of maney of them, they all appear to be friendly this spring as they cannot bluff me off.

Noyes was secure in the owner's trust following a run to Chicago in July 1842. With more than twenty passengers aboard, including the owner and his wife, Noyes's vessel was beset by a gale. The young master worked the vessel out of harm's way and laid her up "under closereefd foresale" until the storm blew itself out, and then safely made Chicago with his relieved charges.[8]

Even after commerce was well established on Lake Michigan, there was a constant flow of saltwater sailors into the ranks of lake mariners. Timothy Kelley, who grew up in Manitowoc during the 1850s, looked up to the saltwater men for their skill and experience. "They made A1 seamen of the boys," he recalled, "and every branch of the sailor's craft was thoroughly ground into us not at all uncommonly with the aid of the traditional rope's end." Kelley particularly identified this group as likely to produce the vessel's "fo'c'sle lawyer whose talk, to his own satisfaction at least, showed a more intimate knowledge of sailor's rights that any admiralty lawyer could boast." Although Kelley believed that saltwater sailors made up a "large part of the crews of the big sailing boats," there is no direct evidence to either support or contradict that assertion. Historian Jay Martin has estimated, based on a statistical sample of biographies, that just under 14 percent of

81

vessel officers had saltwater experience. Certainly, as the nineteenth century reached its end and sailing ships declined, the need for an influx of saltwater seamen all but vanished.[9]

Who Were Lake Michigan Sailors?

During the peak years of Lake Michigan sail, the flow of saltwater mariners onto schooners was greatly augmented by emigration from Norway. Emigrants were Norway's leading export during the nineteenth century. A largely agrarian nation, yet with only 3 to 4 percent of its land tillable, Norway had a tradition of supplementing farming with fishing and trade. Many Norwegians, forced out of their own country by poverty, came to the Great Lakes with useful maritime skills. The first Norwegian to sign on a Lake Michigan ship was David Johnson of Chicago in 1834. Thousands followed Johnson onto the schooners. According to the 1870 census, Scandinavians (Norwegians, Swedes, and Danes) made up 12 percent of all Great Lakes seamen. On Lake Michigan the percentage was just under 25 percent, but because Norwegians were loath to work on steam vessels, their percentage of the schooner crews was likely much larger. One historian estimates that half of all schooner sailors on Lake Michigan were Norwegian. This figure, even if Swedes and Danes were included, would be too high. The Scandinavians likely made up at least a third of Lake Michigan schoonermen.[10]

Norwegians were a common immigrant group on Lake Michigan schooners, but they shared the forecastle with other newcomers. The Germans and the Irish were the two largest immigrant groups in antebellum America, and naturally they found their way onto the decks of Great Lakes sailing ships. The fact that Ireland was an island, with the entire country no more than a few days' journey to the sea, may have inclined the Irish to become more involved in sailing than the Germans. Perhaps more significant was the poverty of Irish immigrants, particularly during the decade following the Great Famine, 1845–55. Their desperate plight made the Irish willing applicants for any difficult, dirty, and dangerous job. As stevedores and canal diggers, they worked on the fringes of the schooner trade. Only for the Irish immigrant would the job of able seaman be a step up the social ladder. By 1860, 34 percent of sailors based in Chicago, on steamers and schooners alike, were Irish-born. While the Norwegians would replace them as the single largest group before the mast by the 1880s, the Irish remained a significant part of the population pool from which ship crews were drawn. Timothy Kelley, the famed Manitowoc mariner, was the son of famine immigrants. He took to the lakes after struggling in a parish school in which German was the official language. Germans represented only 3 percent of Chicago-based sailors in 1860, although this number climbed to better than 11 percent by 1900. Immigrants from the British Isles made up an important element as well, with better than 13 percent of Chicago sailors in 1860 and 15 percent in 1900.[11]

In 1844, when Mary Per Lee took passage on the schooner *St. Joseph* out of Chicago, she observed that "the sailors are all foreigners." The large percentage of immigrants on the lakes could sometimes result in tragedy. Orders barked out in an emergency could easily be misunderstood by crew members yet to perfect their command of English. Two young Germans died when a November gale drove their schooner against the Sleeping Bear Dunes. As the ship helplessly neared the sandy cliff, the captain ordered them to put on all of their clothing. They did not comprehend him and instead climbed into the rigging "only half-dressed." Before the storm eased enough for the crew to make its way ashore, the German lads were dead: "the cold took them."[12]

American-born sailors also were also present on Lake Michigan sailing ships, but they seldom represented more than a minority. A review of Chicago-based sailors in 1860 indicates that only 20 percent were born in the United States. These men generally hailed from the East Coast or the lower Great Lakes. "I am now a sailor," wrote Luke Sherwin, a Green Mountain farm boy, to his brother in 1818. Sherwin shipped aboard the schooner *Hercules* as a way to see the western lakes. But before the season ended the *Hercules* was wrecked and Sherwin's battered body was washed up on Lake Michigan's duned shore. Less typical was the Harvard graduate whom Isaac Stephenson met while sailing from Milwaukee to Escanaba. The man had caught the spell of the sea while on a whaling voyage after graduation and then gravitated to Lake Michigan, where he worked as a common seaman for sixteen dollars a month.

The crew of the logging schooner *Joses* at the Milwaukee Western dock. The three men on the left side of the picture wear the leather vests of "lumber-shovers." Historical Collections of the Great Lakes, Bowling Green State University.

In strong contrast to Scandinavian mariners, who preferred sailing ships, American-born lakemen were more likely to work on steam-powered ships. The American-born mariners may have been less prejudiced toward the new technology than men more deeply rooted in a maritime culture. During the antebellum period, lake ports like Oswego and Buffalo supplied sailors for Milwaukee and Chicago. By 1900, when the schooner era was nearly done, United States–born mariners constituted 51 percent of the Chicago sample. More than half of these men were Midwesterners. By the time steam finally eclipsed sail on the inland seas, a genuine maritime culture had been established in the communities around the lake.[13]

For all Great Lakes sailors, a berth on a schooner was only seasonal labor, since ice and winter storms closed Lake Michigan to shipping from the first of December to the end of April. Saltwater sailors, either from Europe or the East Coast, revealed how firmly they were tethered to the foam if they took that occasion to return to the sea. This annual winter migration of sailors from the lakes to the ocean, and their return in the spring, maintained a connection between these two divisions of the maritime world. "It was a delight," one young sailor recalled, "to be on watch with one or more of these 'old salts.' The yarns they spun of weird things in distant seas was a never ending delight to us. We knew the names and reputations of the New York–Liverpool clipper masters who were notorious for brutality to the seamen. We heard and believed (then) tales of wonderous things in the South and China seas."[14]

Sailors from the shores of Lake Michigan or the other lakes were likely to turn to seasonal labor within their home region. Logging was a popular source of winter employment, and pine logging was conducted almost exclusively during the winter. The foremen of lumber camps were just beginning their operations when the navigation season closed. Farmers fresh from their harvest and idled sawmill hands were more important sources of logging crews than sailors, but the beached schooner crews also found their way into the woods. "There are farmers, sailors, likewise mechanics, too, And all sorts of tradesmen, found in a lumber crew," according to the lyrics of "The Shanty-Boys Song," a traditional Michigan ballad. "Sailing a ship was not unlike blazing a way through the forest," contended Isaac Stephenson, because each required estimating distance and location without reliable maps or charts. In 1848 Stephenson tried to convince his mentor to let him pursue a sailor's rather than a logger's career, but a few weeks' work as a common sailor convinced him that "I had my fill of sailing, at least as an occupant of the forecastle." The *Milwaukee Sentinel* reported in 1877: "The close of this port [Kenosha] will necessarily throw many out of employment. But the great mass of mariners invariably go north to the woods, and work in the great timber fields." One of Manistee's early settlers followed the typical pattern. He sailed the lakes from 1844 to 1846. After the 1846 season he went to work as a lumberjack near Escanaba, Michigan. When spring came he hiked the Wisconsin shore to Milwaukee, where he signed on with the brig *Solomon Juneau*. When winter came he again "hired out" to work as a logger, this time near Manistee.[15]

Among the other trades sailors turned their hands to during the off season was shipbuilding. Crew members did maintenance on ships during voyages and had firsthand knowledge of what made vessels work well. Captains were regularly involved in fitting out newly constructed vessels. While work was generally available during the winter, there were sailors who simply chose to live off their summer earnings, which during good years could be more than adequate. In 1851 the crew of the schooner *Madeline*, after spending the season coasting the shore of northern Michigan for cargoes of fresh fish, repaired to an isolated anchorage at Old Mission Point, near Grand Traverse Bay. The remote location was purposely chosen. The captain and crew hired a seventeen-year-old secondary school graduate to teach them the rudiments of spelling, reading, writing, and arithmetic. Three of the crewmen were brothers, a fourth was a close friend, and the cook signed on to provide meals over the winter in return for free tuition. They all wanted to be educated but feared the ridicule of joining seven- and eight-year-olds in a traditional school. The hold of the ship was transformed into a school, kitchen, and sleeping quarters. The men's desire to learn paid off handsomely. According to the teacher, nearly all of them rose to positions of responsibility in business or maritime affairs.[16]

The diversity of men serving on Lake Michigan vessels mirrored that of the Lake Michigan basin. Swedish, Dutch, French, and even Hungarian could be heard in the forecastle. African Americans had been part of the maritime frontier of the Great Lakes since the era of the fur trade and therefore played a role in the history of the schooner. Jean-Baptiste Point DuSable, Chicago's first settler, was not the only man of color involved in the trade with Native Americans. During the schooner *Felicity*'s 1779 cruise of Lake Michigan, she encountered a group of "Negro" traders at the mouth of the Muskegon River. Blacks served on the crew of the *Porcupine*, one of the early U.S. Army schooners on the lakes. The vicious Captain Packer owned the ship's cook, Harry, as his personal slave, and once had him whipped because the meat for the captain's table was undercooked. The job of ship's cook was a niche for runaway slaves or men without families. The schooner *St. Mary*, lost with all hands in 1860, had a black cook. John Malvin, a freed slave, could find no work in Cleveland, since "my color was an obstacle," but eventually he managed "to obtain employment as a cook on the schooner *Aurora* that sailed . . . between Mackinac and Buffalo." Malvin went on to become the first African American vessel owner on the Great Lakes.[17]

Women on Lake Michigan Schooners

Women also served as cooks on sailing ships. Historian Theodore Charrney has estimated that as many as a quarter of the schooner cooks were women. In April 1883, as the masters of the vast grain fleet wintering at Chicago began to fit out their ships and fill out the crew, there was a run on female cooks. A good cook went a long way toward making for a happy, stable crew, and in the competition for good seamen, the majority of captains seemed to have decided that a female cook was an essential asset. After more than fifty vessels signed on women, the labor supply in Chicago was exhausted. Rather than hire male cooks, the masters advertised for women, preferably "country girls." This sudden increase in the number of women in the grain fleet drew the scrutiny of the press. The *Chicago Inter-Ocean,* locked in a circulation battle with the city's other dailies, put a salacious spin on the story, intimating that since the cook on most schooners was bunked in a stateroom off the cabin, near the captain and the mates, the women provided more than hot meals. This would cause dissention, the writer claimed, because "the mate wants to love the woman cook as well as the captain does, and there is often trouble between these commanding officers." One outraged captain tried to quash the "slander" by threatening the *Inter-Ocean*'s marine reporter: "I swear by all that's good and great that if he prints me, I'll kill him." The newspaper also drew a quick reaction from captains' wives, one of whom condemned the practice of allowing women on ships and contended that "if the wives would be a little more watchful, they might drive these women from the fleet themselves." Several vessel owners shared with the newspaper their orders to put the female cooks ashore. Little sympathy was expressed for the working women who lost their jobs.[18]

Saltwater men were sometimes shocked to find women aboard Great Lakes schooners. "To my astonishment," recalled Captain John Kenlon of the 1870s, "when I went on board, I found that they were shipping a women cook." The master turned to the mate and demanded, "what the h—— is that woman doing on board?" When the saltwater man tried to fire the woman, he was informed that the rest of the crew would quit in protest. Kenlon backed down and contented himself with closely observing how she conducted her duties. He was impressed that she "took her part with the rest of the crew." When two of the men dropped a bag of potatoes, Kenlon was amused to hear her give "vent to a string of profanity highly artistic." Nor was the reality of a competent ship's cook in keeping with the newspapers' insinuations of erotic encounters between women and a schooner's officers. Kenlon described his cook as "what I might term 'canal-boat built,' broad-shouldered, wide faced and had she been dressed as a man there would have been no question about her sex so far as appearance went. Her hair was short, and her hands red and sufficiently large enough to take care of herself in almost any emergency." When about her duties, it was not uncommon for her to chew tobacco, although when she spied that the captain had a box of quality cigars aboard she liberated a considerable number for her own use. The captain had no idea what happened to his "smokes" until the mate opened the door to "Mrs. Cook's cabin" and "showed me a line of 'butts' on her table." This incident aside, Captain Kenlon had to admit that "she certainly did her work well; the meals were hot, plentiful and clean," although "she had a rather brusque way of serving them with an air of finality, and he would be a bold man, indeed, even for a sailor, who would make a complaint or, like Oliver Twist, ask for more."[19]

Occasionally the newspapers of lake ports printed a story that revealed the danger and isolation of women operating in the male maritime world. In October 1875 men on board the *Fessenden,* a U.S. revenue cutter, heard a woman calling for help from the schooner *Harvest Home.* The cook, Jennie Simmons, was being beaten by the vessel's intoxicated master. Her appeal for help from the schooner's mates was met with laughter. The officers of the *Fessenden* intervened to take Simmons off the schooner, but they declined to take any action against the guilty captain. The suicide of Mary Gorman, the pretty young cook on the *Harvey Bissell* in 1882, also points to the dark side of women's lives in the schooner trade. Gorman was a widow who worked to support her child's room and board at a Detroit industrial school. Her death was hastily determined by a justice of the peace in Escanaba, Michigan, to have been self-inflicted, in spite of physical evidence that pointed to a struggle. In Kenosha that same year the female cook of the sailing packet *Maria* deserted her post after the vessel's captain became enamored with her. The master responded by going on a bender and then jumping his own ship to search for the cook in Chicago.[20]

Of course, such incidents were the exception to the much more mundane challenges most female cooks faced. By the light of one or two gimballed lamps in a cramped galley, the cook would be up before dawn to start the men's breakfast. A wood-fired, cast-iron stove with a rail around the top (to keep pots from slipping to the floor with every pitch of the ship) was the focus of much of the cook's waking life. When not cooking over its radiating hot surface or heating water to clean dishes, the cook was obliged to stoke the stove with firewood and clean out its ash-filled firebox. While the sailor's life was indentured to the sails—setting them, reefing them, taking them in, even mending the canvas—a female crew member was bound to the stove.

There is at least one case of a woman, disguised as a man, working as an able seaman. Frank Chambers of Chicago seemed like a regular tar. He smoked, chewed tobacco, and did his dangerous job aloft. But the deception ended where it began dockside on the Chicago River. The indigent skipper had noticed Chambers's belly swelling at an alarming rate and became suspicious. He had Chambers turned over to the police, who forced her into a dress. Brought before a judge, she was slapped with a fifty-dollar fine, perhaps for falsely signing her articles of employment. Unable to pay, the woman was thrown into Bridewell, the city's notorious jail. What drove her to become a sailor, whether simple poverty or a desire for adventure, is not known. After six weeks' confinement in Bridewell, "Frank" gave birth to a "fine healthy baby." In June 1878, Captain William Turner of the lumber barge *George Dunbar* discovered that the smooth-faced young man named Ben who had served as cook on the vessel was actually a woman. Although he admitted that she had been "performing successfully" in her position, Turner had "the ambitious female" immediately put ashore. While such incidents were not common, it is not unlikely that there always was a small complement of women secretly working on Great Lakes vessels.[21]

A crew member in foul-weather gear mans the helm of the *Lyman Davis* under the watchful gaze of the vessel's master, who is nattily attired in a vest and bowler hat. Ivan H. Walton Collection, Bentley Historical Society, University of Michigan.

Schooner captains and sometimes even mates would occasionally take their wives and children along for a trip. "This is the season of the year when the wives of vessel captains turn out in full force and take possession of cabins," the *Inter-Ocean* reported in July 1884. Children relished such visits, "tripping over deck loads of lumber seeking the best amusement they could find," while "the proud fathers carry their youngest and introduc[e] them to their friends." In 1872, when he first became a vessel master, Timothy Kelley took advantage of the good weather in June and brought his wife along for a run. Mary Ames, wife of the master of the schooner *Pride,* took a trip with her husband from Saugatuck to Chicago. With virtually no wind, the run took three days and she labeled the whole business a bore. Often the lake's unpredictable weather would cause seasickness or worse. In July 1891 the scow schooner *Silver Cloud* was lost near Sheboygan. A northeast gale raised rib-cracking heavy seas, and the old scow fast took on water. When the captain went down to the cabin to see to his wife and child, the swamped vessel suddenly capsized. Had they been on deck they might have scrambled into the rigging, as did the crew, and survive. As it was, the family perished in the cabin. A mother and three children trapped in the cabin of the schooner *Experiment* survived after the captain and crew were swept away to their deaths. An air pocket formed in the cabin, and for twenty-four hours the mother tried to keep hold of her children in the icy blackness. Her infant was at one point washed out of her arms. The other children were rescued when curiosity seekers rowed out to the upturned ship and, after hearing the mother's pounding on the planks, chopped a hole through the hull. While some masters, particularly those who owned their own ships, wanted to share with their families at least a part of their sailing life, most captains would have agreed with the marine reporter who argued that in a storm "a woman is only in the way, or worse, for she often unnerves the crew by her very presence and alarm." With only a few exceptions, the deck of a schooner was a male preserve.[22]

Life on a Lake Michigan Schooner

The romantic image of a life before the mast is quickly banished by the grim details of a sailor's everyday existence. "The sailor's home on board ship," recalled lakeman Nels Palmer, "was up in the forecastle, a dark and dirty hole, with bunks in the wings, like in lumber camps." On most schooners the forecastle was a small triangular room located below the deck, near the bow of the ship. Far from being a snug berth, the forecastle was often cold, wet, and smelly. "The air was so bad that a lamp would scarcely burn, and there was not a single room sufficiently tight to keep water out in a head sea or when it rained," claimed Thomas Murray, who sailed on schooners in the 1870s. "When heavy seas were encountered or it rained the men went to bed with their oil skins on to keep dry." Late-season voyages could be truly miserable in an unheated forecastle. "A stove was out of the ordinary, and in all my sailing I can state that I have never been shipmate with a stove," claimed Palmer. "In stormy weather you could hear the wind play Yankee Doodle and see the water coming through her seams." To complete the wretched picture, only seldom was a water closet provided for the crew. A slop bucket was placed in the forecastle for the men to expel their bowels.[23]

The size of the crew could vary widely. Timothy Kelley once shipped as the single crew member on the schooner *Two Brothers*. It was supposed to be a short trip from Chicago to South Haven, but the schooner encountered easterly breezes blowing a gale. Rather than trust his anchor to hold the ship off the Wisconsin shore, the captain stayed in the middle of the lake and worked his way north. Neither he nor Kelley got any sleep until they reached the lee of Plum Island near the Door Peninsula. In contrast, a large grain schooner would have a crew of six to eight, a cook, two mates, and the captain. Arthur B. Strough, a sailor on the lower lakes, contended that a square-rigged laker required a complement of eight "foremastmen," while a schooner needed only six. As Strough indicated, the key to the size of the crew was how a ship was rigged. The schooner *St. Mary* had a crew of five, a single mate, the captain, and a cook. A schooner with two masts could make do nicely with such a complement. The key was to have enough men to make sail and to stand watch.

The routine of shipboard life was divided into watches, each of four hours' duration. A mate and at least two seamen made up a watch. Seamen were kept busy with tasks all the while a ship was under way during the day, whether on watch or not. During the evening, unless an emergency arose, sailors were free to do as they pleased at the conclusion of their watch. Reading, talking, and—most popular of all—sleeping passed the time off duty. Sailors on night watch were likely to become drowsy, so a good mate varied their duties. On the *City of Grand Haven,* still under sail in 1925, men alternated between taking the helm, walking the deck, and standing lookout. This routine, one sailor recalled, "got pretty tiresome," but the frequent alteration in tasks kept boredom at bay.[24]

Making sail was a strenuous activity that required the cooperation and teamwork of the entire crew. "When making sail on the large vessels, two sailors get on top the jaw of the gaff and when almost up close would jump off the gaff, hang on the halliard going down," recalled Nels Palmer. "The weight of these men would help in the pulls, and [with] two [more sailors] on the junk barrel and the rest on deck, this gave every man a chance to pull. It was a real hard job to dress one of these old windjammers, carrying gaff topsails, main top mast staysail, raffee and some with a big squaresail. Then the fore, main, and mizzen sails and all jibs and staysails." One argument against having a female cook was her inability to help with this exhausting work, which male cooks were generally expected to do.[25]

Because activities such as hauling up the anchor and setting sail required the coordinated strength of the entire crew, they lent themselves to use of work songs, known as chanteys. Favorite songs for hauling up the anchor were "Shenandoah," "Leave Her Johnny," and "Homeward Bound." For raising sail the crew might sing "Haul Away Joe." A specified chanteyman led the crew in the singing. A popular short-haul chantey was "Reuben Ranzo":

Oh, poor old Roving Ranzo,
Hey, Ranzo, boys, a Ranzo!
Oh, poor old Roving Ranzo,
Ranzo, boys, a Ranzo!

The crew working the halyard would know that each time the name "Ranzo" was sung they were supposed to heave hard. Chanteys brought a spirit of teamwork to drudgery and provided an opportunity for humor and self-expression within a disciplined, task-oriented framework. A good chanteyman, a sailor later explained, "would give it to the old man sometimes and also to the mate—but they never let on." The chanteyman, like a military drill sergeant, set the cadence of work, and through his changes in the lyrics could cast jibes at individuals, as well as make a group of individuals come together as a crew. Wise captains knew the value of a good chanteyman and would pay him a bit extra to stay on the ship.[26]

The most dangerous part of a sailor's life was going aloft to tend the topsails or, where present, the square sail. A hundred feet above the deck of a pitching sailing ship, with only a couple of ropes for support, was where the mariner was separated from the landlubbers. In addition to the mainsails, topsails, and jibs, some captains deployed staysails, triangular sheets set from the stays (ropes that helped to hold the masts firmly in place). A poorly maintained ship could not make use of staysails because they would strain the rigging. Nels Palmer had a nightmarish experience with a staysail when he shipped out of Chicago on the *Ellen Williams*. To keep the schooner cracking-on

93

A typical lake schooner

The Great Lakes schooner was a distinctive adaptation to the requirements of the maritime frontier. The crudely improved harbors of the region and the short distance between ports account for the shallowness of the schooner's hull. Frequent trips with modest cargoes were the hallmark of the schooner trade. Note the drop centerboard that provided stability on the open lake, yet could be raised to allow access to to a frontier port. Unfortunately, the centerboard, housed in a watertight box, took up valuable cargo space.

A schooner was both a workplace and a home for its crew. The living quarters of the crew had to be sandwiched in between the specialized equipment needed to sail the three-master. The cross-section view illustrates the location of the crew's quarters, the forecastle, in the bow of the vessel; the cargo hold amidships; and the deckhouse and rudder mechanism in the stern.

The deckhouse held the quarters of the master, mate, and cook, as well as the galley. It was where all of the crew would take their meals.

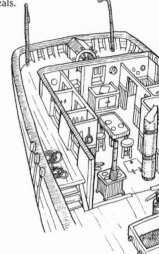

Ship's wheel. The steering mechanism was operated either by a rope and pulley or an iron worm gear.

Hand-operated bilge pump

The deck windlass served to help raise the sails and unload cargo. By the 1880s some schooners were equipped with a steam donkey engine to speed the work.

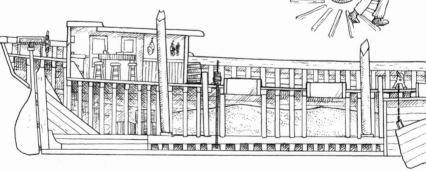

The forecastle or crew's quarters were located in the crowded, damp bow of the ship. A lucky crew would have the benefit of a small stove to ward off the cold on a spring or autumn run.

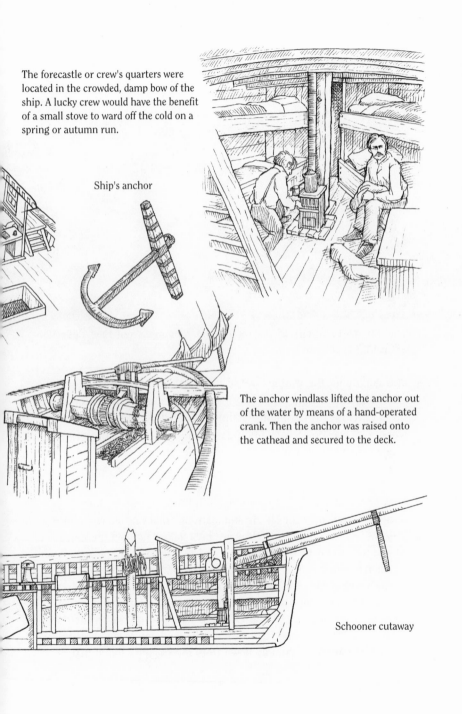

Ship's anchor

The anchor windlass lifted the anchor out of the water by means of a hand-operated crank. Then the anchor was raised onto the cathead and secured to the deck.

Schooner cutaway

The entrance to the forecastle of the *Lucia A. Simpson,* about 1908. Collection of the Chicago Maritime Society.

at a good clip, the captain would order set every inch of canvas she could stand. His "lucky sail" was a topmast staysail. "This sail was way up aloft, close to the moon," Palmer recalled. As the *Ellen Williams* worked its way down Lake Michigan, tacking against a contrary wind, a crew member had to go aloft and take in and reset the topmast staysail after each tack:

> We came about west of South Manitou Island. It was my turn to go aloft to shift over the sheets and a strong wind was blowing, but I went and out on the triangle stays. I got a good hold on the staysail and was about to throw the sail and her sheet over the top stay when a strong puff of wind lifted the sail up in the air like a balloon, me hanging on to the sheets, was lifted up in the air and off the stay I went. I was a long way from home dangling between heaven and earth. Here again the Good Lord was with me, the sail made one great sweep and came back very gentile [*sic*] and landed me close to the topmast . . . coming down from the rigging I found that my

Making sail on the *Lyman Davis*, 1913. Ivan H. Walton Collection, Bentley Historical Library, University of Michigan.

knees were shaking and shivering to let me known how close I had been to the Davy Jones Locker.

When Palmer discovered that several of his shipmates had had similar encounters setting the dangerous sail, they conspired to cut its line and let the wind shred it to pieces.[27]

Staysails were one of the ways good captains squeezed a little extra speed out of their vessels. Working in the "crosstrees," as the small platform between the lower masts and topmasts were called, was a risky business, particularly among the grain ships. Typical of the brief notices that regularly appeared in Chicago, Milwaukee, and Green Bay newspapers was the death of Wes Chambers in August 1860. As his ship *L. B. Crocker* left the mouth of the Chicago River, "Chambers was sent aloft to lose the main gaff top sail, when by some means he

97

The crew of the *City of Grand Haven*. Michigan Maritime Museum.

lost his footing and fell to the deck, killing him instantly. The schooner at once returned and brought back the body. Deceased was about 23 years of age, and belonging in Smith's Falls, Canada West [Ontario]." The most traumatic incident in Captain Timothy Kelley's nautical life came when his young nephew, Eddie Egan, fell to his death from the topmast of a ship under Kelley's command. Grief stricken, he blamed himself, as the man who ordered him aloft, for the boy's death.[28]

Death waited for sailors in open hatches, the crash of broken rigging, the sudden shift of a heavy deck cargo, or slowly, through ice and cold's erosion of strength and judgment, and of course, in hundreds of different variations on the theme of drowning. On April 28, 1860, the *Chicago Tribune* reported: "The schooner *Fred Bill* which cleared for Buffalo Tuesday evening with wheat, encountered very heavy weather, and ran back last night, having lost a man overboard, Emil Dietrichson, a resident of the Eighth Ward. He left a wife and child." Any sailor lost overboard during a early- or late-season voyage was a dead man owing to the frigid temperature of the lake water. A seaman lost overboard in a squall, regardless of the time of year, was also unlikely to survive, even if a good swimmer, because of the difficulty of maneuvering a ship to retrieve a crewman in a storm. In August 1860 two schooners collided in the middle of the lake during a sudden squall, the impact throwing two sailors from their ships. Although "boats were lowered and every exertion made to save them they sank before they could be reached." Many sailors drowned dockside, returning from a drunk or by being knocked overboard while loading cargo. Stephen Doyle, a twenty-five-year-old Chicago seaman, drowned in Traverse Bay as he readied the schooner *Grapeshot* for her first voyage of the season. He attempted to reach the schooner from shore over the ice when he broke through. Death nearly claimed Captain Kelley on a spring evening as he sat on the mizzen sheet, trying to gauge the vessel's speed, and not thinking about the wind, "when the sail filled away and threw me overboard at 11 P.M." Fortunately, as he hit the water Kelley was able to grab a chain on the rudder and hold on for dear life until he was pulled back on deck: "It was a very narrow escape from drowning for me, but thank God I am saved."[29]

The smell most lakemen associated with their days before the mast was that of tar. "Many an hour and many a day have I spent midst our shipping," a Milwaukee mariner recalled, "and the aroma from pitch

Sailing a schooner

The schooner rig dominated Great Lakes sailing ships because it was well suited to inshore waters. The fore-and-aft sails of a schooner allowed it to sail closer to the wind than a square-rigged ship. The dominant winds on Lake Michigan were the southwest breeze and the northeast breeze. When the wind was in their favor, schooner sailors had an easy journey. Yet, if a schooner entered the lake bound for Milwaukee and it encountered winds from the southwest, the sailors were in for a long, hard day tacking against the breeze. Topsails, which had to be trimmed and reset on each tack, constituted three-quarters of the work of sailing a schooner. How well they managed this difficult, dangerous task was the measure of both master and crew.

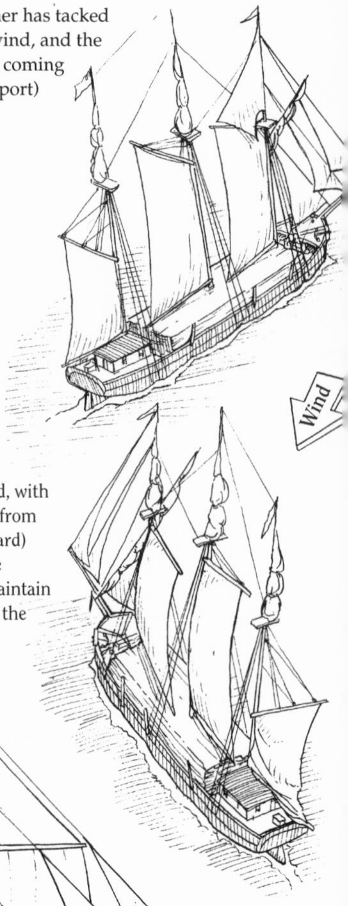

ii) The schooner has tacked through the wind, and the breeze is now coming from the left (port) tack.

Wind

i) Sailing upwind, with a breeze coming from the right (starboard) tack, the sails are trimmed in to maintain an angle close to the wind.

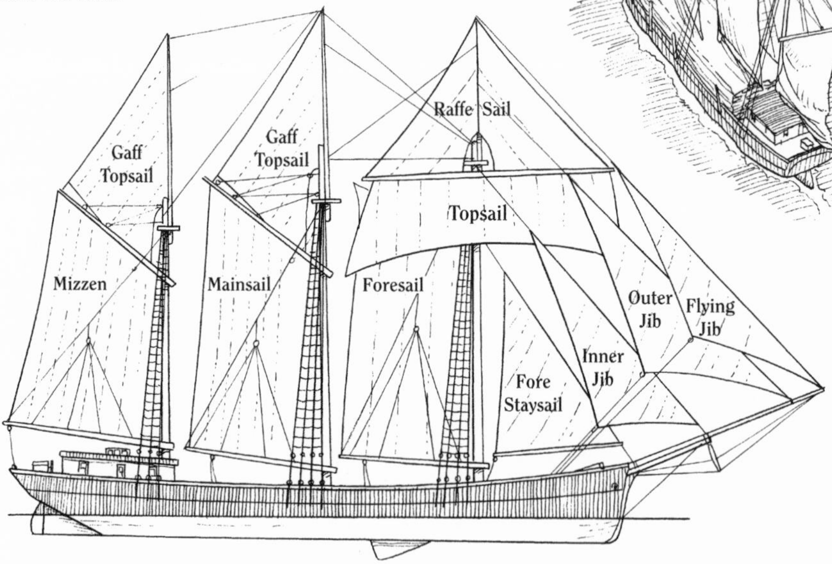

Gaff Topsail

Gaff Topsail

Raffe Sail

Topsail

Mizzen

Mainsail

Foresail

Outer Jib

Flying Jib

Inner Jib

Fore Staysail

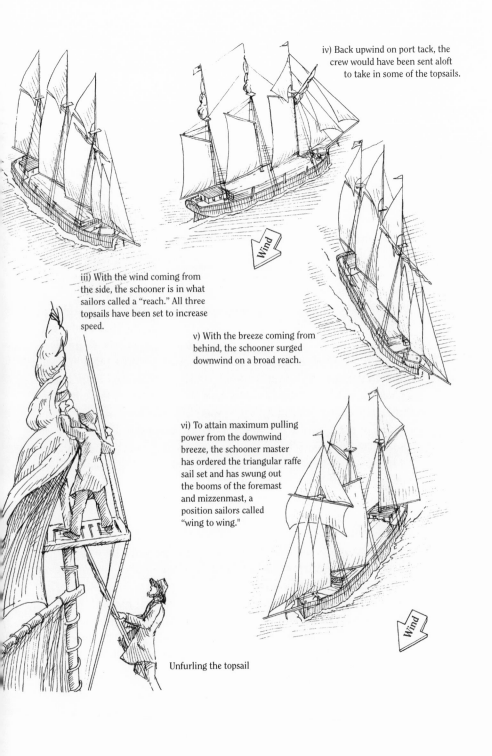

iv) Back upwind on port tack, the crew would have been sent aloft to take in some of the topsails.

iii) With the wind coming from the side, the schooner is in what sailors called a "reach." All three topsails have been set to increase speed.

v) With the breeze coming from behind, the schooner surged downwind on a broad reach.

vi) To attain maximum pulling power from the downwind breeze, the schooner master has ordered the triangular raffe sail set and has swung out the booms of the foremast and mizzenmast, a position sailors called "wing to wing."

Wind

Wind

Unfurling the topsail

and tar is as sweet smelling today as in days of youth." Tar was used in a variety of concoctions to help seal the seams of the hull and deck and to preserve the masts and bulwarks. In 1878 the captain of the schooner *Wells Burt* mixed up "a composition of tar, benzene, oakum, and other material" to caulk the deck of his ship. The presence of a toxic hydrocarbon like benzene on the ship indicates another, hidden danger to sailors, even when they were doing simple maintenance. During the 1870s it was possible for ships to obtain all the coal tar they wanted from municipal gasworks in large towns such as Milwaukee or Chicago. Tar was used so extensively in vessel upkeep that it sometimes looked as if the schooners were glued together by the stuff.[30]

While danger was part of the sailor's life, most of his time was spent in tedious drudgery. Scraping, painting, and polishing were the day-in, day-out duties of an able seaman. Indeed, it was the mindless repetition of these tasks that likely made men embrace the danger and thrill of fighting a gale or working aloft. So good were officers at keeping the crew busy that few Great Lakes vessels did not look neater and cleaner after a trip than before. While most of the busywork involved scraping, washing, and painting, good mariners learned how to conduct even more serious repairs while under way. On the *City of Grand Haven* the mate showed the crew how to plug leaks in the old ship's hull while under full sail. Old rope was chopped into small pieces and placed in a bushel basket, and the basket was then pushed by long poles over the leaky planks. The inrushing water sucked the fragments of hemp out of the basket and into the seam, caulking it temporarily. Among the other ordinary tasks that consumed a sailor's day were patching sails, helping the cook peel potatoes, and oiling the windlass.[31]

Discipline on Great Lakes ships bore little resemblance to what took place on oceangoing ships. Ordering a seaman who was slow or sloppy with his duties to be lashed was neither an option nor a necessity for the captains of Lake Michigan schooners. A problem sailor could be discharged within a matter of days, sometimes within hours. The small size of the ships and crews on the Great Lakes bred a much greater degree of familiarity between officers and crew. This generally worked to smooth relations between the ranks, but it also meant that sometimes an officer had to be prepared to enforce his will with his fists. Isaac Stephenson, a sometime schooner captain, enforced discipline among his lumberjacks with "a strong arm and a heavy fist." While there are documented cases of vessel masters doing the same, such as in 1885, when the captain of the *H. P. Murray* settled a labor dispute with his crew with his fists, it was not generally necessary. Timothy Kelley remembered mates and experienced seamen employing "the traditional rope's end" on boys slow to learn their job. Most Great Lakes officers seem to have tried to avoid physical punishment yet insisted upon a sailor's obedience and respect. Seaman Duncan McLeod recalled that his skippers invariably were referred to as "Sir" and the mate as "Mr."[32]

The most persistent cause of problems between officers and crew on Great Lakes vessels was the abuse of alcohol. Heavy drinking was part of the culture of Great Lakes sailors. Like construction workers and lumberjacks, sailors lived in a male subculture that valued physical prowess aboard and conviviality when in port. The popular Great Lakes ballad "The Cruise of the *Bigler*" concludes with sailors celebrating in a typical manner:

Now the *Bigler* she's arrived at Buffalo port at last,
And under Reed's elevator the *Bigler* she's made fast,
And in some lager-beer saloon we'll take a social glass,
We'll all be jolly shipmates, and we'll let the bottle pass.

Drinking was hard for a sailor to avoid, since saloons were an integral part of the shore-based marine establishment. It was at a saloon that a sailor new to a port could locate a boardinghouse or leave messages for friends. Saloons served "free" bar meals for drinkers, and most important of all, they were the best location for landing a berth on an outgoing ship. "The sailors had two headquarters those days," recalled one Chicago schoonerman, "one was the saloon at the South Water Market dock, operated by a large and powerful Norwegian, [and] the other was the sailors' Union Hall. The saloon at South Water Market was a real home for the sailors, and you could obtain a berth on some vessel in need of a sailor or two."[33]

Crews raised in a saloon were often a challenge to the captain, as the test of wills that took place on the *Ellen Williams* indicates. Nels Palmer was one of a group of six sailors hired out of a Chicago dive. "Some of the old-time sailors noticed that the captain was very anxious to get a crew and they took advantage by making the captain buy the drinks." When he finally convinced them to head for the *Ellen Williams,* they insisted that he get a wagon in which they could ride. "We all piled on the dray and started to sing some of the old-time sailor songs." Even though Captain Alver Swanson waited until the next afternoon to leave port, many of the men were still roaring drunk. In trying to raise the mainsail, several of the inebriates hauled on a line when they should have stopped and fell in a tumble on the cook, who was lending a hand. The cook was injured seriously enough that it was necessary to have the ship towed back into the Chicago River so he could be sent to the Marine Hospital. Needless to say, this made Captain Swanson "real sore" and he "promised he was going to sober the boys up." All the way down Lake Michigan he drove the men hard, demanding that every possible piece of canvas be set. Palmer and another crew member retaliated by cutting a line on one of the topsails. "We waited as long as we could to give the wind a good chance to do a good job ripping up the sail." The skipper suspected what had happened, and after dressing down Palmer and his accomplice he ordered them to spend their time off watch mending every rent in the canvas. By the time the *Ellen Williams* reached Manistique, "the whole bunch of us were sore to the core, and we were all going to jump ship." But here the magic of drink worked to Swanson's advantage. After helping to load the ship with lumber, the crew repaired to a saloon. Several other crews were also in port, and the men "met many of our old-time sailing pals and friends." After a "few cans of beer" the men "forgot all about their sorrows and troubles." Not only did none of the men quit, but Palmer decided "I admired the captain, he sure knew how to handle men and also knew how to get the best off his men."[34]

The experience of the *Ellen Williams* reveals the latitude sailors had within the disciplined framework of shipboard life. Rather than openly defying an officer, disgruntled sailors could resort to sabotage or simply a work slowdown to vent their anger. On the other hand, sailors took pride in their skills as seamen, and by extension in the sailing qualities of their ship and the skill of the captain. Although a hard-driving captain might be a source of complaint among the crew during a run, he would be something to boast about in a saloon afterward.

For most of the schooner era on Lake Michigan, the relationship between officers and crew was structured by federally mandated "Articles of Agreement." Articles were a written contract between the vessel master and a seaman that specified how much the man was to be paid, where the ship was going, and what the sailor's duties were. They generally listed certain prohibited activities as well, such as fighting, drinking, and sleeping on watch. A master could purchase books of blank articles, so that all he had to enter was the date, wage, and destination. Then the sailor had only to sign his name or make his mark. Articles were a legal contract and could be enforced by police action. In October 1860, Martin Busher, master of the schooner *Rapid,* had five of his crew tracked down and arrested for deserting the ship. After the men were behind bars, Busher had no trouble convincing them to return to the ship. Earlier that year, in Chicago, the master of the brig *Walbridge* had the city police arrest seaman James Gerot "for refusing to do his duty in violation of the articles which he had signed." In spite of the law, however, the use of articles was by no means universal on Great Lakes ships, as evidenced by the Milwaukee Board of Trade's 1856 issuance of a special resolution condemning masters who did not require articles.[35]

The failure of many Lake Michigan captains to make use of Articles of Agreement reflects the fluidity of the labor situation during the schooner era. Some ships seem to have gathered a new crew for every run. "Plenty of sailors and plenty of ships in those days," one sailor recalled. If a sailor who had not signed articles wanted a few days off or wished to go on another ship, he would simply grab his seabag and leave as soon as he got to port. Captains arriving at busy ports also liked having the freedom to discharge the bulk of the crew. Lumber ships entering the Chicago River frequently had to wait for dock space at the Lumber Market, and rather than keep the whole crew under pay for two or three idle days, a master would better serve the owners by discharging the men and then hiring a new crew for the return run. Nor did sailors seem to mind this tactic, since they preferred to hit the bars or find another ship rather than mope about a ship in port. Yet this rapid turnover must have hurt the efficiency of a crew's performance in a crisis and placed a tiresome responsibility on the master of a ship ready to leave port. In July 1881, Captain Timothy Kelley was ready to be towed out of the Chicago harbor when he discovered that his cook had jumped ship. He made fast his schooner, the *Lottie Wolf,* near the Lake Street bridge and went ashore to hunt up a cook. When he came back the entire crew had deserted (perhaps they were thirsty). Leaving the new cook, Kelley set off in search of a crew. Failing to find a single man, he returned to the *Lottie Wolf,* only to find that the new cook had also jumped ship![36]

Cooks were generally among the more steady members of a ship's crew. A ship between cargoes still needed a cook, and besides, a good cook was such a boost to morale that a smart captain would try to keep him or her aboard. As a rule, the food aboard schooners was good. "The fare or living provided by the cook under the captain's orders, was in most instances of good quality," recalled Arthur Strough. "Most captains provided liberally for the living of their crews and the men generally lived better than when at home." At the start of the season, ships put up stores of dried fruit, cured or salted meats, and bags of flour, coffee, and sugar. They also made occasional purchases of fresh meats, vegetables, and stove wood at ports along the way. "Salt Pork and Lob-Scow was the main menu," Nels Palmer recalled. "Lob-Scow was sailor's dish, you could call it stew or hash. This was the leftovers with everything put in one pot and warmed for supper."[37]

A conscientious cook had one of the most demanding jobs on the ship. All meals had to be prepared from scratch on a small wood-burning stove on a vessel that was usually in motion. Although the stoves in most schooner galleys were equipped with a short railing to prevent cooking food from sliding off, the cook needed experience to know how much liquid each pot could hold before it would "slop over." Another trick of the trade was to soak the tablecloth before setting the table for dinner, since plates would not slide off the wet fabric. In addition to breakfast, dinner, and supper, the cook was expected to provide sandwiches for the men coming off their night watches. One former sailor remembered "bread and seaman's salt horse" and cups of black coffee when fresh off duty. Sometimes schooners—particularly those captained by Swedes or Norwegians—seemed to float on a sea of black coffee. The day started with a large pot of strong black brew, and a pot was always ready at any time during the remainder of the day. Before the cook went to bed at night, his last job was to put a fresh pot at the ready for the night watches. A candle placed under the pot kept the coffee warm without risking a night fire in the stove. "The schoonermen did not know what milk and cream looked like," recalled Nels Palmer. "Black coffee, and I have been on some of them that never cleaned out the coffee pot from spring to fall."[38]

All meals were taken aft in the galley. The captain presided at the table, or if he was on deck, the mate. "In the galley the captain sat at the head of the table," remembered one sailor. "The mate was next at his right and the boy in the crew was at the lower end of the table." If a certain formality prevailed on some vessels regarding seating at the table, the very fact that the officers and men ate at the same table was a significant departure from the custom of ocean vessels and perhaps provides the reason why the crews ate better on the Great Lakes. "You have only to go below into the cabin and listen to the conversation which passes around the table," a journalist observed in 1884, "to hear the sailor and the master discuss abstruse questions of politics and religion, science or social life, and the interjected comments of the remainder of the company, to know you are in the midst of a good-tempered family. Social distinctions, there are none at the table, but the meal over and the routine business of the vessel resumed, all is changed. The Captain is again the autocrat for six hours, the lapse of time between meals." Some captains would send the cook to take the helm so that all the officers could share in a meal together.[39]

The pay of a schooner sailor during the peak years of the 1870s and 1880s was about $1.25 per day. Considering that the wage included room and board, it was good pay, and more than a man could make at any other wage labor job, save perhaps as a teamster. Lumberjacks, working at an even more dangerous job, were paid considerably less, between twenty and thirty dollars a month. When the sailor's job became more dangerous during the late-season runs, from September to December, wages were substantially increased, and it was not unusual for an able seaman to earn $2.50 a day. However, the going wage for sailors fluctuated according to the demand for grain or lumber as well as the availability of seamen. There was a built-in elasticity in the supply of Lake Michigan sailors. Saltwater men moved freely back and forth from the lakes to the ocean depending on the wages and personal whim. Sailors resident in the Great Lakes region had ample opportunities for shore work when they did not want to go before the mast. William Callaway, who gave up a career in the British Merchant Marine for a life on lake schooners, also worked for long stints in a wholesale fruit store. Other sailors were experienced at carpentry through work in shipbuilding and fitting. High wages could expand the pool of available experienced seamen on the lakes. This elasticity in the workforce probably depressed the growth in wage rates for Lake Michigan sailors.[40]

Sailors on Strike

Both vessel owners and sailors sought collective action as a means to control wages. What ensued was a sort of tug-of-war that extended through the shipping season. Early in April, masters and vessel owners in major ports like Chicago and Milwaukee would meet and try to establish uniform rates. Sailors, anxious for work at the start of the season, would accept the usually modest wages offered. In 1860, for example, masters of grain vessels from Buffalo, Cleveland, Oswego, Detroit, and Chicago met in the latter city and resolved to pay seamen twenty-five dollars per month. To enforce this agreement, they also resolved that all hiring of sailors would be done through the port shipping office. These nonbinding terms would be challenged during the course of the season. A rise in the price of wheat would encourage a captain anxious to get under way as soon as possible to offer a higher wage and to seek his crew at a waterfront saloon, not at the shipping office. Nor were masters the only ones paying attention to the freight rates. Savvy seamen responded to a jump in rates with a demand for higher wages. The dockside was the scene of numerous ad hoc negotiations and calculations based on the latest news. Nor were disputes always settled peacefully. In 1874, with a national depression slowing shipping to a trickle, a Lake Michigan–bound schooner, the *Annie Vaught,* was stopped at a Buffalo wharf by a gang of fifty sailors who had heard that the captain had signed on his crew for $1.25 per day. The men contended that $1.50 had been the going rate in the port and would not allow a lower wage. A "parley" ensued, after which the master of the *Annie Vaught* raised the pay of his crew and was allowed to make sail. Wildcat strikes, set in motion by mobs of sailors surging over the docks and stripping ships of their crews, were common in the 1860s and 1870s. The master of a schooner at a Cleveland wharf in 1874 defended at gunpoint his ship and loyal crew from a mob of wildcatters.[41]

The most successful of the early attempts of sailors to organize was the Seamen's Mutual Benevolent Society, formed in Chicago in September 1860. Initially the society's orientation was similar to that of many other antebellum social welfare organizations. While sailors were behind the creation of the society, it was headed by a board "composed of some of the best men of the city." Its purpose was not higher wages but the "moral, mental and mutual improvement of the members." To that end, monthly meetings were held at which a hundred or more sailors heard sermons from local ministers. The society opened a reading room at Clark and Lake Streets which was kept open at all hours for sailors between ships to have a place of resort more wholesome than the saloons of South Water Street. Through dues and solicitations, the society also began a fund for the care of sailors' widows and orphans.[42]

The Seamen's Mutual Benevolent Society existed as a philanthropic organization until the tumultuous strikes of 1877, which raised the class consciousness of workers all across the United States. Beginning as a railroad job action in West Virginia, the Great Strike gradually spread across the country. In Chicago it involved not only railroad workers but a broad alliance of wage laborers. For three days—July 24, 25, and 26—the city was all but shut down by throngs of workers closing the streets and battling the police. Although dockworkers played a leading role in the unrest, sailors did not. Sailors considered themselves skilled workers, and issues such as the eight-hour day had little relevance to them. Yet the Great Strike of 1877 did give impetus to the creation of effective worker organizations. The Knights of Labor, the most important union in the nineteenth century, was born in Chicago. Longshoremen were among the first to organize to set wages and hours. Inspired by the success of the longshoremen, the sailors of Chicago reorganized their self-help society as the Chicago Seamen's Benevolent Union, with the new objective of aiding its members' "mental, moral and financial improvement."[43]

By 1878, when the economy climbed out of depression, the demand for shipping was high. Vessels taken out of service in 1876 or 1877 were pressed into the grain or lumber fleets. The Chicago Seamen's Benevolent Union, which had organized the majority of the more than one thousand mariners based in the city, found itself in a position to dictate wage rates to vessel owners. Branches of the union were formed in Buffalo, Cleveland, Milwaukee, and other major lake ports. Unfortunately, instead of working toward a trade agreement that

109

would set a seasonal standard for the entire industry, the union tried to manage a floating rate that reflected rising freight rates. Union sailors were forbidden from signing articles for a round trip to any other union port, since the union chapter in each port constantly adjusted the standard wage. So a sailor might make a run from Chicago to Buffalo for $1.75 and find that the union members in Buffalo had gathered and voted a 25-cent raise. As a result, he would work the trip back to Chicago for $2.00 per day. The trouble was, members were quicker to vote rate increases when demand for freight was high than they were to cut wages when shipping rates fell. This resulted in numerous dockside disputes and left vessel captains irritated by their suddenly idled ships.[44]

Between 1878 and 1880, when the union was strong, non-union sailors were all but forced off of the lakes. Union men were forbidden from serving on ships that employed "scabs." The union's growing power was checked first in Cleveland in 1881 when an owners association, headed by an experienced strikebreaker, defeated the union's attempt to set wages. The sailors union remained stronger on Lake Michigan, where it was joined to the Knights of Labor from 1886 to 1891. But the sailors made a critical error when they decided to limit their membership to men who worked on sailing ships. To sailing men, steamboaters were deckhands or coal shovelers; since they knew nothing about working aloft in the crosstrees, they could not be counted as real mariners. To underscore that point they coined the phrase "Wooden boats, iron men; iron boats, wooden men." Fortunately for the union, the vessel owners were also divided. Some tried to follow the tactics of Cleveland, such as recruiting non-union crews on the Atlantic coast. Others, particularly the large steamship companies who did not see the union as a major threat, organized the Lake Carriers Association and went after government aid to navigation. The tide began to turn in favor of the vessel owners in 1892 when the Lake Carriers Association was reorganized to appeal to all vessel owners, from the master who owned his own schooner to the capitalist with a fleet of steamships. When hard times hit again in 1893, the owners were united and organized, while the sailors were divided between steamboat and sailing men. Desperate for work, sailors found themselves with little leverage. Able seaman who in 1893 were making between thirty and thirty-seven dollars per month found their pay reduced by one-third. "There was poor times among the sailors in every seaport," Captain Soren Kristiansen noted in his diary, "and the money made and spent during days gone by would have been of important benefit to a multitude of idle sailors." The lower rates held until nearly the end of the century.[45]

Schooner Captains

When the Seaman's Mutual Benevolent Society was organized in Chicago in 1860, vessel masters played a leading role. The gulf between captain and crew on Great Lakes ships was fairly narrow during the schooner era. Most masters had themselves been sailors, and many sailors aspired to become a mate or captain. Certainly it was a long, slow process: perhaps after "five or six years . . . if he has kept his record clean and shown the requisite ability," a sailor would be appointed mate. Generally it took twenty years of hard work and good judgment to earn the title "Captain." The dynamic of the sailing era—many ships of relatively small capacity—supported an egalitarian atmosphere in the industry and upward mobility among the ranks. By the time the Lake Carriers Association was formed the trend was clearly in the direction of fewer and fewer ships of greater and greater capacity. In such an industry not only were fewer sailors needed, but the opportunity to rise from the ranks was also severely circumscribed. The large steel ships that began to dominate the lakes by the end of the nineteenth century represented large capital investments, and the industry eventually moved in the direction of professionally trained officers. The integration of ships with railroads and large shore-based industries took autonomy away from both the crews and the captains of Great Lakes vessels. Masters were reduced to a slot in the matrix of corporate management, and crews were simply employees.[46]

Modern commercial shipping is a far cry from the feeling inspired by the tug of the wheel in a master's hands as a schooner bounded over waves and jack-tars scrambled aloft to set topsails. Most men who rose to the rank of master during the schooner era had a zest for sailing. Runs from port to port were not simply cargo transportation; in the words of a former lakeman, they had "the character of a race

Two schooner masters in the lumber trade, relaxed and in port, share a pipe. Courtesy of the Wisconsin Maritime Museum.

filled with the thrills of rivalry and sportsmanship." A good captain was a man who was confident of his skills and eager to take up any challenge. Not at all unusual was the notice in the *Buffalo Express* of June 6, 1876: "Captain Jannisson of the schooner *C. G. Breed* desires us to announce that he will sail the *Cortez* for $1,000 a side, or schooner for schooner." A less formal method of challenge was for the master of a good taut ship, when approaching a rival vessel, to send a man aloft to wave a broom from the crosstrees. The broom was the signal of a challenge and had much the same effect as a red flag on a bull.[47]

Captains were esteemed for their ability to get as much as possible out of their ships. Along the docks of Lake Michigan, the sailing qualities of masters and ships were fiercely debated. Alver Swanson, for example, was known as "a Swede from the old school and a real sailorman." His 321-ton, three-masted schooner, *Ellen Williams,* was known as "a heavy-weather vessel," which meant that it "seldom laid in for bad weather." The master of the *Annie Peterson* named his ship after his daughter, and with a father's pride he never could bear any ship's getting the best of her. He permanently kept a broom tied to his mainmast to signal his willingness to challenge all comers to a test of speed. According to the dockside scuttlebutt, he too was "a good weather man," meaning he could get the most speed out of any wind conditions. Captain Peterson's aggressive spirit sometimes got the better of his judgment. Once, just outside the Chicago River, Peterson raised the broom to the schooner *Gassliaf.* The ships were neck and neck all the way down the lake. When they reached the Sturgeon Bay channel, both schooners were still clipping with all sails set. Neither captain would "give way" for the other, and as the ships tried to maneuver in the confined space of the channel their yards became entangled. To the sickening chorus of splintering wood and ripping canvas, the duel came to an inglorious end with "much damage" done to each vessel. Such lapses of judgment, however, were tolerated in a skipper whose regular devotion to good sailing might mean one or two more runs per season. A master's zeal for speed could also infect his crew and rally them to extra exertion. William Houghton, helmsman on the schooner *Mechanic,* remembered staying at the wheel for two straight watches as his ship passed every downbound vessel "one after the next." To encourage speed, the shipping establishment often awarded prizes to the first vessel to enter the harbor at the start of the season.

113

Silk hats or new suits frequently were garnered by the winning masters.[48]

During the heyday of the Lake Michigan schooner, masters were men esteemed by the community. "When we saw the captains of these vessels standing on the quarter deck," recalled a boy growing up in Manitowoc, "sailing into the narrow entrance of the river in a breeze of wind, it was the delight of us boys, all of whom hoped that some day they might occupy like positions." Even in large and diverse cities like Chicago and Milwaukee, former schooner captains often served in important public posts. Andrew B. Johnson spent most of his life at the helm of Lake Michigan lumber schooners. As his income rose he purchased several vessels and became active in politics. Johnson became president of the Chicago Board of Education and the head of the powerful Cook County Board. Norwegian-born John Anderson used the profits from his years as a schooner skipper to invest in Chicago real estate. He later became a Chicago alderman. S. T. Gunderson, one of three brothers who rose to the rank of captain, also served in the Chicago City Council. Through his calm, capable exercise of authority, a good vessel captain inspired trust even among landsmen. "Captain [Augustus] Pickering was so esteemed," recalled a passenger on the schooner *Illinois,* "that our pioneers felt secure and in the hands of a capable navigator and watchful guardian, who could be trusted to lead them to their new homes." An associate of Pickering's described him as "embued with a spirit of adventure and enterprise that charged his whole nature."[49]

Schooner masters were confident men who sought to control every facet of their trade. Frequently they would seek input in the building and fitting out of vessels. Most sought an ownership share of the ships they commanded and looked for a free hand in the management of the ship. A. P. Dutton, one of Racine's pioneer merchants, recalled a resolution passed by a council of schooner masters in the 1850s: "The 'court' held that when a man had once been appointed master of a craft the owner had nothing to do or say about the vessel until she laid up in the fall and that the master was the sole director of the vessel in and out of port. The masters declared that they had the right to insure, hold all funds, give no trip sheet, or send in any statements until they settled up after the vessel went into winter quarters." While masters may have sought this type of complete authority, it was generally achieved only by men who owned their own vessels outright. More typically owners used telegraph or messenger services to convey to captains special instructions regarding what cargoes to take and at what rates.[50]

The business side of operating a schooner could be the most challenging aspect of command. The fixed costs of operating a vessel—wages, provisions, towing, insurance, unloading—constantly had to be balanced against the rates paid for bulk cargoes. In the early days of sailing on Lake Michigan, locating cargoes could be a real challenge. In 1842, Captain William Burton found his ship idled in Racine, where he learned that the low price for grain had induced farmers not to harvest. Exasperated, Burton finally took his crew inland to the wheat fields. In return for every tenth bushel, he offered to thresh the grain himself. The advent of grain elevators in the major grain ports of the lake meant that masters would not have to resort to Captain Burton's desperate measure of harvesting his own cargo; rather, they needed to maintain an accurate knowledge of the fluctuating prices for grain, lumber, and iron ore. Grain merchants used their elevator capacity to hold grain not only for its best wholesale price in the East but in order to obtain cheap freight rates from the schooner captains desperate for a cargo. Conversely, a good master might dock his vessel for several days and wait for an advance in rates. The key was to be able to properly anticipate a rate change. Among the things a veteran skipper in the grain fleet might calculate would be the strength of the lumber and ore markets. Lumber hookers or ore boats might seek grain cargoes if their normal trade was depressed, and this would drive down grain freight rates. Another factor would be how close the elevators were to capacity. If the elevators were full and more crop was on its way, merchants would grow anxious to move the grain and the rates would advance.[51]

The strain on masters of managing their boats, crews, and trade was often extreme. Captain Augustus Pickering, who in 1834 had been the toast of Chicago as the man who brought the first ship into the Chicago River, is an example of a master who broke under the pressure. In 1844 Pickering supervised the building of a new schooner, the *Columbia*, at Sackets Harbor, New York. To reach its Lake Michigan destination, the *Columbia* needed to use the Welland Canal. With his new ship loaded with 130 western immigrants, Pickering discovered to his mortification that he had built the vessel one inch too wide to fit in the canal locks. Amid a chorus of complaints from the westbound settlers, he set about the arduous process of planing an inch off the sides of the schooner. As the work dragged on and the complaints mounted, Pickering's nerve broke. Although he was the father of six, the forty-year-old captain walked into the woods along the canal and fatally cut his throat. In the fall of 1875, another Lake Michigan captain took his own life. William C. Rothwell was an English immigrant who rose through the ranks to the position of master. After years serving as a mate in the lumber fleet of Charles Hackley, he was entrusted with the charge of the schooner *Rouse Simmons*. One week after taking the helm, Rothwell's ship collided with another schooner in heavy fog off Grand Haven. After a lengthy layup the *Rouse Simmons* was back to work, although heavy weather caused repeated damage to her rigging. Finally, after a stormy November passage from Muskegon to Chicago, the ownership became exasperated with Rothwell's management. The *Simmons* had lost her mainsail off Manitowoc, collided with the pier at the mouth of the Chicago River, and lost her anchor. When he was relieved of command, Rothwell hit bottom. He checked into the Sherman House hotel, downed a bottle of morphine, turned on the gas in his room, and lay down in his bed with a brand-new revolver and a razor. The latter were unnecessary, as he was found dead of an overdose the next morning. Even a dispirited master was careful and thorough.[52]

Masters like the unfortunate Captain Rothwell did not last long on the quarterdeck. The shipping season was too short for owners to long tolerate mishaps that kept their schooners off the lake. Captain A. L. Huntley of the schooner *Merrill* learned this lesson in 1849. A Congregational minister, George Nelson Smith, was a one-quarter owner of the *Merrill*. When Huntley reported a $100 debt at the end of the season, the reverend felt impelled to investigate his conduct. Smith discovered that "The hands say he is drunk in port, goes to the theater . . . and cares not whether he sails or beaches or what, often sleeps during his watch." Huntley was sacked. While Rothwell may have simply been guilty of bad luck and Huntley the victim of sailors' gossip, such was the lot of the master who did not own at least a share of his vessel. Captain Samuel Ward, who in 1825 took the first ship from Lake Michigan through the Erie Canal, would not have inspired most owners with confidence. He had a distinctly non-nautical bearing and "might have been taken for a prosperous country merchant," a friend recalled. He did not relish life aboard ship, and preferred to stay in hotels while in port. Nor was he a particularly attentive master. He once ordered his men to set all the sails, only to discover that he had yet to order the crew to raise the anchor. Nonetheless, Samuel Ward was a gifted manager of the business of chartering and marketing cargoes, and as master of his own ships he never had to brook criticism for his shortcomings as a sailor.[53]

Skippering a schooner was one means to the end of making a fortune on the Lake Michigan frontier, and it was not uncommon for a master to be a businessman first and a sailor second. Leonard Noyes, who came to Grand Haven from Massachusetts with saltwater experience, disliked the life of a sailor but understood he could do quite well as a vessel master. "This is a wild Place to live," he wrote of Michigan in the 1840s, "but I can stand it [if] I can make Money." Noyes was constantly on the watch for other investment opportunities. For a time he thought about trying his hand at fur trading with the Native Americans or marketing grain. He did sell lumber for a while and even tried his hand at marketing salted shellfish from New England. Finally, he left schooners to operate a freighting business on the Chicago River. With a partner he bought a steamboat for $3,500. Each man put up a $500, with the rest due in a year. Noyes went deeper into the hole to have a new canal boat built at a cost of $400. His timing, however, was excellent. The Illinois and Michigan Canal, after twelve years of on-and-off construction, opened that summer. Noyes's new canal boat was suddenly worth $1,000, and his passenger and freight business between Chicago and Bridgeport boomed.[54]

Vessel ownership was the key to independence for the schooner master, and it was within the grasp of most captains. The cost of a new schooner was generally too high for anyone living on wages. The schooner *Rouse Simmons,* a typical lumber hooker, cost $17,000 at the time it was built, in 1869. Yet because wooden ships rapidly depreciated in value, older schooners could be purchased at modest prices. William Callaway, the saltwater sailor who had been drawn to the lakes by the vision of meat three times a day, became a vessel owner in 1862. He was approached by the mate of a grain schooner on which he had just completed a run from Buffalo to Milwaukee:

> "Bill, let you and I buy a vessel of our own." I asked him how much money he had and he said: "A hundred dollars." I had the same amount. Our united resources did not seem a sum that would go

far toward the purchase of a vessel, but "where there's a will there's a way." We started out, got as far as Division Street bridge, and there saw a smart little schooner called the *Mariner*. We asked the captain if he knew of a small vessel for sale, and he told us the *Mariner* was for sale . . . the next day we bought the vessel for $850, paying $200 down and giving our notes for the balance—$100 to be paid each month for five months and $150 in the following July.

The whole venture "looked rather risky" to Callaway, but he and his partner managed to pay all the notes as they came due and in less than a year were profiting from the venture.[55]

Callaway's $100 was his entry ticket to a new world of risk and opportunity. As owner of a schooner, he rose to the rank of master. He

The *Lucia A. Simpson* tied up in the Chicago River. In this photograph, the weathered vessel, likely in need of an overhaul, is near the end of her career. Collection of the Chicago Maritime Society.

was sought out by other men of business to participate in a variety of ventures. With those investments he moved from being a laborer to being a capitalist. It was an entry into a world inviting in its prospect of profit yet with the potential of disaster looming with the approach of every weather front. In the spring of 1850 Racine vessel owners and investors expected great profits in the grain trade and were confident enough in their vessels to place wagers up to $200 on which schooner would win the race to Buffalo. Yet within twenty-four hours of the start of the season a fierce snow squall had scattered the fleet. Most escaped with only the loss of a few spars, but the *Outward Bound* was swallowed by the lake with all hands and the *Tempest* was driven ashore near Sleeping Bear Dunes. To refloat the *Tempest* the crew had to throw overboard her entire cargo of 2,400 bushels of wheat, with the result that the owners of the ship lost nearly $4,000. Since vessels were frequently underinsured by schoonermen who wanted to reduce their fixed costs, fortunes won over years of hard work and good luck were not infrequently blown away by a single gale. Asahel P. Lyman, one of Sheboygan's leading merchants, had his share of marine misfortunes. His first ship, the schooner *Morning Star,* into which he had invested years of savings, went to the bottom with its entire cargo of wheat on its maiden voyage. Within a few years Lyman recovered his fortune and again invested in the shipping business, only to again meet with disaster. In June 1868 his clipper bark *Cortland* collided with a passenger steamer also bearing the ill-fated name *Morning Star.* In the cold and confusion, three hundred lives were lost. Lyman paid $85,000 in damages and retired from all further involvement with sailing ships.[56]

One way to lessen the risks inherent in Great Lakes sailing was to only own a partial share in a vessel. Even the master of a ship who could afford to own the ship outright might prefer to own a half or quarter interest in the ship he commanded and invest a portion of his profits in a share of another ship. Many schooner masters may have persisted in their jobs out of pure love for sailing, but it did not hurt that the potential for considerable profit was ever-present.

Samuel Ward's 1825 voyage from Green Bay through the Erie Canal to New York was said to have netted him $6,000 profit, but that sort of windfall was not typical. Captain Arthur N. Nelson, a Norwegian mariner based in Chicago, reported that during the prosperous years before the Panic of 1873 he was able to net earnings of $6,000 per year for his small schooner *White Mary*. In 1887 the *City of Grand Haven* grossed an estimated $4,281 for ten trips between Muskegon and Chicago during a two-month period. At that rate, a vessel could pay for itself within three years of being launched. In hard years, however, vessel profits could dwindle to a few hundred dollars. Although some dedicated mariners would operate their ships as tramps, hunting up a cargo wherever it could be found, smart owners understood it was not wise to risk a vessel when the rates did not pay, so they would lay up the ship for the season, or until the rates recovered. The low cost of maintaining a schooner in port, as well as its modest operating costs, gave sailing ships an edge over their steam competition. In his study of the schooner *Rouse Simmons*, Theodore Charrney argued that due to the high cost of steamer personnel, insurance, and fuel, a $1,000 schooner often earned a higher profit margin, in proportion, than a $100,000 steamer.[57]

Since most masters would at some point have had an opportunity to share in the profits of vessel ownership, the key to social and economic mobility for sailors was to rise through the ranks. Sailors who perceived and accepted this challenge were easily identified by their willingness to learn and their acceptance of responsibility. They tended to avoid the expense and emotional ties of marriage until they had at least obtained the rank of mate. Timothy Kelley did not marry until he was a mate, although his decision to help his sister at the time of the Great Fire in Chicago rather than stay with his ship cost him his job. But aside from that incident Kelley had made a good name for himself, and within a year he attained his goal of being named captain, at the tender age of twenty-two.[58]

The relationship between master and mate was critical in the management of the vessel and in the training of future captains. A good skipper was a role model and an invaluable employment reference. As mate of the *Annie Sherwood* in 1870, Timothy Kelley had a cordial relationship with Captain Henry Reed. On one occasion when Reed was away from the ship visiting his wife, the vessel's owner suddenly visited the ship at a Buffalo pier and ordered Kelley to immediately set sail. Kelley did so but doubled back and, unbeknownst to the impatient owner, quietly picked up the captain. The young mate could have used the opportunity to try his hand as master, but either affection for the captain or desire for his approbation persuaded him to disobey the owner instead. In his later years Kelley liked to tell the story of a master and mate who did not get along. One day, after relieving the mate, the master discovered that the mate had made an entry in the log: "The Captain's drunk today." Outraged, the captain added his own entry: "Mate sober today." Some officers formed close bonds of trust and friendship and sailed together for years. The unfortunate William Rothwell, who later failed as a vessel master when finally given his chance, had served long and well as second in command to Captain Seth Lee on a number of Hackley lumber schooners.[59]

Many men made the decision to follow a life before the mast at an early age. Kelley began his sailing career at the age of thirteen, signing on as a cabin boy on the schooner *Ellen*. This was not unusual for men who rose through the ranks. Alfred Ackerman, a notable skipper in Kenosha, began on the lakes at age fourteen as an able seaman. By age eighteen he was a mate, and before reaching twenty he was master of the schooner *Herald*. The last rung on the ladder for Ackerman, vessel ownership, took a much longer time—not until he was thirty-seven years old.[60]

The Ship's Boy

Boys were found frequently on ships. Referred to as "ship's boy" or "cabin boy," they generally worked to assist the cook and serve as a "gofer" for the captain. Former lakeman P. J. Blantom recalled that "boy stowaways were frequent." A lad eager enough to stow away on a ship was usually given a chance to prove himself as a member of the crew. One captain made a practice of impressing on the boys the danger of a sailor's life. When a young stowaway was discovered he always told them that they could stay if they could hang their hat on the main-topmast. Usually they would get about halfway up the ratlines, take a look at the pitching deck below, and give up. "I recall one boy about 10–12," Bantom later said, "who went up to the top of a 132 ft mast, Mount Blanc, furled his cap there and stayed up enjoying the show for a time before he came down. The Captain, when he saw the boy was about to stand up on the main topmast called him to come down, but he kept on going while we all stood around breathless. When he finally did come down nothing aboard was too good for him and he stayed on as 'boy' all season."[61]

The ship's boy or a greenhorn sailor was the favorite butt of sailors' pranks. Before leaving port they would send the greenhorn to get oil for the ship's running lights, with the caution to be sure and get green oil for the starboard lamp and red oil for the port lamp. Another favorite was to tell an earnest young fellow, caught up in the excitement of setting sail, to "let go and haul." Boys were warned that it was their job to keep the captain happy and that they would be responsible if he ever got mad. Shark watch was another of the cabin boy's duties. A favorite anecdote of old-time sailors concerned the novice helmsmen. The captain gave the fellow a star to steer by and went below for coffee. "In a short time he called the Captain and said he was past that star and asked for another."[62]

Sailor Lore

The biggest mistake a greenhorn could make was to violate one of the numerous sailor taboos or superstitions. Joseph Hendricks told of an entire crew abandoning ship when someone accidentally dropped a hatch cover support down into the hold. If the accident had happened when the ship got into port or was unloading there would have been no problem, but for it to happen while the crew was battening down the hatches prior to beginning a run it was a very bad omen. Other bad omens were a black dog or any cat on a ship. A common superstition was that ships named after living people would not long outlive their namesakes. The strongest of the lake sailors' superstitions, however, was that of the danger of beginning a voyage on a Friday. In April 1883, a large portion of the grain fleet remained in the Chicago River rather than embark on a Friday. Masters pointed to the case of the schooner *Van Valkenberg*, which opened the season on a Friday and suffered a chain of mishaps before finally sinking with all hands. Some owners, impatient with such dawdling, ordered their ships to sail. "No matter what the orders are," the *Chicago Inter-Ocean* reported, "there is always something to do, or something out of shape so that it is after midnight when the craft starts." On another occasion, the captain of a newly launched schooner respected the wishes of his crew and held off leaving port until after midnight. They caught a fair breeze and a day later came across a schooner that had violated the taboo. The vessel's flag was at half mast. The captain had fallen, hit his head, and died. To the sailors this "proved the point."[63]

Superstition gave sailors a sense of control over the great natural forces with which they contended on a daily basis. A vast folklore grew up among sailors that reflects their understandable obsession with weather. Sayings such as "Red sky at night, sailor's delight; red sky at morning, sailor take warning" were very common. Longtime lakeman also used the verse "Evening gray and morning red, Put on your hat or you'll wet your head." Some rhymes conveyed important navigational advice, such as when passing a ship at night: "Green to green, red to red; Perfect safety, go ahead."[64]

Some sailors watched the gulls for a clue to the weather. When they were low in the sky it was a sign of fair weather. Gulls were often fed by sailors off the stern, with the birds taking scraps of toast or old bread from their fingers. Some old salts believed that gulls were the reincarnated souls of dead mariners. One fellow even claimed he could recognize former shipmates, but he probably was just lonely.[65]

Conclusion: A Life before the Mast

Loneliness was something many sailors experienced. Even though Lake Michigan sailors' voyages were measured in days and weeks, not months and years, they were plagued by a longing for home and loved ones. Portbound by a gale in November 1872, Captain Timothy Kelley wrote in his diary, "Awful lonesome." He was anxious to complete the last run of the season and get home, but the next morning the gale continued to blow across Georgian Bay, causing the master to write: "Never so lonesome and Discouraged." Able seamen experienced the same sentiment. John Treiber, a German immigrant sailor on a Lake Michigan schooner, wrote his wife: "Dear Darling and how ar you weall I hope and thinging of mea I hope for I am thinging of you all the thime and the tim that I shall sea you." Great Lakes sailors had more opportunities than their saltwater counterparts to visit family between voyages, but such reunions were made difficult by the variable schedule and changing destination of schooners. Sea-

The schooner *Granger* tied up in the Chicago River, east of Rush Street, in 1888. Courtesy of the Wisconsin Maritime Museum.

man John Treiber tried to arrange a visit with his wife in Chicago during the middle of the season. Unfortunately, his ship took its next cargo to Milwaukee and the reunion had to be canceled. The fact that "it takes money to stop in Chicago" prevented him from arranging another rendezvous. He wrote his wife, "I will have to make A Nothir trip in the same vesil I Dont No Whear she is going yeat eather Bufalo or Thruw the Canall." New Englander Leonard Noyes constantly looked for opportunities to get out of sailing and home to Massachusetts. "I can do as well here at sailing as aney where and Propably better," he wrote his brother in 1845, "but it kills me by inches, I can not stand it." In 1879 Timothy Kelley was able to make a brief stop at his home in Manitowoc during the middle of the season. After the overnight visit he wrote: "I am awful lonesome leaving Manitowoc this evening. I wish I could stay at home. I do hate this sailing business and hope I can give it up this fall."[66]

Kelley did not give up the sailor's life. Instead, he spent sixty-one years sailing the freshwater sea. Loneliness, like foul weather, was an occupational hazard, and lakemen weathered those depressions like they weathered autumn low-pressure systems, watch by watch, doing their duty and earning their pay. When the season finally came to an end the sailors would stuff their possessions into their white seabags, join shipmates for a parting glass, and repair to family or friends. Some, like John Treiber, did not "want to sahle any more if I can help it." More common was William Houghton's recollection: "Those were the days. We had to work like hell, and at all hours, but we always went back the next season as long as the old schooners lasted."[67]

4

Schooner City: The Life and Times of the Chicago River Port

In 1871, the year of Chicago's Great Fire, more ships arrived in that city than in New York, San Francisco, Philadelphia, Baltimore, Charleston, and Mobile combined. The port of Chicago was not only the entrepôt of the Great Lakes; it was one of the greatest ports in the world. Before Chicago was known as the "Windy City," before it was called "the city that works," before Carl Sandburg had dubbed it the city with "big shoulders," Chicago was known as the "Queen of the Lakes." It was as a port city that Chicago grew to prominence, and it was its maritime industries that shaped the character of the nineteenth-century city. Milwaukee, Racine, Green Bay, Muskegon, and the other ports of Lake Michigan, while significant in their own right, were subsidiary to Chicago in terms of influence over shipping on Lake Michigan. Three-quarters of all cargoes shipped out of Lake Michigan came from the Chicago harbor. Nineteenth-century historian James Parton accurately, if rather grandiloquently, captured the nature of this relationship when he referred to Chicago as the "Marseilles of our Mediterranean."[1]

It is axiomatic in Chicago history that the city's destiny was shaped by the economic opportunities resulting from its geographic location at the meeting of the prairie and the lake. The ability to provide cargoes for sailing ships was the seed from which grew Chicago's endur-

The mouth of the Chicago River, ca. 1893. Collection of the Chicago Maritime Society.

ing commodity markets. The need to manage the daily flow of scores of ships in and out of the Chicago River was one of the first and most persistent challenges to the city's urban infrastructure. Supplying sailors and stevedores, as well as drovers and railroaders, with shelter, refreshment, and entertainment made Chicago the vice capital of the lakes as well. Chicago's status as a port did much to give the city its frantic, intense nineteenth-century image. "Here on the shores of Lake Michigan," wrote a much impressed visitor, "has risen a great and growing city, worthy to bear the title of the Empire City of the West."[2]

The strength and weakness of the port of Chicago was the Chicago River, which Theodore Dreiser praised as "the smallest and busiest river in the world." The river's most obvious asset was its ample sheltered dockage, which was increased by dredging throughout the nineteenth century, along the short main branch of the river and up the north and south forks. The Chicago River weaved its way through the heart of the city. Ships could sail right up to grain elevators, lumberyards, or railroad sidings; sailors could make a dash for hundreds of saloons and bordellos, or, depending upon their predilection, the YMCA and a complete range of churches. The river was the hub around which life revolved in the nineteenth-century city. That was

The Chicago River from the Clark Street Bridge. Reprinted from Alfred T. Andreas, *History of Chicago* (Chicago: A. T. Andreas, 1884–86). Collection of the Chicago Maritime Society.

also the rub. To move a hundred or more ships a day in and out of the bustling heart of a city was to invite chaos.[3]

"Bridged" in the Heart of the City

Chicagoans embraced that chaos for half a century. "The blackened waters of the river," wrote Frank Norris in his novel *The Pit*, "disappeared under fleets of tugs, of lake steamers, of lumber barges from Sheboygan and Mackinac, of grain boats from Duluth, of coal scows that filled the air with impalpable dust, of cumbersome schooners laden with produce, of grimy rowboats dodging the prows and paddles of larger craft, while on all sides, blocking the horizon, red in color and designated by Brobdingnag letters, towered the hump-shouldered elevators." By the 1870s the busy stream that divided the

129

business district was bridged by twenty-seven spans that pivoted on piers sunk in the center of the river. Designed to facilitate both maritime and pedestrian access to the central city, these swing bridges were the bane of both. The bridge piers reduced the already narrow river channel to a needle's-eye passage. The bridges' constant opening and closing maddened the masters of vessels moving upriver and left pedestrians, suddenly cut off from their business across the river, stomping their feet with frustration. On a single day in 1854 a total of 24,000 pedestrians and 6,000 teams of horses crossed the Clark Street bridge. Yet during that same day 100 boats passed Clark Street and the bridge was opened for a total of three hours.[4]

In 1856 an anonymous journalist aptly captured Chicagoans' irritation with the way arriving and clearing ships brought all surface traffic to a halt. He penned a satiric story titled "Success Triumphant, or The Lover at Clark Street Bridge." The story concerns a wealthy if incon-

A pair of two-masted schooners, *Conquest* and *Helen Pratt,* in the Chicago River near the Wells Street bridge in 1888. The two passing steamers make for a tight fit on the crowded Chicago River. Courtesy of the Wisconsin Maritime Museum.

stant young woman who pledges herself to marry two men at the same day and time. One lover races to the wedding from his residence on the west side of the city, while the hero, a southsider, strives to beat him to the church on the north side of the Chicago River. As they near the church from opposite directions, both are "bridged" by passing ship traffic. The southsider, however,

> makes a stern resolve. One steam-tug, the *Fairy Belle,* is coming up stream, another, the *Zekel Barnes,* is going down. He seizes the auspicious moment; he leaps for his life. He only knows that he leaps for a wife. With one bound he is on the *Fairy Belle,* with another on the bridge now swinging in the middle of the stream; again he leaps, and scarce touching the *Zekel Barnes,* a fourth bound lands him on the north side. With a shout of defiance to his despairing rival, he rushes forward, while boat-men and bridge-tenders suspend their labors, and stand transfixed with breathless astonishment at the surpassing feat.

The hero wins the girl, her fortune, and a six-story house on a quarter-section lot. In old age, the humorist concludes, he "relates to a numerous and still increasing family, the fearful legend of the Clark Street Bridge."[5]

All Chicagoans could shake their heads knowingly about the frustrations of being "bridged." Traffic was not infrequently backed up a quarter mile. "There was a great deal of scolding on such occasions," reported a journalist, "and—alas for human nature!—sometimes I fear, a slight degree of profanity." In 1887 a doe-eyed Frank Lloyd Wright, fresh off a train from rural Wisconsin, took an unscheduled ride on the Wells Street bridge. He was staring dreamily at the river when he "suddenly [heard] the clanging of a bell. The crowd began to run. I wondered why: found myself alone and realized why in time to get off, but stayed on as the bridge swung out with me into the channel and a tug, puffing clouds of steam came pushing along below pulling an enormous iron grain boat, towing it slowly through the gap. Stood there studying the river-sights in the drizzling rain. . . . Later, I never crossed the river without being charmed by somber beauty." Less aesthetically inclined Chicagoans took foolish risks to avoid such delays.[6]

It became common for pedestrians to remain on the bridges as they

Frustrated pedestrians await the passage of another ship in the congested Chicago River. *Harper's Weekly,* May 28, 1887.

swung open. This reduced their delay somewhat, as they could at least walk to the other end of the bridge while the ships were passing. Last-minute leaps from the street to the turning bridge were a regular part of a nineteenth-century Chicagoan's commute to work. In November 1863 such tactics had tragic results on the Rush Street bridge. A drover moving a herd of cattle to a northside stockyard tried to hurry his beeves onto the span as it swung open for an approaching ship. The bridgetender could have stopped opening the span, but experience had taught him that only by moving the bridge away from the street could he stop traffic. Unfortunately, the cattle were not experienced commuters. Panicked by a tugboat whistle and the moving of the bridge, the drove stampeded to one end of the span, where its weight caused the span to tilt and then break in half. The cattle and a handful of terrified pedestrians on the bridge were thrown into the filthy, cold water. For a moment the perturbed commuters were rendered motionless by the sudden disaster. There followed a mad rush to get boards down to the drowning people and rescue boats into the water. A young girl, the sister of the reckless cowboy, was killed, and the bridge, valued at $50,000, was a total loss.[7]

An even worse accident had occurred at the same site just seven years before. Prior to erecting the swing bridge, the city facilitated crossings at Rush Street by means of a hand-operated ferry. On September 19, 1856, a ferry filled with workers, including a large number of boys, ran afoul of a schooner. According to regulation, the schooner signaled its approach and the ferry operator, who pulled hand over hand on a rope to power the ferry, dropped the rope. By doing so the schooner could safely pass over the ferry line. But the commuters, impatient to reach their jobs, took up the line themselves and began to pull for shore. Unfortunately, the schooner snagged on the elevated rope, and the ferry was spun around and in an instant capsized. Fifteen people drowned.[8]

The Chicago City Council struggled to manage the conflict between busy street traffic and a burgeoning port. In 1867 an ordinance was passed which established that no bridge could be open for more than ten minutes at a time. Bridgetenders were given a large red ball, lowered by a rope, to signal approaching vessels that the span would swing closed. In 1881, "much to the satisfaction of tens of thousands who work down-town every day," the city council made it unlawful to open a bridge during the morning (6:00–7:00 A.M.) and evening

Chicago's river-harbor was spanned by more bridges than any other port in the world. Tall-masted schooners had to run a gauntlet of more than twenty bridges to ascend the river. Note the bridgetender's house atop the swing bridge. From this perch the tender was master of his portion of both the road and the river. Photography by Crater's, ca. 1865. Negative no. ICHi-03762, Chicago Historical Society.

(5:30–6:30 P.M.) rush hours. Among the most controversial ordinances was the regulation that tugboats be designed so that their smoke-stacks were lower than the eighteen-foot clearance afforded by the bridges. In this way tugs pulling canal boats or tugs returning from towing sailing ships would not require bridges to open. This was too much for the volatile tug skippers, who immediately went out on strike. An economic nightmare was avoided only when a clever citizen invented a hinged stack that could be quickly raised or lowered.[9]

The most loathed sight for a tugboat skipper was the bridgetender's red-ball signal that the span was about to swing shut. To the tugmen the bridgetenders were petty tyrants perched atop the spans solely to frustrate their livelihood. The post of bridgetender was a patronage plum, doled out more as a reward for faithful party service than for temperament, marine background, or sobriety. The Republican *Chicago Tribune,* never missing an opportunity to strike a partisan blow, delighted in portraying a Democratic, usually Irish bridgetender as the cause of most accidents or traffic delays on the river. It was a high-profile, high-pay job. During the hard times of the 1890s, Chicago bridgetenders were paid a lavish $2,700 for eight months' work. True, the operators of the first swing bridges had to open and close their spans by means of a hand crank, but once the spans were electrified the tender was relieved of manual labor. Journalist Peter Finley Dunne, best known for his colloquial stories about the Bridgeport neighborhood, described the importance of the bridgetender in a May 1897 story: "In Archer road the command of the 'red bridge' is a matter of infinite concern. There are aldermen and members of the legislature in Archer road, clerks of the courts and deputy sheriffs, but their duties do not affect the daily life of the road. Whereas the commander of the bridge is a person of much consideration, for every citizen sees him day by day; it is part of his routine to chat loftily with the wayfarer, and the children help him to turn the bridge." Through his fictional character, Mr. Dooley, an Irish saloonkeeper, Dunne spoofed Irish anxiety over the rise of other immigrant groups in the patronage system:

"They have put a Polacker on th' r-red bridge," said Mr. Dooley.

"A what?" gasped Mr. Hennessy.

"A Polacker," repeated Mr. Dooley. "A Polacker be th' name iv Kazminski."

"Dear, oh dear," said Hennessy, "an' is this what Lawrence McGann [alderman] an' young Carther [Mayor Carter Harrison, Jr.] have done f'r us? A Polacker on th' r-red bridge! 'Tis but a step fr'm that to a Swede loot at Deerin' sthreet an' a Bohemian aldherman. I niver thought I'd live to see th' day."[10]

One of the complaints Mr. Dooley had about putting an Eastern European in such a lofty position was that no one on the river would be able to swear at him and "be answered dacintly." The cussing between tugmen and bridgetenders was legend in nineteenth-century Chicago. "From 9 o'clock until 11 a blue haze hung over the river near the Lake Street bridge as a result of the promiscuous profanity which the captains and sailors exchanged with the bridge-tenders," recorded the *Chicago Daily News* on December 1, 1893. The bridge's power system had gone out, and a considerable backup of ship traffic resulted. "Pedestrians stood on the bridge and listened in awe to the strange oaths, known only to river men, which the boatmen and bridge-tenders hurled at each other."[11]

Nor was the tension between tenders and tugmen always dissipated with profanity. Feuds would grow over the course of a season. The tugs were paid by the tow, and since time spent waiting for bridges meant fewer tows, the tugmen tended to "high ball it" when they saw a bridge open. Since it was impossible to bring a tug and tow to an immediate stop, they tried to put the tenders in a position of having to hold the span open for them. Bridgetenders who were quick to lower the red-ball signal could risk serious accidents. But to the irritation of the tug skipper, it was the boats that usually got the worst of any collision. The tugs were responsible for any damage to a vessel in tow. Since the cost of fouled rigging or a snapped jibboom came out of the skipper's hide, resentment of tenders ran high. Historian Theodore Charrney, who has done the most original work on this subject, estimated that a hundred or more such incidents occurred each season. The sailors got their revenge through late-night (when tenders were asleep) bumps or "rubs" that left the spans mysteriously bruised the next morning. More commonly, sailors on the tugs would content themselves with pelting the tender with coal when he was not looking. Tenders returned the favor by accidentally dropping scraps of wood or coal from their high perch as their rivals passed below. "At Dearborn Street," noted a waterborne *Tribune* reporter in April 1895, "an evil-minded bridge-tender emptied a barrel of ashes into the boat, and a loud, emphatic exchange of compliments shocked casual passers by." Peter Finley Dunne played off these petty rivalries in a "Mr. Dooley" column in which a bridgetender and a boat captain feud became so heated that the tender simply resolved never to open for the offending boat until the tug skipper stood up on his cabin and cried out three times: "Hurrah f'r Mike Dooley, the king iv Connock."[12]

Tugs: The Workhorses of the Harbor

The tugboats were vital to the operation of the Chicago River. In the early days of the harbor, ships occasionally would try to navigate the river under sail. After a string of collisions with municipal bridges, however, the city ruled, in September 1855, that all ships must use tugs when passing bridges. About thirty tugs were based in the port in its heyday. Competition for tows could be intense, and rivalries between tug lines resulted in occasional price wars and frequent acts of intimidation between crews. Vessels only required a tow to or from the breakwater at the mouth of the harbor. Before that point schooners or steamships required no assistance, yet when business was slow tugs would scour the waters around Chicago looking for incoming vessels. It was not unusual for tugs to steam out fifteen or twenty miles in search of tows. During the 1890s, when the sailing fleet's numbers began to plummet, tugs desperate for work ranged as far north as Milwaukee. These industrious tug skippers tried to offset the extra expense in coal by bringing two or three schooners in tow.[13]

The leading tugboat men during the heyday of the port of Chicago were the partnership of Mosher and Dunham. Albert Mosher, a millionaire lumberman from Bay City, Michigan, got involved with tugs as a result of his need to transport large amounts of lumber to Chicago and the great lumber port on the eastern Great Lakes, Tonawanda, New York. James S. Dunham began his maritime career at the age of fourteen, working as a ship's cook. Three years later he came to Chicago and found work on one of Mosher's Chicago tugs, the *A. B. Ward*. When the Panic of 1857 slowed commerce on the lakes, Mosher entrusted Dunham with the task of taking two of the Chicago tugs down the Mississippi to find work on the Gulf. It is good that Dunham earned considerable profits during his first years in Dixie, because in 1861 the vessels were seized by the Confederacy. Dunham returned to Chicago and, as Mosher's partner, reentered the towing and wrecking business. By 1883 the firm had five schooners and four tugs, all based in Chicago.[14]

Tug captains like James Dunham had the unenviable task of trying to maneuver quickly and safely within the confines of the crowded, twisting river. Although the Chicago River was by nature a sluggish stream, its currents could be quite tricky. Bends and narrows, where the current was confined or pushed toward the far bank, were the most difficult places to navigate. Since the city's sewers emptied directly into the river, a thunderstorm could suddenly cause the current to quicken and the level to rise. The river's current was particularly troublesome for vessels "red balled" by a closed bridge. It took great skill to keep a schooner from drifting out of the channel while waiting for a bridge to open. One technique required the ship being towed to

The tug *S. P. Hall* pulls a fully loaded lumber schooner into Chicago's outer harbor, ca. 1893. Collection of the Chicago Maritime Society.

drag its anchor, just off the bottom of the river, from the stern of the vessel. If the tug had to stop, the anchor could be lowered to the bottom and act as a break, what sailors called a "way-check." Dragging anchor in the congested river, as can be imagined, was not without its dangers. Anchors could and did become entangled; more commonly, the sharp flukes of the anchor stove in passing vessels.[15]

The tugboats enjoyed a mixed reputation with schoonermen. Their service was indispensable to the operation of a sailing vessel, and the

As a tug pulls a two-masted schooner into the Chicago River, horse-drawn wagons and carriages begin to back up at the Rush Street bridge. Note a second tug with a schooner in tow straining to catch the bridge while it is open. Pedestrians on the bridge slouch in a relaxed fashion, knowing from experience that the bridge will not be closing anytime soon. Photograph by Carbutt, 1869. Negative no. ICHi-03731, Chicago Historical Society.

tugmen often played a heroic role in rescuing men from distressed vessels. On the other hand, tugboat skippers could be unscrupulous. Before tow rates were fixed in the mid-1870s, tugs looked for opportunities to take advantage of the sailing men. Woe to the schooner master who did not agree to a firm price for a tow before tying onto a tug. After the fact, the master had little choice but to pay what was asked.

In June 1891, Captain Soren Kristiansen witnessed a particularly artful fleecing of an inexperienced master. A Sheboygan tugboat skipper spied the three-masted schooner *Costhwaite* anchored about a mile off the harbor entrance, waiting out the fog. Determined to create some business for himself on a slow morning, he told his crew to let him do the talking as they steamed out to the schooner. He then told the schooner master that a storm was coming and that the bottom at that part of the lake would not hold an anchor. The panicked captain handed over his towline "without making a bargain." Therefore the tow, which was not needed in the first place, cost the master of the *Costhwaite* double the usual fee. "That is the way vessel men is [*sic*] treated by Sheboygan tug men," Captain Kristiansen brooded.[16]

Another source of tension with the tugs was their desire to return as quickly as possible to the lake for another tow. For lumber schooners this led to problems because dockage near the Chicago lumber market, at the forks of the river and South Water Street, was always in demand. Rather than wait for a berth to open up, tugs preferred to let the schooner tie up farther downstream, necessitating a second tow for the sailing ship when space opened up at the lumber market. It was not uncommon for a ship to require the services of three or four tugs during a single visit to Chicago harbor. These short pulls, moving a schooner from one dock to another to unload or take on cargo, cost no more that five or six dollars, but together with the longer tow from the breakwater, which cost between twenty-five and thirty dollars, the fees added up to a considerable amount. For Michigan lumber hookers the Chicago towing fees might be the most expensive single cost of a round-trip schooner passage. If a careless or impatient tugboat captain crashed a schooner into a bridge or bank, exasperation with the little steamboats reached its peak. The tugs were responsible for the cost of repairs, yet while that was taking place the schooner was out of service, often losing the opportunity to make one of the twenty to thirty runs the short shipping season allowed.

The Harbor Master

The overlord of the crowded, often chaotic Chicago river port was the harbor master. Generally a veteran sailing master, he had the difficult job of keeping traffic moving on the congested river. An assistant was stationed atop the lighthouse, which in the nineteenth century stood at the mouth of the river. When he spotted ships approaching the river mouth, the assistant telegraphed (later telephoned) a request for a tug to a central dispatch office. Meanwhile, the harbor master himself patrolled the river. At congested points like the lumber market, where vessels liked to tie on three or four deep, he would order schooners to move to a less crowded location lest they block the channel. When disputes between bridgetenders and tugs became too heated, he intervened, to their mutual dissatisfaction. Abandoned and decrepit vessels taking up space in the river and liable to sink and impede commerce were taken in tow by the harbor master and sunk in the deep water beyond the breakwater.[17]

One of the banes of the harbor master's life was the tunnels under the Chicago River. These structures were built to allow horse-drawn vehicles unimpeded access to the other side of the river. The first one was completed at Washington Street in 1868 at a cost of more than half a million dollars, and a second was added at LaSalle Street a year later. These projects were carried out by private companies empowered by the city. Later a third tunnel was added at Van Buren Street under the south branch of the river. While the tunnels succeeded in their primary purpose of giving "bridged" traffic an alternative route across the river, they also contributed to congestion on the waterway. During the 1870s the size of vessels on Lake Michigan began to increase. By the end of the decade the larger ships visiting the city began to run aground on the top of the tunnels, particularly when the water level was low. Usually the tugs could nudge their consort off the tunnel, but some groundings lasted for days and all but closed traffic in and out of Chicago. These vessels would have to be completely unloaded, and if that failed to refloat them, they would remain grounded until the river's level rose. By 1900 the larger steel vessels on the river were grounding on the tunnels almost weekly, and the marine community cried loudly for the tunnels to be eliminated. It was not until 1906 that shipping interests, with the backing of the U.S. Army Corps of Engineers, were able to force the tunnel owners to lower the obstructions and allow for a clear channel twenty-one feet deep.[18]

The irony of the port of Chicago in the nineteenth century was that its weaknesses were its strengths. The narrow little river that limited the flow of ship traffic wound its way through virtually all parts of the city. The congested river-harbor beset with thirty-seven navigation-

141

A steam barge surges up the Chicago River, while to the left the schooner *Winnie Wing* discharges her cargo of lumber, ca. 1890. Collection of the Chicago Maritime Society.

inhibiting bridges was located in the heart of the business district. Bulk cargoes shipped to Chicago required less handling in its port than in many larger natural harbors. Ships sent to Chicago, particularly the adaptable schooners, could use the river to directly access northside distilleries, southside slaughterhouses, or westside lumberyards.

142

The Lumber Market: From Sail to Rail

Lumber hookers were forced to run the gauntlet of bridges along the main branch of the river, turn up the south branch and its string of bridges, pass the densely developed central business district, where river frontage was among the most expensive real estate in the Midwest, and finally enter the empire of wood. At Eighteenth Street, where the south branch bent gently to the west, the lumberyards began to line the banks. "The timber yards are a considerable part of the city's surface," reported an English visitor, "there appearing to be enough boards and planks piled up to supply a half-dozen States." The lumberyards were packed densely along the banks of the river, and the numerous slips and canals, many over a quarter mile long, reached north into the city. Affordable real estate and access to the Illinois and Michigan Canal dictated the district's location. Originally the canal had played an important role in bringing lumber to and from Chicago, but by the 1860s railroads became the favored conveyance to reach the Chicago market's expanding network. Side tracks were extended along each slip. By 1896 more than $10 million worth of dockage improvements had been made in the lumber district. Once a schooner docked in the district its cargo could be easily unloaded, to be sorted and stored in Chicago or immediately shipped by rail to a distant siding on the barren plains.[19]

While it was at the lumber market near Wolf's Point that lumber cargoes were inspected and sold, it was to the westside lumber district that schooner captains had to deliver virtually all their cargoes. It was access to the railroads that made Great Lakes lumber gravitate to Chicago. Lumber sold for a higher price in Milwaukee or Detroit than in Chicago—if you could find a buyer. Chicago offered lower prices but always had a buyer because its merchants were backed by a transportation system that could reach customers across the country. The limited rail networks supporting the substantial ports of Milwaukee and Detroit prevented lumber merchants in those cities from being able to market forest products as extensively as Chicago. In 1898, Windy City lumber merchants boasted that "80,000 miles of Railroad have terminals on the Chicago River."[20]

W olf Point was the most congested portion of the Great Lakes' busiest port. Formed where the Chicago River split into its north and south branches, Wolf Point was also the site of the lumber market, where all cargoes of lumber were inspected, graded, and sold. Grain ships loading at the giant Air Line Elevator added to the congestion. Chicago's importance as a transshipment point is illustrated by the numerous rail lines that ran directly to the water's edge and the numerous canal boats awaiting a tow back to the Illinois and Michigan Canal.

Farmers' produce wagons and vendors' stalls crowd the streets behind the lumber market. South Water Street was Chicago's great outdoor market and the site of many sailors' dives. Swing bridges at Lake and Wells Streets open to allow ships to pass and in the process create one of the innumerable traffic jams that beset nineteenth-century Chicago.

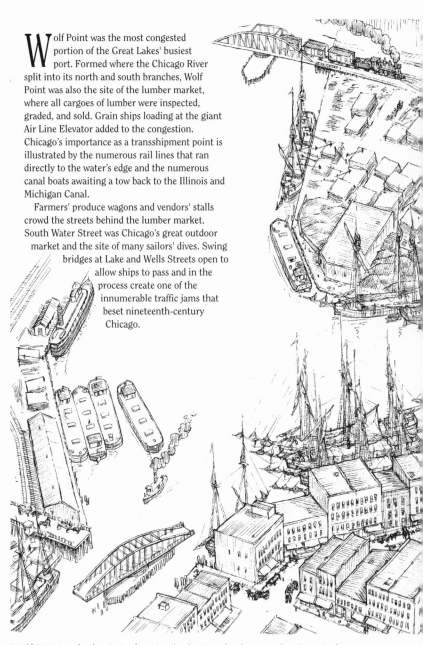

Wolf Point—the busiest place in the busiest harbor on the Great Lakes.

The larger lumber companies in Michigan and Wisconsin operated their own yards in Chicago. The smaller lumbermen resorted to the use of commission merchants who for a percentage of the sale would find a buyer for a schooner-load of wood. The commission merchants had an incentive both to move the cargo fast and to charge as high a price as possible. But best of all, from the perspective of a lumberman weighed down with investments in forestlands, sawmills, schooners, and labor, the commission merchants paid cash for the cargo. Liquidity was a rare thing in a seasonal business like lumber. Lumbermen had to pay bills with no income coming in from October to April. When the first schooners of the season were loaded with cut boards, the lumberman was determined to send them where they would be guaranteed an immediate cash sale.

The Lumbershovers and Grain Trimmers

At any point during its late-nineteenth-century heyday, the vast lumber district on Chicago's west side might be holding over 400 million board feet of wood. To maintain such an inventory, about nine thousand lumber schooners needed to be unloaded every year. While the crew of a schooner was expected to lend a hand loading the vessel in Manistique or Oconto, they were spared the task of unloading in Chicago. The lumber district supported a small army of stevedores, known in the city as "lumbershovers." Their arduous work was done entirely in the outdoors, in driving rain or grilling sun, with ship captains anxious to leave port urging them to make haste. On hot afternoons a wise master invested in a barrel of beer to offer as an incentive for fast work. Stripped to their union suits and sporting leather aprons over their chest and thighs, the lumbershovers ignored slivers and sweat to quickly empty a schooner. They worked in cohesive gangs, between four and a dozen men, headed by a foreman who negotiated with a vessel master for the amount to be paid to the gang for the job. Sometimes the gangs would be based at a nearby saloon and the saloonkeeper would act as the foreman, making money both off the workers through his increased beer sales and by taking a cut of their pay. Some might even operate a boardinghouse at the saloon and require the gang to lodge there. Such a business agent could, however, negotiate set contracts with vessel masters or lumber companies that guaranteed the gang steady work. Without such a deal, a skipper might have to comb the docks to find a crew to unload his ship during a busy season. On the other hand, during slack times gangs would surround a docking schooner and brawls would break out over who had the right to negotiate first with the master. Under these circumstances a shrewd captain could demand a reduced rate.[21]

Seaman Nels Palmer frequented the docks of the lumber district at the turn of the century. He remembered that "each gang had their own waterboy, each man had his own can, which the boy would take care of, and it was nothing new those days to see the boy with 15 to 20 cans of beer at one time. These he carried on two poles and he knew each man's can. All the stevedores would have on would be a pair of short trunks and a leather apron, and on a hot day it would be very hard work. These men are a very hardy bunch and real men." The association of these men with saloons, their intermittent work regimen, their imposing appearance, and their loyalty to their gang made them attractive foot soldiers for the corrupt politicos of Chicago's notorious First Ward.[22]

Initially the Irish were the most prominent group among the lumbershovers. The work was seasonal and hard, and the pay anything but steady. Nonetheless, Irish stevedores fought hard throughout the Civil War to keep African American freedmen from gaining a foothold on the docks. Between 1862 and 1864 riots and brawls were frequently the result of attempts by blacks to find work unloading vessels. Typical was the August 1862 affray at the Twelfth Street docks. The schooner *Meridian* had tied up, and her captain anxiously sought a gang to unload her cargo. The usual charge for a ship of the *Meridian*'s size was $15, but due to the shortage of workers the stevedores demanded, according the not unbiased *Chicago Tribune*, $75. Finally they agreed to a price of $45. But before the lumbershovers began to unload, the captain found a gang of African American dockworkers who agreed to do the job for $13. The captain tried to mollify the first group of lumbershovers by pointing out the approach of another vessel, but the men "became indignant and immediately set upon the negroes, when a general riot ensued." In a July 1864 incident the entire waterfront was aroused. Charles Mears, a Michigan lumberman of staunch Republican principles, had hired a dozen African Americans to unload

147

one of his schooners. A delegation of Irish lumbershovers visited Mears and demanded that he discharge the blacks because "it was degrading to them to see blacks working upon an equality with themselves." Mears, whose Michigan mill towns were named Lincoln, Hamlin, and Freesoil, gave them no satisfaction. Unfortunately, they returned with several hundred fellow stevedores and forced the blacks to flee for their lives.[23]

By the 1870s the Irish longshoremen were forced to share the wharfs with immigrants from Bohemia. The neighborhood north of the lumberyards took on the name Pilsen, after the famous Czech brewery town. Even more than the Irish lumbershovers, the Bohemians were inclined to socialism and unionism. The evidence also suggests that they were less a part of a male bachelor subculture and tended to contain more family men. As their numbers increased on the Chicago River docks, the instances of organized collective action became more frequent. In April 1877 they joined with other groups to organize the Chicago Lumber Vessel Unloaders' Union, Local No. 19 of the International Longshoremen's Association, affiliated with the American Federation of Labor. The union worked to impose a standard rate on the docks as well as bring labor discipline to its members.[24]

The Great Strike of 1877 rocked Chicago largely because the dockworkers took as their own cause the national railroad strike. On July 25 a group of six hundred to eight hundred Bohemian and Polish lumbershovers closed down the docks. When they attempted to carry their movement to the McCormick Reaper Plant, police intervened. To resist their leaders' arrest, the lumbershovers bombarded the police with stones. The panicked police replied by firing into the crowd, wounding two men and putting the rest to flight. The next day, pitched battles between mobs of workers and police rocked the city. Eventually three thousand troops, many straight from combat in the Great Sioux War, were deployed in the city. In the end, thirty workers were killed and at least two hundred wounded. The chaotic uprising was beyond the union's control, although, after peace was restored on July 27, the union was astute enough to impose a rate increase. Masters who balked at paying more to have their schooners unloaded found their boats idled and were forced to knuckle under.[25]

The lumbershovers' ability to mobilize for collective action and their instinct for labor organization brought a degree of order and labor solidarity to the teeming Chicago waterfront. In 1878 the Chicago

Lumbershovers unload a two-masted schooner. More than nine thousand lumber schooners were unloaded annually at the massive lumber district on the west side of Chicago. Note the railroad tracks on the far side of the river and the canal boats on the right—key elements in the distribution system that made Chicago America's leading lumber center in the nineteenth century. Photograph by Barnes and Crosby, 1900. Negative no. ICHi-05415, Chicago Historical Society.

Seamen's Union was organized in cooperation with the lumbershovers at a meeting in Bohemian Hall. The union segregated out the duties of sailors, lumbershovers, and grain trimmers in the port. For example, sailors were forbidden to in any way aid in unloading a ship. In return, the lumbershovers and grain trimmers agreed to end the practice of helping to move vessels up and down the river during the loading or unloading process, as this allowed masters to do completely without sailors while in port.[26]

On the north branch of the Chicago River, factories and grain elevators lined the banks. Here the dockside workers were grain and coal trimmers. Drawn from the Irish ghetto near Goose Island, the grain trimmers performed a dreary task. In the early 1840s the grain trade demanded large numbers of grain handlers. Using hand-carried baskets, a labor gang would take an entire backbreaking day to load a single schooner with seven thousand bushels. The introduction of steam-powered elevators in 1848 reduced the needed workforce to several men. The trimmers had the unenviable task of working with a shovel in a railcar or in the hold of a ship as the golden stream of grain poured from the elevator. Their job was to ensure that it spread equally throughout the cargo bay. To reduce the amount of dust and grain they breathed in, they wore moistened bandannas across their mouths. Coal trimmers had a more difficult and dirty task. Through most of the nineteenth century they unloaded schooners laden with coal by means of wheelbarrows. Black with coal dust and stiff-muscled at the end of the day, they looked with envy on the relatively clean labor of the lumbershovers. On at least an annual basis, the grain trimmers would walk off the job and demand higher wages. Often with a bagpiper at their head, they would parade along the docks until the increase was granted.[27]

The grain elevators were the wonder of nineteenth-century Chicago. Until William Le Baron Jenney invented the skyscraper in 1885, the grain elevators dominated Chicago's skyline. Seventeen hulking brick buildings cast dark shadows over the north side of the city. Visitors from throughout the world came to gawk at the giant vertical bins of grain. As with the lumber business, Chicago dominated the grain trade because its port efficiently brought together railroad and maritime transportation. By the 1890s the larger elevators could unload hundreds of railroad cars per day. In a single hour a schooner could be loaded with 300,000 bushels of grain. Throughout the navigation season, grain left Chicago by both train and ship. Nonetheless, when winter closed the lakes for the year the grain elevators in Chicago were so full that it was often necessary to utilize as reserve storage the holds of the hundreds of ships wintering in the river.[28]

A "Shockingly Offensive Bayou": Pollution of the Chicago Harbor

The abundance of grain gathered in Chicago created the opportunity for a vital by-products industry. By the 1860s merchants in the city began to mill some of the grain into flour, thereby economizing on transportation costs. Distilleries also were established along the north branch to tap the bounty of the harvest. The distilleries were among the most obnoxious plants along the river. They built large

Schooners unload much-needed cargoes of lumber in Chicago after the Great Fire of 1871. Collection of the Chicago Maritime Society.

hog feed lots next to each distillery in order to take advantage of the waste from whiskey production. The manure from the swine was then washed into the river. In the vicinity of the distilleries the river was said to be "nearly the consistency of dough; its surface completely covered with manure, its lower depths made up of—Heaven only knows what." The doughlike crud was said to extend to a depth of six to ten feet, leading the *Chicago Tribune* in 1860 to refer to the north branch as a "shockingly offensive bayou of reeking filth." The industrial character of the narrow stream was further reinforced by the growth of by-products industries tied to the grain surplus, lumber, and the stockyards.[29]

After the Civil War, furniture factories, dye works, and hide tanneries were packed along the water's edge. Left to nature, the north branch would not have been able to serve a commercial purpose for much more than a quarter mile from the river's forks. But by the turn of the nineteenth century, dredging had extended ship traffic several miles north, as far as Western Avenue. While the city of Chicago did have the main river dredged for navigation purposes, the north branch was improved by brick manufacturers, whose plants along the stream required a steady supply of good-quality clay. As the demand for brick, ceramic fixtures, and terra-cotta ornamentation grew, so too did the extent of navigation on the north branch.[30]

A French traveler entering the city by ship in 1886 was horrified at the picture presented by its dense piling of commerce and industry. As the steamship pushed past the open bridges, "stirring up the infectious and muddy waters," he was struck by a noxious smell that grabbed "at the throat." That odor was the result of a toxic stew produced by the businesses sharing the banks of the river-harbor: the lumberyards contributed sawdust; coal dust washed in from the vast storage areas along the stream; breweries and distilleries offered their waste wort and hog offal; gasworks added deadly coal tar; dye works and tanneries released acid; and the stream of fats, organs, and carcasses from the stockyards proved that much more than a "squeal" escaped Chicago's pork and beef kings.[31]

The principal source of the latter pollution was an arm of the Chicago River called "Bubbly Creek." Upton Sinclair, in his 1906 novel *The Jungle,* left a memorable description of the hundred-foot-wide stream:

The grease and chemicals that are poured into it undergo all sorts of strange transformations, which are the cause of its name; it is constantly in motion, as if huge fish were feeding in it, or great leviathans were disporting themselves in its depths. Bubbles of carbonic acid gas will rise to the surface and burst, and make rings two or three feet wide. Here and there the grease and filth have caked solid, and the creek looks like a bed of lava; chickens walk about on it, feeding, and many times an unwary stranger has started to stroll across and vanished temporarily.

The stream of waste from the stockyards was always the most noticeable pollution to the river. Blood from the butcher's knife often dyed the river red as far as Clark Street. Such was the river's odor that when a Chicago teacher once asked a boy to define the word *river* he answered, "A body of water that has a very bad smell." A reporter for the *Chicago Times* lamented that even "birds which attempt to fly over it are intoxicated by its exhilarating perfume, and fall into it and die."[32]

So thick did the river become with waste that nineteenth-century Chicago developed an urban folklore about its being thick enough to walk upon. "It might be deemed extravagant to state that a small boy crossed the river on the scum at Madison street yesterday," the *Tribune* wrote in October 1860, "but some of them may be trying it." Accounts of the river's catching fire, however, were no exaggeration. The Chicago River caught fire so regularly that the city had to establish a fleet of fireboats to prevent the blazes from damaging ships and wharfs. "The news that it occasionally caught fire," *Century Magazine* wrote of the river in 1902, "has been more widely circulated than the fact that it ranks well up among the greatest ports of the world." Peter Finley Dunne's "Mr. Dooley" delighted in the river's pyrotechnics: "'Twas th' prettiest river f'r to look at that ye'll iver see . . . down on th' Miller dock some night . . . see th' flames blazin' on th' wather an' th' lights dancin', green at th' sausage facthry, blue at th' soap facthry, yellow at th' tannery, ye'd no trade it f'r anything. . . . It burned like a pitcher-frame facthry." According to Dooley, the Irish firemen decided that the best way to put out such fires was to "Tur-rn th' river upside down."[33]

Out-of-state journalists thought it was a "huge joke" that the river caught fire, but the Chicago City Council was not laughing. Beginning

153

in the 1860s they tried to solve this problem. One temporary expedient was to turn on the pumps that sent water from the south branch of the river into the Illinois and Michigan Canal. When operated for several days, these pumps could temporarily reverse the flow of the river. Instead of slowly sending the pollution into Lake Michigan, where the city derived its drinking water, the pumps could make the river flow toward the canal and draw fresh, clean lake water into the river. What the city needed was a new, deep sanitation canal that would effect permanently what the pumps could do only occasionally. An attempt was made in 1863 to con the federal government into building Chicago's great drain by dubbing the proposal the "National Ship Canal" and selling it was a vital element in defending the Great Lakes from British attack. But even during the Civil War that tub would not hold water. Not until the late 1880s did the city face the unpleasant truth that if it wanted to clean the river it would have to come up with the funds itself.[34]

In the meantime, city officials struggled to curb pollution of the river. A strong ordinance requiring the elimination of most packing-house and distillery pollution was passed in December 1862. The city also acted to ban the sale of Chicago River ice, which hundreds of households unwittingly purchased for their family iceboxes. "It is not enough that you have inhaled the odor [of the river] all summer," the *Tribune* editorialized. "You must now have it served up for you in solid cubes, to cool and flavor your butter, to impregnate your steaks, to dissolve into your drinking water." The ice monopoly and the large meatpackers launched vigorous protests. The packers downplayed the extent of their pollution and hit the city where it was most vulnerable by blaming the bulk of the problem on the city's 1855 decision to empty its municipal sewers into the Chicago River. The press supported the packers and distillers on this point. "The drains add their freight of mud, offal and impure liquid compounds in regular dismal discharges," wrote the *Tribune*. "How many bags of kittens are at this moment rotting in the muddy depths of the basin? Old hats, old boots, old tin pans, decaying fish, old pipes, slime, swill, ordure, and those shapeless evidences of human sin and shame which abound in every great city, add their effuvials [sic] to the water." Rather than put the burden of expense on those who did business along the river, the newspapers argued that cleaning the Chicago River was a general good that was in the best interest of the entire city. The *Tribune* advocated damming the Des Plaines River and diverting its waters through Mud Lake to the south branch of the Chicago River. This would increase the current in the south branch and main channel so that all of the filth would have been washed into Lake Michigan. What this would do to the city's drinking supply was left unstated by the geniuses at the editorial desk.[35]

What Chicago eventually did to clean its river-harbor was the opposite of what the *Tribune* suggested. A deep canal was dug parallel to the old Illinois and Michigan Canal, and Lake Michigan's clean water was permanently drawn into the river, sending the city's filth to Peoria and St. Louis. Unfortunately, it took a series of calamitous cholera and typhoid outbreaks to convince the city to undertake this massive engineering effort. An 1885 storm raised the level of the Chicago River and propelled its polluted waters out far enough into Lake Michigan to reach the city's water intake cribs. Approximately 12 percent of Chicagoans took sick or died from waterborne disease. By 1892, when the new canal was being planned, Chicago's death rate from typhoid fever was a staggering 174 out of every 100,000 people. The opening of the Chicago Sanitary and Ship Canal in 1900 was a bold undertaking carried out over the objections of other Great Lakes ports who feared that Chicago's diversion of Lake Michigan waters would lower harbor water levels throughout the basin. By creating a new regional authority, the Metropolitan Sanitary District, Chicagoans of the 1890s discovered the means to overcome the financial and political roadblocks that had prevented the city from solving the problem for more than a generation.[36]

"Beastly Sensuality and the Darkest Crimes": The Chicago Harbor after Dark

V ice was another type of pollution that was linked to Chicago's busy port. Most nineteenth-century cities had vice districts where sexual services and gambling opportunities were openly hawked. The port of Milwaukee had its infamous River Street district, and the twin ports of Menominee and Marinette had the brothels of Frenchtown. Escanaba's Ludington Street was so densely packed with saloons and related dens that there was one joint for every thirty-five men who lived in the city. Sailors docking in Muskegon resorted to Sawdust Flats, six blocks of "unspeakable whoredom and violence." But Chicago offered drink, sex, and gaming on a grander scale and was the most popular port of call for wayward sailors.[37]

Chicago's popularity stemmed from the wide variety of vice it could offer. As early as the 1860s, the city boasted more than two hundred houses of prostitution, and streetwalkers in the thousands. Vice on this scale was sustained by the large number of people passing through the city at any one time. The transient population included businessmen and professionals in the city's best downtown hotels; drummers and farmers in town to secure supplies before quickly returning to the countryside; railroad men operating the trains or repairing the track; canal boat crews; and armies of the Midwest's seasonal labor force: harvest hands, lumberjacks, and packinghouse workers. All saw Chicago as a place in which to let off steam, reward themselves for a job well done, and, for those without scruples, momentarily escape the normal bounds of behavior. Chicago's vibrant port acted as the sustaining element in all of Chicago's nineteenth-century vice districts. The several thousand Lake Michigan sailors based in the city and at least an equal number of stevedores were core groups of rough and ready clients for the city's gamblers, saloonkeepers, and prostitutes. From the notorious Sands, Chicago's first vice district, to the Levee, arguably the city last true red-light commune, Chicago vice was tied to its river-port.[38]

On the north bank of the Chicago River, at the current site of the stately Michigan Avenue bridge and the soaring Wrigley and Tribune towers, was the Sands, Chicago's first underworld haunt. The location was perfectly matched to its purpose. The land was originally dune and beach terrain unsuited for permanent construction. The building of the harbor piers, however, had led to the annual deposit of acres of new ground on the north side. Before the business community realized what was happening, a string of boardinghouses, bordellos, and gaming establishments had been erected on this no-man's-land. All ships entering Chicago had to pass the Sands, so even before a ship docked a sailor's patronage could be solicited by the denizens of the district.[39]

Travelers' accounts of Chicago, usually so careful in their description of the imposing grain elevators and sprawling lumberyards, were generally mute about the Sands. Even if gaming or whoring was on the agenda for a Victorian traveler, the Sands would have proved alluring to only the most adventurous libertine. The district was unvarnished and ramshackle. Genteel gaming could be found at a few posh houses on Randolph Street. The Sands offered its sport undiluted, and it appealed to hardy lakemen or coal heavers. The *Tribune* proclaimed it the "vilest and most dangerous place in Chicago." Bare-knuckle brawls vied with rattings among the district's sporting set. The latter pitted a terrier against several bags of rats, with the betting focusing on the number and speed with which the rodents could be dispatched. The bleeding but victorious dog would be rewarded with a bowl of ale. Mike O'Brien, one of the district's leading impresarios, would roll up his sleeves and take on all comers himself if he was short an attraction on a crowded night. Even the bawds of the Sands fought. "Gentle Anne" Stafford once cleared out the Prairie Queen brothel when one of her girls defected to that rival. She thrashed Madame Herrick and drove the rest of the whores through the streets back to her bagnio. Years later "Gentle Anne" brought a reluctant suitor to the altar by chasing him out of his bedroom and into the street with a leather bullwhip.[40]

Sailors who boarded or sported in the Sands awoke to an unpleasant noise on the morning of July 17, 1857. The mayor of Chicago, hulking six-foot, seven-inch "Long John" Wentworth, a squad of police, and a posse of aroused citizens descended on the patch. At the head of this army of virtue was the agent of William B. Ogden, the city's leading real estate investor. Ogden, who had long coveted the prime land near the mouth of the river, overcame the problem of the Sands's nebulous legal status by forming a partnership with the most prominent men of Chicago and Springfield and securing a state charter to develop the area. The mayor served the writs of eviction, and one by one the grogshops and brothels were torn down. After nine buildings were systematically broken up with hooks and chains, a fire mysteriously broke out. By evening the Sands was no more.[41]

While Chicago lost its district of "the most beastly sensuality and the darkest crimes," it did not lose its taste for the same. Two nodes of corruption replaced the one. On the southern fringe of the central business district, on Madison and adjacent streets leading east from the Chicago River, arose one vice district. In 1862 one block in this area boasted fourteen brothels. "After nightfall the street was thronged with cyprians," a journalist recorded. "They stood in the doorways, bedizened in tawdry fineries and dressed to a degree of indecency which disgusted every respectable person." A second district was found on Clark Street, just north of the river. This area was fully exposed to the unrelenting odor of the north branch of the Chicago River and adjacent to Kilgubbin—a wretched Irish ghetto celebrated in the press for "crimes, brawls and drunkenness," but more likely proof of the power of poverty, substance abuse, and prejudice to breed social disorganization.[42]

The near southside district developed into the infamous Levee, Chicago's largest and longest-lived red-light district. In 1893, with the World's Columbian Exposition in the city, the Levee was at its peak of popularity. A notorious corner of the Levee was Custom House Place. Detective Clifton Wooldridge described it in lurid fashion:

> Here at all hours of the day and night women could be seen at the doors and windows, frequently half-clad, making an exhibition of themselves and using vulgar and obscene language. At almost all of these places there were sliding windows, or windows that were hung on hinges and swung inside. These . . . were used by the women to invite pedestrians on the street to enter these places. . . . It was not unusual in those days to see from fifty to one hundred women lounging in the doors and windows in this one block at one time . . . the habitues of this place embraced every nationality, both black and white, their ages ranging from eighteen to fifty years. The costumes worn by these people embraced every kind known to the human race, from that of the Hottentot to the belle of the ball.

With much of the property in the Levee owned by some of the city's most illustrious citizens and rented to the brothels at fantastic rates, the vice trade developed a protected status in late-nineteenth-century Chicago. In 1896, for example, after a much publicized inspection of the district by moral Chicagoans, Mayor George B. Swift took "stern" action: he ordered the brothels to keep their windows closed.[43]

Chicago's wide-open port posed more than a moral or venial threat to incautious sailors. One of the unsavory barmen of the Levee was the legendary Mickey Finn. Part pickpocket, part thug, and part publican, Finn developed a special knockout drink composed of grain alcohol, snuff water, hydrate of chloral, and perhaps morphine. Working

158

with streetwalkers and party girls, he set up sailors and other men newly paid off to be easily rolled. Dock rats and footpads waited in the dark for any sailor foolish enough to conclude his spree alone. Morning always found men slumped in the alleyways or, all to frequently, floating facedown in the river.[44]

During the day the wharfs along the Chicago River bustled with commerce, the sound of chanteys mixing with the cursing of teamsters, and the street vendors' pitches drowning out the vessel captains' call for stevedores. At night the docks were draped in silence and shadows, disturbed only by the clip-clop of a midnight carriage across a bridge or the scurrying of rats along the wharf. In the darkness Chicago's waterfront became the haunt of criminal gangs graced by the city's newspapers with the gaudy name "river pirates": "All along the Chicago River, crouching beneath the wharves, digging between the pilings, or dozing in the lumber yards by day, pillaging, sandbagging, murdering by night, are these fiends of darkness and the oozing water," wrote the *Tribune* in 1895. Beginning in the 1860s the port was periodically beset by gangs that used swift rowboats to rob warehouses and docked vessels. In July 1860 a police task force assigned the job of curtailing such crime made three arrests. Two of the culprits turned out to be sailors. Sailors were also the most frequent victims of the river pirates. In November 1876 the master of the schooner *E. M. Portch*, which had been robbed several times already, assigned two seamen to stand watch on the vessel. Just before midnight a boat with four thieves pulled alongside the schooner. When they scrambled aboard they were surprised to find the sailors with their sleeves rolled up, ready to defend the schooner. Unfortunately, the river pirates were armed with revolvers, and the sailors were forced to jump into the river, where one of them drowned. Once on a schooner the pirates would take anything that was left unattached on the deck as well as try and break into the cabin. Towropes (which could cost as much as forty dollars), lanterns, compasses, and yawls were favorite targets because they could be easily fenced. Left undisturbed, the pirates would strip a ship of every ounce of brass. Warehouses built out over the water on pilings could be broken into by taking a boat under the building and tearing open the floor.[45]

If the ships or warehouses offered no good picking, the pirates would turn their attention to rolling sailors returning to their vessels. "Those wharves are the most dangerous places in the world," complained Captain Fred A. Bailey in 1895. "One doesn't know the moment when he will be knocked senseless, robbed of all he has on his person, and flung into the river." Bailey always carried a pistol when on the Chicago docks. Even so, "Several of my men," he told the *Tribune,* "have reported to me that they have been assaulted when about to come aboard, and I have often seen strange men clamber hastily over the side in coming from my cabin." As the police captain charged with protecting the docks along the south branch observed, "It would be folly and sure death for an unarmed man to venture along the river anywhere between Van Buren and Twenty-second streets." Even his patrolmen would not venture unaccompanied onto the docks at night.[46]

In 1883 the *Chicago Times,* always on the lookout for a lurid story, sent a reporter on a midnight tour of the docks. He left a memorable picture of the wharfs, embroidered in colorful Victorian prose: ". . . a narrow rotten footway, ill-lighted and unpoliced, the abode of vermin, biped and quadruped. Occasionally a drunken sailor or wharf rat is passed and at rare intervals the solitude is broken by the brawling of some inebriated dock-walloper who is making [the] night hideous in one of the many low doggeries that abound." The reporter referred to climbing the stairs up from the river as returning to "civilization." But he did not do so until he had "recoiled with an ejaculation of horror" at the discovery of a dead body floating in the water.[47]

Crime along the river was particularly troubling during the winter. When the navigation season drew to a close, between two hundred and five hundred schooners, steamers, and canal boats would tie up in the river and prepare to winter in the port. Sails would be stripped and sent to a sail loft for storage, the rigging would be secured below, and the schooner could be turned over to a shipkeeper. Keepers were particularly vulnerable to the riverside thugs as they spent a winter alone on a ship. At the same time, the number of pirates and other wharf rats increased as the seasonal jobs of sailors and stevedores ended. "Look out for river thieves," the *Chicago Inter-Ocean* warned in November 1876. "We will have from 2,000 to 3,000 idle sailors in Chicago this coming winter and the desperadoes among them, will, without doubt, work the fleet of fine large vessels laid up in the harbor."[48]

A Christmas tree ship, possibly the *Arendal*, open for business in the Chicago River near Clark Street. Collection of the Chicago Maritime Society.

Frozen Shut: The Harbor in Winter

A maritime village, a distinct neighborhood within the city, existed every winter along the frozen Chicago River. Wintering vessels were tied up three and four deep with gangways linking them to the dockside. Postmen delivered mail directly to the ship each day. Most of this community's residents were shipkeepers, veteran seamen. The job gave them a small income, but more importantly, it saved them from having to shell out money for a boardinghouse during the winter. Keepers did light chores about the ship, such as shoveling off the snow, as well as minor repairs. Masters who owned their own

161

vessels would sometimes move their families in for the winter. Heated with a potbellied stove, the cabin of a schooner could be a snug, if somewhat cramped, winter quarters. When the river froze over, adults and children alike took to their skates. Adventurous skaters would follow the iced river as far west as Riverside, ten miles away. The less youthful would gather around the stove to read newspapers or to share checkers, cards, songs, and stories.[49]

The last schooners to join the winter community were the Christmas tree ships and the potato boats. Mariners desperate or daring enough to sail without insurance, the cost of which became prohibi-

The schooner *Mishicott* idled for the winter. Lake Michigan harbors that bustled with activity during the shipping season were transformed into quiet neighborhoods during the winter. Schooners were tended by shipkeepers or occupied by the vessel owner and his family and became winter residences. Here a hockey game is under way at South Haven in the 1890s. Michigan Maritime Museum.

tive with the end of November, would try one last voyage to northern Wisconsin or Michigan. The sale of Christmas trees directly from a schooner became a Chicago tradition during the late nineteenth and early twentieth century. At the Clark Street bridge the ships would tie up and do a happy December business. The potato boats would arrive in November. In 1900 a reporter observed: "With the increasing likelihood of storms as the season draws to a close, some schooners are taken out of the lumber trade, and the owner, who is usually the captain of the boat, invests a part of the season's earnings in a cargo of potatoes at some port in the potato raising district of northern Michigan. The cargoes are then brought to Chicago and retailed direct from the boat, while the work of putting the vessel in winter quarters goes on." Theodore Charrney discovered the memoir of Henry Brandt, a young man who wintered on the schooner *A. M. Beers* in 1900–1901. Brandt recalled how "Every weekday morning, horse drawn trucks from the commission houses would pull up besides the *Beers*." A shipboard boom would then load bags of potatoes onto the truck. Stoves in the hold of the ship kept the cargo from freezing during the winter.[50]

During the winter many of the unemployed sailors would head north to the lumber camps of Michigan and Wisconsin, while men with carpentry skills could find work in Chicago's thriving shipyards. The shipyards resounded with the bang of caulking hammers throughout the winter as older vessels were repaired and new commissions executed. In the depths of winter the shipyards took advantage of the numerous unemployed in the city by paying their carpenters and caulkers a modest wage ($1.75 per day in 1861), but as outdoor work increased in February and March the wages of skilled ship workers rose (to $2.00 per day and more in 1861). The leading shipbuilder in Chicago during the schooner era was the Miller Brothers shipyard. Located on the north branch of the Chicago River, just above the Chicago Avenue bridge, Miller Brothers had the largest dry dock in the harbor during the 1860s and 1870s. They frequently had two ships on the stocks at the same time and built propellers, tugs, and schooners. Smaller shipyards dotted the banks of the north and south branches of the river, many merely undertaking ship repair, others specializing in canal and small boat construction. John Wesley Powell purchased the hardy boats that descended the Colorado River from one such Chicago yard. Even more important than the dry docks and shipbuilders were the ship chandleries. Gilbert Hubbard & Company dominated the ship supply business in Chicago. Their stock of sails, cordage, and flags was the largest on Lake Michigan, and many ships built in Wisconsin or Michigan came to Chicago to be fitted out with Hubbard's rope, canvas, tackle blocks, and anchors.[51]

Safe Harbors for Wayward Sailors

To repair broken sailors, Chicago had a substantial maritime hospital. In an early, and historically neglected, example of government health care, Congress created the United States Marine Hospital Service in 1798. Port duties and a special tax paid by seamen provided a system of medical care for sailors. The larger ports boasted actual hospitals run by the Marine Hospital Service, while in lesser ports the service arranged with preferred private care providers. Chicago's first Marine Hospital was established in 1852 at the site of the old Fort Dearborn. As grain elevators and warehouses began to crowd along the river and the need for a larger facility became obvious, the hospital was moved up to then suburban Lakeview. For a good portion of the nineteenth century the Marine Hospital the was best of the handful of medical institutions in the city.[52]

There were various safe harbors to which a sailor in need of spiritual care could repair. The first Seamen's Bethel Church was erected in 1844. Joseph H. Leonard, a vigorous Methodist minister, made the spiritual care of Chicago's sailors his personal mission. His zealous, revivalistic methods made him a popular figure among the tars. By 1860 there was an interdenominational seamen's church on Wells Street. During the winter its chaplain held Sunday school for mariners as well as regular services. Another recourse was provided by the programs of the Seamen's Mutual Benevolent Society, a self-help organization that cooperated with a number of the city's ministers. Ministers encouraged masters to offer first employment to the "praying sailors" as a way to encourage good behavior among the thousands of rough, seasonally idle men in the city.[53]

Another revivalist popular among Lake Michigan sailors was Captain Henry Bundy. An ordained minister associated with the Bethel Society, Bundy made the entire Great Lakes his ministry. His first

The Miller Brothers shipyard and dry dock. Located on the north branch of the Chicago River at Goose Island, Miller Brothers was the premier shipbuilder of nineteenth-century Chicago. Photographer and date unknown. Negative no. ICHi-01874, Chicago Historical Society.

vessel, the *Glad Tidings,* was a mere yacht of three tons. By the 1870s Bundy's ministry was able to support the second *Glad Tidings,* a two-masted schooner of thirty-three tons. Finally, in 1883 Captain Bundy was the proud pastor of the third *Glad Tidings,* a sixty-ton vessel. This progression he used as evidence of the growth of his ministry. Bundy took as his charge the spiritual welfare of lake mariners as well as the isolated settlers, fisherfolk, and lighthouse keepers of the region. In 1876 he informed the *Kewaunee Enterprise* that his goal was to "cruise about Lake Michigan and Green Bay, supplying destitute

165

families with bibles, tracts, etc." When he came to Chicago, Bundy always drew considerable press attention. The Reverend Captain's favorite place to preach in the port was on the congested docks of the lumber exchange, where he could not help but draw a large crowd.[54]

The port of Chicago boasted another benevolent institution, the hospital ship. Although not directed toward sailors, it was a popular summer attraction that was much beloved within the marine establishment. The hospital ship was moored at the south end of the breakwater, far from the stench of the inner harbor, where pleasant lake breezes were constant. The aim of the ship was to provide ill or impoverished children with a fun and healthy afternoon outing. Every year a schooner (usually three hundred or so tons) was leased for that purpose. The children would gather eagerly at the Clark Street bridge. There volunteers would take charge, one for every three children, and direct them onto a steam launch for the trip to the outer harbor. The schooner would be prepared for the youthful visitors with awnings stretched and cots, chairs, swings, and baby-jumpers positioned about the deck. "The object of the Hospital Association," the *Tribune* noted, "is to furnish the children with patent medicine free—said medicine consisting of fresh air and sunlight." The kids romped about the vessel snacking on crackers and milk. Between ten thousand and fifteen thousand children would visit the ship each season. A reporter wisely observed that "the mothers of the children seem to derive as much gratification from the rest and fresh air as do their infant charges."[55]

Decline of the Port of Chicago

O ver the course of the last decades of the nineteenth century, the port of Chicago became a victim of its own success. The city that had grown up at the nexus of rail yards and wharfs increasingly had no room for either in the central business district. Urban planners, commuters, and even many of the business community wanted to see freight traffic banished from the heart of Chicago. Mayor DeWitt Cregier, a pliant member of the Democratic machine, called for filling in the river. He was seconded by Carter Harrison the elder. More ominous, however, than the pronouncements of mere politicians was the intention of street railway magnate Charles Yerkes. Through his judicious disbursement of funds, Yerkes was the power behind Chicago's corrupt aldermanic form of government. Coveting control over the streets of the city, he masked his vision of a paved-over river covered with his cable cars by advocating the construction of a massive new outer harbor at the mouth of the river. Yerkes's vision did not arouse the general public. The Chicago River, a federal official noted, "one of the indispensable arteries of commerce upon which is based the eminence among American cities obtained by Chicago was regarded by nine-tenths of the population not interested directly in commerce as a nuisance to be abated."[56]

The disdain that Chicago's citizens and politicos felt toward the hardworking river was translated into neglect. While early in its history Chicago had sought to manage wharfing rights and keep the river dredged, these good intentions had been forgotten by the 1880s. Since the river was a vital economic asset to the businesses along its banks and to the maritime community, the city basically left dock and dredging matters up to the private sector. When river muck became thick enough to impede ships' docking, the owner of a riverfront warehouse would pay to have his frontage dredged. If a dock owner wished to extend his wharf out into the river he simply did so, regardless of the inconvenience caused by the narrowed channel. In places the Chicago River was so crowded by wharfs built out into the stream that the channel was reduced to half its natural size. As a result, Chicago had become, in the words of Captain William Marshall of the U.S. Army Corps of Engineers, "in capacity, depth and width of navigation . . . a third class port." By the 1890s lake trade began to shift to Waukegan, Milwaukee, and South Chicago.[57]

Riverfront business vigorously resisted efforts to have the downtown harbor further downgraded. For a time they found a powerful ally in the Army Corps of Engineers, which had a congressional mandate to manage the nation's navigable rivers. The corps had cited Chicago's insistence on using the river as a sewer as an excuse not to take a hand in improving the harbor, save for installing breakwaters at the river's mouth and along the shoreline. In 1893, however, the corps began to take a more aggressive posture regarding the inner harbor. The city's determination to construct the Sanitary and Ship Canal had roused the army engineers, who made it their goal to prepare the Chicago River for the new diversion of Lake Michigan water and to

167

improve what it told Congress was "the most important navigable stream of its length in the world."[58]

The army hit the river like gangbusters. Their goal was to create a sixteen-foot channel on the river as far north as Belmont Avenue and as far south as the stockyards. Encroachments on the original banks of the stream were ordered removed at the owner's expense. When one outraged wharf owner complained at a public hearing that "the Lord never intended large boats to go above Canal street," an army engineer replied, "There is no evidence as to that before this body." All told, 106,848 cubic yards of encroachments were removed and the river was relieved of obstructing bends. Turning basins were also constructed at Goose Island on the north branch and at junction of the south and west forks. Older bridges that impeded navigation were ordered removed. The Pennsylvania Railroad appealed to the secretary of war that their bridge did not obstruct ships when it was built, and that it was not their fault that vessels became bigger. But even that clout-heavy railroad was forced to back down and remove the bridge. "All this has had its effect," a journalist explained in 1902. "It is no longer safe to treat the Chicago River with contumely; it now has a guardian who demands respect and fair treatment for it."[59]

But the army engineers could not turn back the clock for Chicago's downtown harbor. In 1889 the harbor handled 11 million tons of cargo, giving it ranking with London, Hamburg, and New York as one of the greatest ports in the world. But 1889 was the peak. Chicago was a schooner city. Its cramped river could be adapted to the comings and goings of the small sailing ships, but no amount of improvements by the Corps of Engineers could make the Chicago River an effective port for the new steel vessels that were beginning to dominate the lakes. The steel cargo vessels being built for the lakes at the turn of the century were between 400 and 500 feet long. At sixty feet in width, they could not navigate the inner harbor. Even the cost of getting 300-foot vessels up the river was becoming prohibitive. To take a vessel of that size upriver as far as the grain elevators at Twenty-second Street required tugboat charges that were the equivalent of one-half the cost of transporting the cargo from Chicago to Buffalo. By the first decade of the twentieth century, even Chicago's politicians had become alarmed at the decline of the port. "It is a notorious fact," intoned Mayor Fred Busse, "that the lake commerce of Chicago, once the pride and boast of this city, has been steadily decreasing for a number of years." In 1908 Busse appointed a Harbor Commission to revive the port.[60]

Chicago's maritime community tried to adapt by moving shipping facilities closer to the mouth of the river, or even outside the river to the outer harbor. The centerpiece of this development was the North Pier complex, built upon the remains of the old Sands vice district. The well-connected Chicago Dock and Canal Trust leased valuable real estate, at annual rates as high as $30,000, to a wide range of clients. The construction of the North Pier Terminal Building (originally the Pugh Warehouse) in 1905 was the most important of these structures, but it was soon joined by scores of others. "As soon as I finished one building there on North Pier," recalled architect Henry Ericsson, "they gave me a contract for another, until new warehouses nearly a half-mile in length and six or seven stories high were stretched along the north bank of the river."[61]

The rapid growth of maritime business along the outer harbor and at North Pier forced Chicago to make a critical decision regarding the future of its port. Mayor Busse's Harbor Commission made its maritime plans at the same time that the city's Commercial Club had sponsored architect Daniel Burnham to develop a comprehensive blueprint for the development of Chicago. Burnham's gleaming beaux arts plan of a city fronted by miles of lakefront parks spellbound Chicagoans. "Make no little plans," Burnham told Chicago, "they have no magic to stir men's blood." The Harbor Commission operated on a more prosaic principle. They rejected the grand vision of Alfred Beirly to build a gigantic canal six hundred to seven hundred feet wide from the forks of the Chicago River to near Western Avenue, where it would turn south to link up with the Sanitary and Ship Canal. Such a plan would give Chicago a commodious new harbor in the center of the city. Instead, they called for the lakefront between Randolph and Chicago Avenues to be reserved for "future harbor development." But the only harbor development Chicago ever built in this area was the one called for in Burnham's plan: Navy Pier.[62]

Navy Pier (originally Municipal Pier) was built between 1913 and 1916 at a cost of $4.5 million. It was designed as a triple-purpose facility. Cargo terminals and sheltered deep-water dockage gave it a commercial purpose. A two-story passenger terminal allowed lake boat excursionists to board their steamers directly, while dinning halls, terraces, and a dance hall made it a public recreation destination. While it was an impressive facility, extending three thousand feet out into the lake, it could not by itself sustain Chicago's declining maritime fortunes. In contrast to Chicago, Milwaukee, which was confronted with a similar crisis, chose to reemphasize its port, and began a major new outer harbor port complex in the 1920s.[63]

When Chicago chose the beauty promised by the Burnham Plan over the commerce of the Harbor Commission, the fate of the Chicago River as a port was sealed. During the late 1880s the Army Corps of Engineers made major improvements to the Calumet River, making it more attractive to navigation by lakegoing vessels. South Chicago harbor, located near the Illinois-Indiana state line, became the scene of a tremendous building boom in the 1890s. New grain elevators, with a capacity dwarfing that of their older Chicago counterparts, began to sprout up along the Calumet. In 1895 Joy Morton & Company received 100,000 tons of salt at their docks along that river. The exodus from the Chicago River gained momentum when the North Chicago Rolling Mill, which had begun life on the Chicago River, relocated to the far south side. By 1900 the steel industry in the Midwest was centered in the Calumet region.[64]

While the Chicago River harbor went into a long but steady decline, South Chicago harbor was built on the "big shoulders" bulk cargoes that had once characterized Chicago: grain, coal, and iron ore. Passenger ships still steamed into the river, although when the *Eastland* rolled over in 1915 and took with her more than eight hundred lives, much of the joy in cruising the lakes went with it. Three years later, Christmas trees were sold for the last time from the deck of a schooner. But even this old tie to the past was a fraud. By 1917 the trees had actually come to the city by rail, and their sale from the schooner was a mere marketing ploy. Into the 1920s lumber vessels still meandered their way up the south branch, but the big woods of the Great Lakes states were nearly all cut by World War I.

A dull pall gradually descended over a river that had gone from congested and dynamic to insipid and still. The gray waters, and perhaps a few graybeards at the mariners hall, alone remembered "the merry sound of the 'Heave-Ho,' the cranking of the windlass, heaving the heavy anchor, and the shaking of the unfurled canvas in the wind, the stentorian voices of the officers giving their various orders, and the 'aye-aye' of the active seamen," the sounds of a schooner making ready to leave Chicago and embrace the broad, blue expanse of the lake. The fate of ports, great and small, their rise and their ebb, rested on the decisions of men. In contrast, on the cold waters of Lake Michigan, the fate of wooden ships, however well built or ably manned, was in the hands of Nature.[65]

5

Lost on Lake Michigan: Wrecks, Rescues, and Navigational Aids

"I wish to put down in this book what I am doing every day, and also how the weather is acting and how the winds are blowing." So Captain Soren Kristiansen began his diary in 1891. As a schooner master he knew that what he did, every day he sailed, was inexorably linked to the weather and winds. Weather sayings are among the most prevalent examples of maritime folklore. "A cloudy sky and dark clouds driving fast under lighter ones," cautioned Captain Edward Carus in his personal notebook, "expect violent gusts of wind." Ship's logs and captain's diaries, to the frustration of researchers, fixate on weather and wind to the exclusion of almost all other topics. Lakemen habitually kept their eyes on the horizon, mulling over and attempting to decode every bit of meteorological evidence not merely because they were dependent on the wind for their headway but because weather was an ever-present threat to the survival of the ship and crew.[1]

Lake Michigan sailors had to be particularly sensitive to the whims of the weather because they navigated a body of water just large enough to develop dangerous heavy seas, yet confined enough to allow little in the way of room to run before the storm. Indeed, the inland character of the lakes made them more treacherous than the oceans as storms developed much more suddenly and the waves, striking at much shorter intervals than ocean swells, were more violent and deadly. Prompt recognition of an approaching change in the weather was as critical as taut stays, weather-tight hatches, and a stout anchor chain in surviving a gale. These facts, together with the heavy volume of commerce on the lake and the scarcity of safe harbors, made the risk of mishap on Lake Michigan very great. Well over two thousand vessels have been wrecked on Lake Michigan. But the lake claims more than merely a high volume of accidents. Lake Michigan has also had more major shipping disasters—those involving large loss of life—than all the other Great Lakes combined. "I have seen the storms of the Channel," wrote the French scientist Francis Comte de Castlenau in 1838, "those of the Ocean, the squalls off the banks of Newfoundland, those of the coasts of America, and the hurricanes of the Gulf of Mexico. Nowhere have I witnessed the fury of the elements comparable to that found on this fresh water sea." Storms, ice, fog, ship design, and economics have all played their part in adding to that doleful toll.[2]

Shipwrecks are to maritime studies what battle stories are to military history. They are a dramatic human-interest narrative replete with heroism and folly, individual seamanship versus the seemingly inexorable exercise of fate. Disaster stories dominate bookstore selves and television documentaries. But the accent on shipwrecks distorts the larger social significance of the subject. The importance of these ships in our history is their thousands of successful voyages, not the tragic end of those that sank. In truth, most shipwrecks were not necessarily moments of high drama. For every *Rouse Simmons* that went down in a winter gale on the open lake, there were five or six Lake Michigan shipwrecks that amounted to no more than a vessel going aground on the lee shore and being refloated again in a matter of days. Nonetheless, in the same way that battle narratives can serve to illuminate issues raised by the new military history, shipwreck stories can isolate for closer appreciation important characteristics of Great Lakes history. What do the particularly stressful circumstances of a shipwreck reveal about the quality or faults of lake marine design? How did the shore-based society promote as well as undermine safety on Lake Michigan? And finally, what do the dire trials of a shipwreck reveal about the qualities, the characteristics, that made a mariner a good lakeman?[3]

In the end, all maritime accidents come down to one of three possible causes: human failure, technical failure, or overwhelming natural forces—an "act of God." For reasons both economic and psychological,

The *Bertha Barnes* shows off her raffe sail. This triangular sail was an innovation of Great Lakes mariners. Set from near the top of the foremast and stretched by a long yard, the raffe gave the schooner some of the superior pulling power of a square-sailed vessel. A following wind, such as the *Bertha Barnes* enjoyed in this photograph, offered the perfect conditions for deploying the raffe sail. Ivan H. Walton Collection, Bentley Historical Library, University of Michigan.

an inquiry into a disaster provides an opportunity to assign blame, assert intellectual control over uncontrollable forces, and learn from past mistakes. In the wake of the disappearance of the first ship on Lake Michigan, the *Griffon,* in 1679, something akin to that process took place. There was a tendency on the part of the ship's owner, La Salle, and the missionary, Hennipen, to blame the pilot of the ship for the loss, while subsequent French agents in the area seem to have doubted the utility of the vessel's design. An inland sea with no charts and no safe harbors was not a place, they concluded, for so expensive a capital investment as a ship. Thereafter, the French chose to rely on canoes to carry furs on Lake Michigan. The loss of the schooner *Wells Burt* in 1883 elicited a similar cycle of reflection. While the *Griffon* was lost at the beginning of the age of sail, the *Wells Burt* was lost at its apogee, and the wreck reveals the strengths and weaknesses of commercial sail at its peak.[4]

The *Wells Burt,* built in Detroit in 1873 and valued at $45,000, was one of the most highly regarded vessels in Chicago's grain fleet. Her sinking off Grosse Point on Chicago's North Shore, amidst a sudden and severe May thunderstorm, stunned Lake Michigan sailors. "There never was wind or sea enough inside that point, to founder the *Wells Burt,"* was the typical reaction. Some old sailing men contended that she had been run down by a careless steamer. Eleven men met their end on the deck of the *Wells Burt.* The press tugged at the heartstrings of their readers by recounting in pathetic detail the reaction of the victims' families. Captain Thomas Fountain, master of the *Burt,* was accompanied on that last voyage by his son Daniel. Another son, Arthur, was at the Chicago waterfront when word came of the disaster. "The tears sprang to his eyes and coursed down his cheeks, but he bore it like a man, and returned home without a word." One of the captain's daughters spent that day plaintively walking the beach, her eyes searching the horizon. J. S. Dunham, the tugboat czar of Chicago and owner of the *Burt,* "turned away in tears" when he received word.[5]

In the weeks following the wreck, the ship received its postmortem. The storm, which had developed suddenly as tornadoes formed over northern Illinois and southern Wisconsin, caught many ships out on the open lake. Forty-six ships were forced to ride out the blow at anchor outside the Chicago harbor as the funnels dissipated over the open water. Although a marine reporter opined that the storm was not "extraordinarily severe," men out on the lake in the midst of the crisis described it as "one of the worst they ever experienced." A week after the sinking, J. S. Dunham sent a diver down on the *Burt*'s wreck to determine if it was possible to salvage the ship, as well as to identify the cause of its demise. Captain Peter Falcon, an experienced mariner, found the ship resting hull-down in sixty feet of water. Falcon postulated that the storm tore away the ship's steering mechanism. This left the vessel at the mercy of the waves until she finally turned broadside, was swamped, and plunged to the bottom.[6]

The debate that followed the loss of the *Wells Burt* focused on two principal critiques: first, that the ship's basic design was flawed and was the reason she was lost with all hands; and second, that the ship was not maintained in proper condition. The design critique focused on the *Burt*'s bulwarks, which were built solid to the rail. When waves broke over the ship and flooded the deck, the water could not readily escape under the rail. Instead, it weighed down the ship and might break through the hatch covers and flood the hold, robbing the vessel of its remaining buoyancy. The maintenance critique stemmed from comments made by Mrs. Fountain after it was known that the storm had torn away the *Burt*'s steering gear. She confided to a marine reporter that her husband, just before his departure on the fateful voyage, said, "I never before felt so reluctant to go out. I hate to go this time. My steering gear ain't all right." That a respected master felt obliged to knowingly set sail with a major defect in his ship called into question the safety standards of the entire sailing fleet. Although nothing conclusive was determined in the case of the *Wells Burt*, the two issues raised by its sinking—vessel design and ship maintenance—remain critical to the work of Great Lakes maritime historians.[7]

In the wake of the loss of the *Wells Burt*, some marine reporters rather loosely referred to schooners as "floating coffins." Perhaps because many of the eight hundred or nine hundred schooners on the lakes at that time had been built in small, sometimes frontier, ports, there was a tendency to think of the ships as jerry-built and poorly constructed. This may have been true of some early ships, and particularly scow schooners, which insurance underwriters regularly gave low ratings because of their inherently "unseaworthy form," but it would be wrong to paint all schooners with that brush. The design and construction of the schooner fleet are varied and complex.[8]

There were seventeen hundred schooners active on the Great Lakes

177

The *J. J. Case* was launched in Manitowoc, Wisconsin, in 1875. For better than ten years she carried grain from Racine to Buffalo. Her hold could handle a cargo of 65,000 bushels of wheat or, on the return run, 1,600 tons of coal. Her normal crew was ten men and two boys. The *Case* was one of the fastest sailing ships of her time. Courtesy of the Wisconsin Maritime Museum.

during the period between the Civil War and the turn of the century. These ships were produced at a wide range of locations and under varying conditions. Scores of small (to some minds "out of the way") locations were involved in building these ships. Peshtigo, Pensaukee, Grand Haven, and Little Sturgeon produced quality Lake Michigan ships. The rise of the port of Little Sturgeon on Green Bay illustrates what was necessary to build quality ships. In August 1862 the *Door County Advocate* called to the "attention of shipbuilders" the fact that in northeastern Wisconsin "oak and other fine timber abounds, and can be obtained and furnished for shipbuilding for one-third the cost than at more distant easterly localities." This fact was not lost on Thomas Spear, a shipwright from the state of Maine. With two sons, one a caulker and the other a carpenter, Spear set out in 1866 to develop a shipyard and lumber operation at Little Sturgeon. Their first effort was to rebuild the bark *F. B. Gardner*. As part of this thorough rebuilding the *Gardner* was changed to a schooner rig, and she sailed as such for the next forty years. Spear's most ambitious project was the *Pensaukee*, a 177-foot bark he built with a $60,000 personal investment. Construction necessitated bringing fourteen ship's carpenters from Canada to augment his crew of local workers. In spite of her humble origins, the *Pensaukee*, was a fast, reliable vessel. That she made a round trip from Chicago to Buffalo in fourteen days speaks to her sailing abilities, while the fact that she was in use as late as 1907 makes clear that she was a stout, well-built ship. The success of Spear, who on salt water and fresh built more than fifty ships during his career, is proof that all that was required to build quality ships on the lakes was the raw material and the know-how.[9]

Of necessity, Lake Michigan shipbuilders of the antebellum period had to be creative. While not all were experienced naval architects, they were not afraid to experiment with new designs in order to adapt shipping to the primitive conditions of an unimproved shore. Captain R. C. Bristol, who in 1844 built Chicago's first steam-powered grain elevator, was responsible for an innovation designed to improve schooners' ability to deliver grain to the Chicago market. In 1849 Bristol wrote:

> As the water at the St. Joseph River (Michigan) would not allow a vessel drawing more than seven feet of water to pass, I determined upon another experiment which was to build another schooner of 130 tons burden with a centerboard expressly for that trade it being better than going to Chicago. . . . [T]he *St. Joseph* was built and took one or two cargoes in 1835. . . . Previous to that time it was not thought that it would answer to build a vessel of more than 50 or 60 tons with a centerboard (or rather with a slip keel then used for shoal water).

179

By 1850 nearly all Great Lakes vessels were built with centerboards (made of oak planks ten to twelve feet long and five to ten feet wide). Of course, not all pioneer experiments were happy ones. In 1851, even the boosterish *Manitowoc Herald* described one of the ships being built in the yard of Norwegian immigrant C. Anderson as "somewhat peculiar." Shipbuilders who lacked the skill to produce a centerboard occasionally resorted to the use of leeboards, ungainly stabilizers deployed off the side of a tacking vessel. These positively medieval devices, however, do not appear to have been widely used on schooners.[10]

Perhaps the best example of the quality of design and execution in ships built even in isolated frontier locations was the early work of William Wallace Bates. Born in Maine in 1827 into a family with deep roots in ship construction, Bates in 1851 established with his father a shipbuilding enterprise known as Bates & Son in Manitowoc, then an unimproved Wisconsin town with only two thousand people and a pier jutting out into Lake Michigan. But Manitowoc did have a foundry to produce metal work, an abundant supply of oak, and a demand for more ships. "The supply of vessels here is no more than half equal to the demand, and the same inconvenience is felt at Two Rivers," the *Manitowoc Herald* noted in 1856. Bates brought to Great Lakes ship design a pragmatic imagination. He was familiar with the latest design concepts from the East Coast, and he quickly learned the needs of Lake Michigan mariners. His design for the *Challenge* in 1851 combined the sharp bow of the great clipper ships with the use of a centerboard, the drop keel that R. C. Bristol and other Great Lakes shipowners had been experimenting with for a generation. The result was a fast ship with a shallow draft and ample cargo space.[11]

Bates undertook his initial Great Lakes designs under conditions much more rigorous than those enjoyed by East Coast architects. Back east it was common for shipbuilders to have a mold loft, a large, out-of-the-way space where the ship's body plans could be laid out full size on the floor. The ship's carpenters could use these scale plans to construct templates for the production of the actual structural members. No such space was available in Manitowoc, and Bates's construction plans had to be laid out on the open ground. In December 1861 heavy snow "obliterated the molders' marks" for one of his designs, and on occasion snowfall could be so heavy that all work had to cease. Fires set to warm workers from the harsh winds of a Wisconsin winter sometimes got out of control, and in 1856 a blaze nearly destroyed the

Miller Brothers shipyard, on the north branch of the Chicago River. Note the rare four-masted schooner in dry dock. These vessels were experimented with in the late 1880s and early 1890s in an effort to compete with the growing number of steam-powered bulk carriers. Chicago's river port was ill-equipped to deal with either the large sailing ships or the even larger new steamers. Photographer and date unknown. Negative no. ICHi-17979, Chicago Historical Society.

hull of the *Stephen Bates*. Nonetheless, the sailing vessels produced by Bates & Son were recognized nationally for design quality. In 1853, when Bates launched the *Mary Stockton*, the design was reviewed in the *Ship Builders Manual and Nautical Referee*. John Willis Griffiths, famed builder of the clipper ship *Sea Witch*, wrote that the *Stockton* had "without a doubt, the finest ends below water of any vessel in her class. . . . She has a large amount of stability, which always, in coasting vessels, exceeds the amount possessed by square rigged vessels. Her light draft of water and unequalled speed, must render her a valuable craft for the trade for which she is designed."[12]

Critical of the "blundering process manifest in every department of

181

shipbuilding since the days of Noah," Bates sought to elevate marine architecture from a trade practiced by local craftsmen to a science based on design principles. In addition to operating a shipyard in Chicago, he devoted his later career to promoting scientific ship design. In 1866, Great Lakes ship insurance underwriters acted on Bates's philosophy and presented a series of rules to be followed in constructing future lakes vessels. Bates himself played a prominent role in the 1874 meeting of Great Lakes shipbuilders that produced the manual *Rules of Shipbuilding.*[13]

Because very little in the way of ship's plans survive from the period before 1880 and the majority of Lake Michigan schooners were built during that time, it is very difficult to generalize about ship design. Preliminary findings from underwater archeological research seem to indicate that while the design of Great Lakes sailing vessels was not generally innovative, the vessels were well built. One thing that is clear from individual vessel studies is that within the basic form there was considerable variety, with each ship possessing its unique features.[14]

In 1986, underwater investigators working for the State Historical Society of Wisconsin investigated the remains of the schooner *Fleetwing.* The schooner had been run ashore following a collision during a gale near the notorious Death's Door passage in 1888. The *Fleetwing* had been built twenty-one years before in Manitowoc by the German-born shipwright Henry Burger. After years of service in the grain trade, the *Fleetwing* made her last voyages as a lumber hooker. The archaeologists were impressed that although the ship was built in a frontier town it exhibited all the characteristics of solid maritime craftsmanship, including the use of standard-dimension sawn frames and members as well as the extensive use of iron fastenings. The spine of the ship, as befit a vessel designed for a career as a bulk carrier, was composed of eight wooden members secured in a pyramid-shaped assembly that ran the length of the ship's 136 feet. By reinforcing the keelson with sisters and riders, the builder prevented her from hogging under the strain of tons of grain or relentless lashing of heavy seas. "These vessels were not constructed haphazardly by backwoods builders," archeologist David Cooper concluded, "but were sturdily built, with particular attention paid to the practicalities of lake commerce, and the requirements of specific cargoes."[15]

The two types of schooners that most frequently came under criticism for poor design were scows and canallers. Scows had squarish ends by design, which made them cranky sailers. As inexpensive, locally built, and locally used coasting vessels, scows tended to be less well rigged than clipper schooners and often manned by smaller, less experienced crews, sometimes harvest hands or lumberjacks. Insurance companies thought so little of their seaworthiness that they would not give even the best-built scows a rating higher than "B," which deterred the owners of valuable cargoes from using the ships. Canallers were a more important part of the Lake Michigan fleet. Their size was determined by the scale of the locks on the Welland Canal, the only way for a vessel to reach Lake Ontario. Like scows, these vessels had flat-bottomed hulls, and unlike clipper schooners, they had no keel to help keep the vessel on its track. When sailing into the wind a canaller tended to slide to the leeward with only the centerboard to check this slippage. This was a particularly dangerous characteristic on the closed waters of Lake Michigan. A cautious shipbuilder might compensate for this defect by installing two or three centerboards, although this merely indicates the inherent difficulties of the design. A string of vessel sinkings during the fall of 1874 caused the *Chicago Tribune* to attack the design of canallers. In October the schooner *Wanderer* was lost. A month later, the schooner *Atlanta* went missing. Then, on November 26, an autumn gale drove the schooner *William Sanderson* against the massive sand cliffs of Empire Bluff on Lake Michigan's east shore. What made this chain of accidents particularly disturbing was that all three ships were lost with all hands. "Strange to say, all of the unfortunate crafts above described were what are styled 'canal built,' " the *Tribune* noted. "This does certainly look as if flat-bottoms were a failure, and no other vessels of that style should hereafter be allowed to float the lakes." The trouble with the *Tribune*'s prescription was that the demand for canallers remained strong throughout the 1870s. The *Tribune* itself regularly ran ads requesting canallers to carry grain or lumber to Canadian or European ports.[16]

Another charge leveled at Great Lakes schooners in the wake of the sinking of the *Wells Burt* was that shipbuilders used inferior materials during construction. It is true that the quality of ship timber varied around the lake, and that builders tended to use what was locally available. In 1887 the *George Nestor* was launched at Baraga, Michigan, on Lake Superior. With little good oak available on the shores of that lake, the ship was made entirely of Norway pine. Yet the *Nestor* was an exception. It was one of a handful of ships made on Lake Superior because of a lack of quality timber. Notable shipbuilding locations like Manitowoc and Saginaw flourished only so long as their supply of oak was plentiful. Larger shipbuilding centers like Milwaukee, Detroit, and Chicago had substantial lumber markets that made quality material available at attractive prices. As the world's most important lumbering region, the Great Lakes region generally offered superb building material. "For flexibility, durability and toughness," historian Walter Havighurst noted, "Michigan oak was equal to the best English oak." While many quality oceangoing vessels, such as clipper ships, were only framed with oak and then planked with pine, most Great Lakes schooners were made almost wholly from stout white oak.[17]

Saltwater sailors were frequently impressed with the sailing qualities of ships built on the inland seas. Captain John Kenlon believed that the three-masted schooner *Resumption* was "one of the fastest vessels I have ever had the pleasure of sailing." The crew he found "a rather unsailorlike looking lot," but they were "very smart" when it came to "handling a ship and obeying orders quickly and capably." He was impressed that less than an hour after leaving Chicago the ship had all of her sails spread before a "spanking southwest breeze." What particularly drew his attention was *The Resumption*'s "mainmast reaching one hundred and forty-seven feet high; the longest spar I had ever seen in my life. The spread of sail on this 'stick' was simply immense." The saltwater man was baffled by the centerboard, which he labeled a "contraption" until the wind shifted and the mate deployed the slip keel. "It was while heading into this wind that I realized the value of our center-board. I was truly surprised to find how close our vessel was able to lay up into the wind." After a night spent heading into a winter gale, Kenlon was amazed to learn that the schooner, instead of being blown back to Chicago, had held her own. "This was a very remarkable accomplishment for a vessel under those conditions," he noted. As Kenlon learned how to use the *Resumption*'s powerful spread of canvas and to let the schooner lean on her centerboard, he found that the vessel could clip along at twelve knots. "I believed I could have put her into a race with yachts of supposedly finer lines and won with ease."[18]

The fact is that Lake Michigan sailing ships, particularly clipper schooners, were generally well designed and built of first-class materials. It was in the areas of vessel maintenance, ship overloading, and crew downsizing that the maritime industry was culpable in promoting dangerous conditions. These economically driven factors, not schooner design, were the preventable causes of Lake Michigan shipwrecks.

Unless meticulously cared for, wooden ships were subject to rapid deterioration. After fifteen years a lakes schooner had seen her best days and generally required a major refitting to retain an "A-1" rating. Historian Theodore Charrney estimated that the grain schooner *Dick Somers* only depreciated 2 percent a year during her first fifteen years of operation. After fifteen years, however, vessel repair was a constant feature of operating an older schooner. For this reason, shipyards were located in virtually every port on Lake Michigan. Certainly, many of these yards produced new ships, but a steady income was provided simply repairing and rebuilding existing ships. If a schooner was carefully kept in repair and given a rebuilding at some point, it could remain a competent commercial vessel for a long time. The *William Aldrich*, built just four years after William Bates's prototypical clipper schooner *Challenge*, remained a working sailing ship for almost sixty years. During that time she was rebuilt twice. The schooner *Our Son* sailed for fifty-five years, the *Lucia A. Simpson* for fifty-four years, and the *Mary Ellen Cook* for forty-eight years.[19]

Most schooners, however, did not last as long as those venerables, since they were not afforded the regular maintenance necessary to keep them safely afloat. In 1883 the *Chicago Times,* aroused by the loss of the *Wells Burt,* editorialized against the sale of the schooner *Watts Sherman.* Built in 1846, the *Sherman* was in scandalous condition. "There is not enough sound wood in her to make a decent load of kindling wood," decried the newspaper. "All her frames are rotted out fore and aft, and her ceiling is so rotten that a hole can be punched through with a walking stick . . . she is not worth the powder to blow her up." What most incensed the *Times* was that the ship's owners, the prosperous Union Dry-Dock Company of Buffalo, were trying to sell a ship that they had for years refused to maintain. "What is needed is a government inspector to condemn such craft and to prevent any persons other than the owners from risking their lives in them."[20]

The trouble was, there was no government regulation of lake vessels, and in many cases it was the owner-masters themselves who chose to sail ships dangerously in need of a refit. The only inspection of ships came from the insurance underwriters. During the winter the insurers usually sent inspectors to the major lake ports—Chicago, Milwaukee, Cleveland, and Buffalo—as between them they held the bulk of the fleet. On the basis of this survey ships were given an insurance rating, ranging from "A-1" for the top-quality ships to "C" for hulks on their last legs. Ships too far gone, like the *Watts Sherman,* were given no rating at all and could not be insured. The system had major flaws. Not every ship was checked each year, and because the inspections themselves were only cursory, paint and tar could go a long way in preserving a ship's rating. Even more of a problem were the owner-masters of deteriorating vessels, who, without adequate investment, tried to extend the life of their ships. This problem grew in the 1880s and 1890s as the schooner fleet aged and the ships lost their niche in lake commerce. "Vessel-owners should raise a fund to buy up all these old coffins and get them out of service," proposed a Chicago shipowner. "The majority of them are owned by poor men who are obliged to run them until they rot down in order to earn a living for themselves and their families." Unfortunately, this proposal was not acted upon. Nor did the ships simply "rot down"; rather, with tragic frequency, they went down with their crews.[21]

In March 1878 the *Chicago Inter-Ocean* and the *Buffalo Express* both complained about the number of unseaworthy vessels operating on the lakes, noting that "there are the [insurance] inspectors say, at least a couple of hundred vessels which should be condemned as utterly unseaworthy." Nonetheless, the majority of these were being fitted out for another year of service, and would likely remain in use "as long as they hold together." The trade of last resort for such vessels, which sailors referred to as "milkers," was lumber. On Lake Michigan lumber ships made short runs, usually no more than two days. As a cargo, lumber would not be damaged by the ship's leaky hull, and even added buoyancy if the vessel foundered. The veteran schooner *Winslow* was no match for a fierce May gale in 1894, yet even though the lake flowed over her gunwales, her cargo of cedar posts kept the ship afloat until a tug could save the crew. Even if a ship was lost, the lumber could easily be salvaged. As long as there were masters willing to run the risk of sailing "a venerable old tub," there would be lumber companies willing to take the risk of using them. When a veteran of fifty-nine seasons, the *William Aldrich,* was lost in 1915 it was taking on a cargo of cedar posts. And when the last Great Lakes schooner sank beneath the waves, the *Our Son* in 1930, it was carrying a cargo of lumber.[22]

Second only to the problem of vessel maintenance was the tendency to overload schooners. Again, lumber vessels were the worst offenders in this regard. Because the runs were relatively short, there was a tendency to check the horizon for storm clouds, then fill the hold and stack the deck with lumber as high as the cabin top. For the owner of an old schooner, too small to economically compete in the trade, the deck cargo became the margin of economic viability. High freight rates could seduce even normally careful masters to overburden their vessels. During the smooth sailing months of June, July, and August the chances of making good the gamble were quite high; not so in autumn. "Many went down during the fall gales because they were overloaded," recalled an experienced lake captain. Canallers, because of their shallow draft, were particularly susceptible to overloading. During the fall, therefore, a lakeman explained, "the mortality among canal schooners became almost epidemic." Although the problem of vessel overloading was widely recognized and investigated in the 1880s by underwriters and by the commissioner of navigation, no legislation regulating overloading was approved during the era of sail.[23]

It was for financial reasons that vessels were overloaded with cargo and their maintenance deferred. The third factor in the economic troika that drove schooners to destruction was smaller crews. Cutting costs to the bone meant reducing the size of the ship's complement. An innovation such as the Grand Haven rig, in which three-masted vessels were rerigged with two masts, was popular because it was a way to increase cargo space and decrease crew size. Virtually all major changes in Lake Michigan sailing ships from the Civil War onward had to do with reducing fixed costs such as labor. The move from square sails to the schooner rig was done in large part to save labor, the addition of donkey engines for raising sail or anchor was done to save time and labor, and even the use of the raffe as opposed to square topsails was done to save labor. In the late 1890s, when the petite eighty-eight-ton *Mary A. Gregory* was put into the "lakeshoring" trade, bumming from harbor to harbor in northern Lake Michigan, she was reduced to a crew of two besides the captain. There were times when she even sailed with only a single seaman. Larger schooners

Ice hangs from the bow of a lumber schooner, perhaps preparing for one last run before winter. The crew stand on the deck cargo, stacked four or five feet high on the heavily loaded little schooner. Note how low she rests in the water, affording little margin for the heavy seas of a November gale. Michigan Maritime Museum.

could not get by with less than four crew members, but even that was half what a ship might have used a half-century before.[24]

As the crew sizes shrank, the quality of men before the mast also diminished. By the 1880s it was clear that the future of the lake marine was with steam-powered steel ships, not wooden sailing craft, and young seamen chose their berths accordingly. Schooners were increasingly left with either unskilled boys or gray-haired tars. In 1894, when the schooner *J. Loomis McLaren* began to break up on a storm-tossed bar off Chicago, bystanders waded out to the wreck to help the crew to shore. The last man taken off was a somewhat befuddled seventy-two-year-old able seaman. Although he had been sailing the lakes for sixty years and clearly knew better, he refused to leave the wreck until he had his luggage in hand. "I've been in many a wreck before," he later told a reporter, "but I never got as wet as this." In her final days, the fifty-year veteran *City of Grand Haven* was reduced to a crew of six adolescent boys averaging seventeen years of age.[25]

Sailing on Lake Michigan was at its most dangerous during the years before the Civil War. With few improved harbors, little in the way of navigational aids, almost no charts, and next to nothing in the way of safety regulations, sailing the inland seas was a hazardous undertaking. In 1850 alone 431 lives were lost on the entire Great Lakes, along with $500,000 worth of ships and cargo. In his annual address to Congress in 1851, President Millard Fillmore pleaded for federal action to improve the lakes: "Great numbers of lives and vast amounts of property are annually lost for want of safe and convenient harbors on the Lakes. None but those who have been exposed to that dangerous navigation can fully appreciate the importance of this subject." Insurance rates on sailing vessels in the 1850s averaged between 8 and 10 percent of the ship's value. The slow response of government, both state and federal, to what amounted to a state of emergency of the lakes was criminal, and did much to move the Great Lakes states securely into the ranks of the more proactive and progressive Republican Party.[26]

Lighthouses were one of the few internal improvements the southern-dominated Democratic Party would approve for the Great Lakes. At the time of President Fillmore's address there were twenty-seven lighthouses built or under construction on Lake Michigan. However, many of the early lighthouses were haphazardly built, equipped with ineffective lenses, and indifferently manned. Reform came after 1852 when the Lighthouse Board was created within the Treasury Department. The new board set about improving the design and maintenance of lighthouses. Army engineers were brought in to design all future lighthouses, and naval officers were assigned the duty of inspecting the operation of the lights. A pair of schooners, appropriately renamed *Lamplighter* and *Watchful*, was purchased to act as lighthouse tenders. French-designed Fresnel lenses were adopted for Lake Michigan,

189

making some of the lights useful to mariners for the first time. Fog signals were another important upgrade. At the time of the Civil War there were only a handful of steam fog signals on all of the Great Lakes, but they gradually became standard at most Lake Michigan lights.[27]

During the post–Civil War era the system was further upgraded when the Lighthouse Board began to pay closer attention to the quality of individuals brought into the Lighthouse Service. Political influence remained a factor in the selection of lightkeepers until they were brought into the civil service in 1896. Nonetheless, many of the keepers and their assistants were conscientious public servants. Former schooner captains, Soren Kristiansen for one, sometimes joined the Lighthouse Service. The depression of 1893 and the growing dominance of steam power on the lakes drove Kristiansen to take up a new trade. "I had spent 25 years sailing on vessels," he noted in his diary, "now I should help to guide our modern merchant fleet safely in and out of harbors." He was much pleased with his new career. The last entry in his diary was the day he took command of Lightship No. 60 guarding Eleven Mile Shoal near Escanaba, Michigan: "In the evening the light was hoisted for the first time, and thus my new life has begun, with perfect gentlemen for superior officers."[28]

But not all Lake Michigan lighthouse keepers were gentlemen. The Beaver Island light was long maintained by women. Peter McKinley was officially the keeper for most of the 1860s, but chronic ill health meant that his wife and daughters were the de facto keepers. After nine years of such an arrangement, Elizabeth Whitney Van Riper came to Beaver Island as the wife of the new keeper. When her husband died trying rescue the crew of a distressed vessel, Mrs. Van Riper was appointed the new keeper. She continued in that job until 1884, when she took the post of keeper at Little Traverse Light. Harriet Colfax was the longest-serving female keeper on Lake Michigan. From 1853 until 1904 she manned the Michigan City Lighthouse, keeping the light in service even in her eighties. One source has estimated that in 1851, when seventy-six lights were in service on the Great Lakes, there were thirty female keepers.[29]

As efficient as the Lighthouse Service was, there were gaps in the system of beacons and navigational aids. The 1883 spring gale that wrecked the *Wells Burt* also wreaked havoc at the mouth of the Chicago River, in part due to a lack of proper lights. At the time of the

Chicago's first lighthouse, ca. 1857. Reprinted from Alfred T. Andreas, *History of Chicago* (Chicago: A. T. Andreas, 1884–86). Collection of the Chicago Maritime Society.

storm there were only low, dim lights on the breakwaters, which had only recently been constructed to create an outer harbor. Ships running before the wind desperately searched the horizon of breakers for the harbor entrance, but the breakwater lights, no more than twenty feet above the water during calm weather, were obscured under pounding surf. As the schooner *Mary E. Cook* approached breakwater, Captain Edward Williams saw a reddish glow and took it to be the entrance light. He steered his reeling ship toward it, only, at the last second, to perceive that the red light was from a lantern on a ship anchored inside the harbor. The *Cook* drove, not into the harbor, but directly toward the breakwater. Fortunately, at the moment of impact the schooner was riding a thirty-foot wave that lifted it up onto the seawall. For a moment the vessel hung on the breakwater. Henry Miller, a passenger who had never before been in a Lake Michigan gale, chose that moment to jump off the vessel and onto the breakwater. As he did, a giant wave broke over them. Miller was swept away to his death, while the breaker lifted the stern of the ship off the wall and deposited the ship neatly on the other side. The next day masters and shipowners in the port circulated a petition to the Lighthouse Board for new lights at the outer harbor.[30]

Long after lighthouses had begun to be built along the lake, mariners still had no accurate charts of the inland seas. As Great Lakes navigation evolved from birchbark canoes to larger and larger schooners and steamships, unmarked shoals and reefs became a greater threat. In the eighteenth century the British government had begun to make charts of their portion of the Great Lakes, but it was not until 1841 that Congress created the United States Lake Survey under the control of the Army Corps of Engineers. The survey was begun in the area at the head of Lake Michigan because this was the great "thoroughfare" of the lakes. While the charts produced by the engineers were painstakingly accurate, they were also slow in being completed. By 1860 charts were available for the dangerous waters near the straits and the heavily used Manitou Passage. The Civil War drew engineers such as future Army of the Potomac commander George G. Meade away from the lakes, and not until 1874 was the preliminary survey of Lake Michigan completed.[31]

While the army engineers went about their work of charting Lake Michigan, some lake mariners scoffed at the idea that the result would be worth the effort. Experience and oral tradition had been the means of navigating schooners for better than a generation, and one master remembered that "the old lake captains ridiculed the idea of looking at one of them for information." Vessel owners, however, may have reacted more positively. When John Kenlon was given command of his first schooner, he was "authorized to go out and buy my own instruments and charts, and provided with a certain amount of money for that purpose." With the "limited amount of money at my disposal," Kenlon was pleased with the "very fine set of charts of the Lakes" he was able to buy. Interestingly, the owner did not seem as concerned about the quality of navigational instruments available to their captain. The best Kenlon could obtain with his remaining funds was "an old sextant, pretty well used up," bought at a pawnshop. A veteran saltwater sailor, Kenlon also wanted to buy a chronometer, but he lacked the funds and had to use his pocket watch for that purpose.

Despite some grumbling from the old-timers, the use of charts seems to have caught on quickly. W. H. Hearding, a veteran of the lakes, contended that "during the year 1859 more than 5,000 were issued from the [Lake Survey] office in Detroit and there is scarce a vessel of any consideration on the lakes which has not a full set of them on board."[32]

The need to do more to aid lake mariners than mark dangerous locations was painfully brought home by a string of disasters on the lakes in the 1869, including one four-day gale that wrecked ninety-seven ships. As the volume of shipping grew after the Civil War, so did the number of accidents. Between 1878 and 1898 almost six thousand ships were wrecked on the lakes. In the period of federal inactivity before the Civil War the government's only gesture toward lifesaving on Lake Michigan was to place twenty-three life boats at the shore of particularly dangerous waters. In 1871 Congress established lifesaving stations manned by full-time professionals. Lake Michigan received ten stations. Some of these were located near hazardous waters, such as Point Betsey and Point Au Sable, while the bulk were established near busy harbors along the lake's east and west shores: Grand Haven, St. Joseph, Chicago, Racine, Milwaukee, Sheboygan, and Two Rivers. Over the next twenty years stations were added at Evanston, Muskegon, Manistee, Kenosha, Pentwater, Frankfort, White River, Holland, Sturgeon Bay, Baileys Harbor, Plum Island, Sleeping Bear Point, and South Manitou Island.[33]

In a short time the men of the Lifesaving Service achieved a heroic stature. They were celebrated in the press as "surf warriors." Actually, the job was one of routine and drill broken by occasional moments of high drama and real danger. Each station was commanded by a keeper and staffed, during the shipping season, by a half dozen surfmen. Their job was to bring crews off distressed or beached vessels. To do so they drilled in the use of their surfboat and the Lyle gun, a small cannon that fired a rescue line several hundred yards. If a storm was too fierce to use the surfboat, they would try to reach a stricken ship with the Lyle gun. On the rescue line they would then deploy a "breeches buoy," essentially a sling in which the crew could be pulled one by one above the waves to safety. In the days before radio, the only way for the crew to know if their services were needed was to be vigilant. In stormy weather the men would man watchtowers or undertake long patrols along the beach to look for vessels in trouble.[34]

The crew of the Jackson Park Lifesaving Station in their surfboat, ca. 1910. The Jackson Park station was one of three Chicago-area stations. The Lifesaving Service manned stations all along the shore of Lake Michigan and earned a reputation for bravery and dedication. Collection of the Chicago Maritime Society.

Typical of the service performed all along the lake was the November 1895 rescue performed by the Evanston lifesaving crew. The Evanston station was unique in one regard: all of the crew were made up of Northwestern University students, and the station was located adjacent to the campus. The keeper, however, was veteran mariner Captain Lawrence O. Lawson. In the teeth of a late-November gale, the steam barge *J. Emory Owen* and her two consorts, the schooners *Elizabeth A. Nicholson* and *Michigan,* were driven aground about five hundred yards from shore. Pounded by the full fury of the storm, the ships were in imminent danger of breaking up. The *Owen* desperately tried to signal for help by blowing its steam whistle, but it was after midnight and the residents of Chicago's posh North Shore communities had all gone to sleep. Several hours passed before word of the wreck reached the Evanston station several miles to the south. The surfboat then had to be laboriously hauled up the shore, through snowdrifts several feet deep. While passing through a woods the boat was jarred from its truck and stove in. Captain Lawson improvised a patch using a raincoat and some barrel staves. Finally, after several hours they reached the site of the wrecks.[35]

It was only with great difficulty that the lifesavers could even the launch their boat. Several times the waves crashing ashore simply tossed the boat back onto the beach. At last they managed a successful launch by wading waist deep into the icy surf. They pulled for the steamer *Owen,* where they found its crew had been joined by the complement of the *Nicholson.* Great difficulty was encountered bringing off Mrs. William Smith, the cook and wife of the master of the *Nicholson,* and her six-month- old infant. All told, the lifesavers made four trips to the *Owen* and two to the *Michigan.* By the end of the first trip the livesavers' oilskin coats had frozen stiff and ice coated the boat. The surfboat completely vanished from sight in the deep swells between waves, and on occasion the crash of the breakers knocked the boys from their seats and threatened to capsize the boat. Suffering from cold, cramps, and fatigue, they did not quit until all thirty-six people had been removed from the wrecks.[36]

Located along the busy shipping lane between Milwaukee and Chicago, the Evanston station effected the rescue of four hundred mariners between 1876 and 1916. But not all rescue efforts were successful or heroic. In May 1894 a gale wrecked eight schooners off Chicago. Thanks to the work of the Chicago Lifesaving Station, local police and citizens, and tugboat operators, most of the crews were saved. The major exception was the ill-fated crew of the little two-masted schooner *Myrtle.*

The *Myrtle* appeared to be safe on the afternoon of May 18. She was securely anchored and riding out the storm when another schooner broke its moorings and slammed into her. Stove in, with her rigging fouled, the *Myrtle* sank to the deck level while the storm pushed her south along the lakefront. The tug *Protection* tried to reach the helpless ship, but the *Myrtle* was so surrounded by spars and cordage that the tug had to turn back for fear of fouling her propeller. The next attempt at rescue was done in cooperation with the Lifesaving Service. The Chicago harbor surfboat was towed out with the idea of letting it drift to the *Myrtle*. But no sooner did the tug clear the breakwater than the heavy seas upset the surfboat, suddenly placing the lifesavers themselves in need of saving. They were in the cold water nearly an hour before all six could be pulled aboard the tug. "When we fished them up they were nearly frozen and unfit for further exertion," recalled Captain William Smith of the *Protection*.[37]

When the tug returned to the lifesaving station, Smith informed the crowd gathered there that the *Myrtle* was doomed: "I am confident nothing can be done to save them, they must be lost." But in the best traditions of the service, Captain Fountain, the Chicago station keeper, refused to give up without one more try. Several of his men were capable of making another effort, and five volunteers were raised from the crowd of onlookers, including the *Chicago Tribune*'s maritime reporter. Captain Fountain told each man that "he would probably not come back alive," but the volunteers were undeterred. Unfortunately, heroic drama gave way to low comedy when, as the men were donning their yellow raincoats and writing their farewell messages, someone offered several bottles of whiskey to fortify them from the cold. Some refused, while others "poured down their throats all they could hold." Unfortunately, "Captain Fountain in particular imbibed so freely that he soon began to stagger." The rescue was canceled when he slipped on the dock, fell, and could not rise. While Fountain slept off the whiskey, the *Myrtle* was lost with all hands.[38]

Apart from the sorry performance of Captain Fountain, the Lifesaving Service was the most impressive example of a substantial federal commitment to marine safety on the Great Lakes. The building of harbors of refuge, the charting of dangerous shoals, the establishment and maintenance of a system of lighthouses, beacons, and buoys, and the creation of the Lifesaving Service itself were accomplishments of the federal government during the schooner era that greatly reduced the loss of lives and property on Lake Michigan. It may have been rugged individualists who first built and sailed schooners on the lake, but the blue-water frontier was conquered only with a considerable amount of government assistance. The United States government had gone from being one of the major reasons for fatalities on the lakes before the Civil War, to being an important force for a safer, more efficient lake marine after the war.

Yet in spite of this federal establishment, schooners remained vulnerable to the elements, and each season on Lake Michigan saw scores of them go down to destruction. The May 1894 gale that sank the *Myrtle* offers some telling clues, beyond vessel design and maintenance, regarding the weaknesses of sailing ships on the inland seas. The 1894 gale cost twenty-seven lives all across the Great Lakes. Although a total of thirty-five ships were sunk or damaged, all of those that perished were schooners. Old-timers referred to the gale as "a real schooner eater," but the sad truth was that any sustained storm was a "schooner eater." While on the open sea a ship in a storm can trim her sails and ride before the wind, that safe course is inhibited on the Great Lakes by the lack of open water. With its north-south expanse of more than three hundred miles, Lake Michigan offers one of the largest stretches of open water on the lakes. Even so, a schooner traveling from Escanaba to Chicago that encountered a northern gale would be able to run before the storm for little more than two days before reaching the southern end of the lake. In the 1894 gale the schooner *Jack Thompson* made such a run. By the time she reached Chicago, her sails were shredded and her pumps broken. She collided with another schooner just outside the breakwater and sank within sight of safety. A rescue crew made up of concerned bystanders helped to save all but one of the six-man crew. Most ships, however, did not have the entire length of the lake as sea room. Within a matter of hours a storm might drive them upon a lee shore.[39]

The most common type of Lake Michigan shipwreck was for a ship to be driven ashore. Depending on the severity of the weather and where the ship went aground, the event could be anything but dramatic. The *Chicago Tribune* reported in May 1860: "The schooner *Whirlwind*, Captain Berga, from Centerville for this port, went ashore this morning, just north of the lighthouse pier. She was lightened of her cargo (91 cords of wood) and got off, without any damage." A big blow might end with several steamships crashing ashore as well, but most of the time those vessels' power source gave them the ability to make headway into the storm and avoid destruction in the shallows. When a schooner was driven ashore in a gale, the great danger was that the pounding of the surf would cause it to break apart. When the decks were awash and the danger of breakup was imminent, the crew had two choices. One was to try to make it ashore in the yawl, although in heavy seas those little boats usually foundered before they could even be launched. The other choice, and hardly more attractive, was to seek refuge in the rigging. Since most wrecks occurred in

spring and fall, climbing soaking wet into the rigging was a frighten-
ing and frigid experience. Frostbite and hypothermia dogged the desperate men. Remarkably, men were known to survive for more than
forty hours in such an exposed position. After that, nothing could be
done but to cut them down. Such was the fate of the schooner *M. J.
Cummings,* which foundered near Milwaukee in May 1894 in eighteen
feet of water. The crew were lashed to the rigging and desperate for
assistance, but the combined efforts of the Milwaukee and Racine lifesaving stations could effect no more than the rescue of a single seaman, the other six crew members perishing from exposure.[40]

The most common place for a schooner to come to grief was not
out on the open lake but near the entrance of one of the lake's narrow-
mouthed harbors. A sailing ship attempting to enter a harbor, particularly in heavy seas, had one approach to get the vessel in properly.
Even a slight miscalculation would slam the schooner against the pier
or drive it ashore. On October 4, 1897, the petite two-master *Addie*
overshot the entrance to Frankfort, washed into the beach, and was
ruined. Because entering a harbor was so difficult, most masters attempted to anchor off the entrance and wait out the storm. This meant
relying on both the anchor to take firm hold on the bottom and on
the chain to hold against the strain. The fate of the schooner *Toledo*
in 1865 is illustrative of the dangers of the situation. After securing a
cargo of lumber from an isolated pier on the Wisconsin shore, the
schooner set sail for Manitowoc, only six miles away. By this time a
southeast gale was ripping across the lake. The *Toledo* could not seek
shelter at Manitowoc because sand still blocked the harbor's mouth.
Captain William Callaway had little choice but to drop anchor inside
Rawley Point. After several hours the *Toledo* began to drag her anchor.
Hoping to avoid a beaching, Captain Callaway discarded part of his
deck cargo, close-reefed the mainsail and foresail, and slipped the anchor. After making several tacks very close to shore, he eventually
managed to work the schooner a mile offshore when the gale carried
away the mainsail. The staysails soon followed, leaving only the foresail to keep them off the lee shore. It was not enough, and the *Toledo*
grounded about a quarter mile from Two Rivers. Thanks to gallant
work by some residents of that town, Callaway and his crew were taken
off the wreck. Of course, that was not the end of the *Toledo.* Although
she was buried up to her bulwarks in sand, Callaway had her refloated

two months later and the ship was lengthened and refitted to sail again.[41]

As was true for the men of the *Myrtle*, death often awaited sailors right outside the harbor. In 1847 the captain of the *H. Merrill*, which was sinking at the Milwaukee pier, tried to jump to the dock. He fell just short and drowned in the heaving water. In 1882 John Dibble died on the schooner *Jesse Martin* when she stranded within sight of the Grand Haven lifesaving station. Dibble had joined a group of sailors determined to refloat the ship after it had gone aground south of the Grand Haven pier a week earlier. They managed to patch and refloat the *Martin*, but the vessel, still sluggish with water, capsized when she turned broadside to the lake comers in an attempt to enter the harbor. Most of the crew made it into the crosstrees, which at least provided a secure hold while the ship thrashed in the water, and awaited rescue from the nearby lifesaving station. Dibble, however, had been in the passageway alongside the main cabin when the ship heaved over, and he was caught in the peak halyards and held under the water.[42]

Wrecks in the open lake were less common but more deadly, since there was little chance of assistance outside the sight of land. The cold temperature of Lake Michigan during most of the navigation season gave men wrecked in the open water only a few hours before they would succumb to the elements. Following a big blow, shipowners would wait anxiously for news of their vessel. Some ships, such as the *Thomas Hume*, set sail and were never seen again. The loss of the *Hume* in May 1891 befuddled everyone. Critics of the sailing fleet had to admit that the *Hume* was a well-maintained vessel with an experienced captain and a full union crew. For nineteen years her owners, the Hackley-Hume Lumber Company, had operated a fleet of schooners without a mishap, not even a grounding. They offered a reward for information on the fate of the ship and dispatched a tug to search the lake between Chicago and Muskegon. Yet nothing was ever found of the *Thomas Hume*—not a hatch cover, not a spar, not a body.[43]

There was much speculation that the *Hume* had been caught with a full spread of sail by a sudden storm, one of Lake Michigan's notorious white squalls, and that before the crew could bring in the canvas the schooner was capsized. In the wake of a big blow it was not uncommon for a schooner to be found floating upside down, abandoned in the middle of the lake. When empty, lake schooners, particularly canallers, were vulnerable to capsizing—what sailors called "turning

A tug maneuvers in heavy surf to save a three-master that ran out of lee room. Such groundings were typical of the majority of Lake Michigan shipwrecks. Collection of the Chicago Maritime Society.

turtle"—because of their shallow draft and high masts. Some of the most hair-raising shipwrecks on Lake Michigan involved capsized vessels.

In May 1853 the schooner *Mary Margaret* set sail from Chicago to Muskegon in quest of a cargo of lumber. Andrew Bergh, the young acting master of the ship, was disappointed to find nothing available in that sawdust city, so he made his way down the shore to Grand Haven. At midnight he reefed his sails and retired for the night, leaving orders with the watch to wake him if the wind came up. It did, at about two o'clock in the morning, but the first Bergh knew of it was when he heard a loud noise on deck. He sprang to his feet and arrived

200

on deck just as the ship rolled over. Caught under the ship, Bergh struggled breathless in the cold, dark chaos to make his way to an air pocket in the overturned cabin. The cook and two members of the crew were also huddled there. Fortunately, after two hours the ship rolled partially over on her beam ends. The trapped men called for their shipmates, but the watch had been swept away when the ship capsized. For a day the four men shivered in the submerged cabin. The cook and one of the seamen, Zachariah Nelson, were the first to yield to hypothermia's debilitating grip. Remarkably, Bergh and another man held on, able to keep only their heads out of the water, for nearly three days. Finally, the schooner *Geo. R. Roberts* spotted their wreck and laboriously cut a whole in the side of the *Mary Margaret* to free the survivors. On the other side of the lake, the same squall that had done in the *Mary Margaret* capsized the brand-new clipper schooner *North Yuba* on her maiden voyage from Manitowoc.[44]

Although Andrew Bergh had endured several days in the frigid darkness of a capsized vessel, his ordeal was by no means an unparalleled case. The record for misery must go to a woman trapped for five days in waist-deep water. The crew had given her up for dead when they abandoned the ship, and when salvers came they did not hear her cries. The men were stunned, then, when she walked up the stairs to the deck after they righted the schooner.[45]

Collisions were another cause of wrecks in the open lake. When both the *Wells Burt* and the *Thomas Hume* were wrecked so mysteriously, schoonermen let it be known that they believed the ships had been run down by a steamship. Such accidents did occur all too frequently. A particularly bad year for such mishaps was 1896, when at least five schooners sank in collisions with steam-powered vessels. The loss of the *Mary D. Ayer* was the worst of the lot. Run down by the steamer *Onoko* in dense fog, the stricken schooner drifted helplessly. For a time the steamer *City of Duluth* was able bring her in tow, but somehow the ships parted company and the *Ayer* was lost along with five lives. In 1892 there was a deadly collision near High Island between a powerful new steamer, the *W. H. Gilcher,* and the fore-and-aft-rigged collier *Ostrich.* What exactly happened is not known, as both ships were lost with all hands.[46]

The worst disaster on Lake Michigan involved a collision between the schooner *Augusta* and the passenger steamer *Lady Elgin.* The *Lady Elgin* was a stately, well-appointed vessel, popular with excursionists and tourists. On the evening of September 7, 1860, she left Chicago harbor with more than four hundred passengers. Many were Irish Democrats from Milwaukee who were returning from a tumultuous rally and torchlight parade in honor of presidential candidate Stephen A. Douglas. The 332-ton, 128-foot-long *Augusta* had only been in the lake trade for five years. Each vessel spotted the other a good ten to fifteen minutes before the accident, yet neither made an effort to modify its course. One reason for the accident was that just after the wheelmen spotted each others' running lights, a violent squall hit and the *Augusta* was nearly thrown on her beams. Captain D. M. Malott, off duty below, came on deck and helped the crew bring in the sails. For the men working on saving the schooner, the approaching steamer was further obscured by the deck cargo of boards piled high as the cabin top. Suddenly, through the rain, the schoonermen saw the running lights of the *Lady Elgin* as the steamer passed directly in front of their bow. "Hard about!" Captain Malott ordered, but the *Augusta* was an unresponsive vessel when fully loaded. The squall had her pitched over on her port side, water dashing past the rail, and Malott's order could not be executed. They hit in a jarring collision, the ships at a ninety-degree angle. The *Augusta*'s jibboom drove deep into one of the *Lady Elgin*'s staterooms. With her bow fouled in the steamer, the *Augusta* was pulled alongside. Seaman William Bonner of the *Augusta* called out for the steamer to throw the sailing ship a line. There was no response, and the ships shortly broke away from one another.[47]

Aboard the *Augusta* there was fear that their bow had been stove in and the ship was lost, so the crew set about letting go the anchor and readying the yawl. Both Captain Malott and the mate expressed the sentiment that "it was hard of the steamer to run away and leave us." But the leaking, while substantial, was not too much for the pumps. Malott had the head gear cleared away and determined that he just might be able to reach Chicago harbor. His only fear for the *Lady Elgin* was that perhaps his jibboom had killed a sleeping passenger.[48]

In the end, somewhere between 279 and 350 people on the *Lady Elgin* were doomed by the collision. Unbeknownst to Captain Malott, the sturdy *Augusta* had pierced the *Lady Elgin* beneath the waterline. As soon as he determined the size of the hole, Jack Wilson, captain of the steamer, immediately headed his ship toward shore seven miles away. The ship was bereft of lifeboats or preservers. Fortunately, when

The *Augusta*'s fatal collision with the steamer *Lady Elgin*. The 1860 accident led to the deaths of more than 279 people. *Frank Leslie's Illustrated Newspaper*, September 22, 1860.

the *Lady Elgin* went down her superstructure broke apart. This allowed the panicked passengers to grab onto stateroom doors and sections of deck as makeshift flotation devices. One section of deck supported more than forty people. Heavy seas drove them toward the Illinois shore near Evanston. It was the pounding surf, at the brink of safety, that exacted the final payment from many of the passengers. The makeshift rafts were dashed to pieces, and their occupants were thrown headfirst into the surging crosscurrents and powerful breakers. Through the early-morning hours the residents of Evanston and Winnetka, roused from their beds by news of the calamity, gathered at the beach. With ropes tied around their waists, brave citizens plunged into the waves to rescue the survivors.[49]

Milwaukee, home of the majority of the dead, was a "scene of wild grief and confusion" as people gradually discovered the fate of their loved ones. The day after the wreck, public buildings and most stores and private homes were draped in black. Although a jury in Chicago determined that both ships had been at fault for the collision, sentiment in Milwaukee naturally was strongly against the *Augusta*. The ship's Detroit-based owners wisely sold the ship, and Captain Malott was assigned to a vessel operating on the lower lakes. Nonetheless, when, eight months after the disaster, the former *Augusta*, sporting a new color and a new name, the *Colonel Cook*, docked in Milwaukee to take on a cargo of wheat, the ship was threatened with mob action. The *Colonel Cook* was kept out of Milwaukee after that, but she did go on to have a long career. More than twenty years after the collision with the *Lady Elgin*, a young woman who had known the vessel in better days spotted the *Colonel Cook* docked in Marquette, Michigan. She looked down at a "ragged waif of a ship with paint cracking off and sadly needing an overhauling," yet easily recognizable by her lines and the scars showing where her jibboom had once been shattered.[50]

Although she was reputed to be a jinxed ship, haunted by the ghosts of the drowned three hundred, the former *Augusta* came to no dramatic end. Like so many other leaky old schooners, she was driven ashore near Cleveland in a storm, abandoned by her crew, and broken up by Erie's pounding waves. Darius Malott, master of the *Augusta* that sorry night, did come to a fateful end. In 1864 he journeyed back to Lake Michigan for the first time since the *Lady Elgin* sank and was at the helm of the *Mojave*, a large new sailing ship. On September 8 he was hailed by a passing schooner, and all seemed well with the ship. Yet she was never seen again. Four years to the day after the disaster, Malott and his ship vanished into Lake Michigan's cold embrace.[51]

The *Lady Elgin* tragedy occurred in the crowded waters off Chicago. More ships were wrecked in these waters than anywhere else on the lake. Northern gales had 320 miles of open water to build the waves they sent crashing on ships heading to Chicago or the other ports near the lower end of the lake. Still, the dominant reason for the large number of wrecks off Chicago was the tremendous volume of shipping that was funneled into that port. There were other graveyards of ships that offered a greater challenge to sailors.

Death's Door, Porte des Morts Strait between the Door Peninsula and Washington Island, was one of the most notorious stretches of water on the lake. A strong current flows through the passage, and tricky, often contrary winds made this channel a challenge to schoonermen. Nonetheless, heavy traffic ran the gauntlet through Death's

Door in order to reach Green Bay and the lumber towns of Peshtigo, Marinette, and Menominee. The first lighthouse established here in 1850 was only a small help because the passage is often draped in fog. The lighthouse keepers, however, were kept busy by the regular shipwrecks in the channel. One keeper noted an average of two wrecks per week between 1872 and 1889. The October 1880 gale, known to history as the *Alpena* gale due to the loss of that steamship with one hundred souls, left thirty ships wrecked in the deadly passage. The 1872 shipping season was the worst for Death's Door. In one week nearly one hundred ships were damaged or wrecked making the passage. Not surprisingly shipping interests supported a plan to avoid Death's Door through the construction of a canal at Sturgeon Bay. The canal was an on-again, off-again project for years until it was finally opened to commerce in December 1881. The tolls charged for the waterway were deemed appropriate by the government, yet many schoonermen, hard pressed to make ends meet, still chose to tempt Death's Door rather than pay the fee. The bones of some of those ships litter the floor of the passage.[52]

The Manitou Passage was another of Lake Michigan's graveyards, though not on the same scale as Death's Door. Located between the Leelanau Peninsula and North and South Manitou Islands, the passage was the scene of an estimated two hundred shipwrecks. For ships bound either up or down the lake, the Manitou Passage posed both a challenge and a respite. The sandy shores of the islands, the offshore shoals of the passage, and the ominous, looming presence of the giant Sleeping Bear Dunes made it a particularly dangerous waterway during fog or in a storm. "We were a plaything of the giant waves that pushed us toward the immense bank of sand," recounted a terrified traveler in 1838. On the other hand, the Manitous offered the only reliable shelter from a gale. South Manitou Island's natural harbor made it a regular stopping place for early Great Lakes steamers seeking shelter and firewood. Captain Timothy Kelley, squallbound there with the *Wells Burt* in November 1880, reflected the impatience of many a mariner in the lee of South Manitou: "I am getting sick, I wish I was in Chicago and the schooner stripped and I would soon be home with the help of God. I have read my wife's last letter again today, have read it about a dozen times altogether, it seems good to read it anyhow." But better the ennui of the harbor than the terror of the gale. The brig *J. Young Scammon* wrecked in 1854 trying to reach the safe anchorage of South Manitou. Heroic work by the keeper of the light-house there saved the lives of the crew. The keeper then took the shipwrecked men to the lighthouse. "We found that during my absence I had been blessed with the arrival of an eight-pound, blue-eyed boy," the lightkeeper recorded. That night "there was a feeling of happiness in the station . . . and I felt satisfied that I had accomplished more that day than on any other day of my previous life."[53]

The other principal danger spot on Lake Michigan was at the head of the lake, the straits region where Lakes Huron and Michigan inter-mingle. Some of the earliest navigational aids on Lake Michigan were dedicated to making this choke point a safe commercial passage. The Ile Aux Galets, or "Island of Pebbles," sits in the middle of Lake Michigan's outlet like a bone in the throat. Known to the schoonermen as Skillagalee, a lighthouse was first placed here in 1850 and one has been maintained there ever since. Skillagalee is made more treacherous by the presence of the Waugoshance Shoal, a seven-mile string of islets which, together with the Waugoshance Point, acts as a barrier forcing shipping twenty miles away from the shore. It is likely that it was upon Waugoshance or Skillagalee that young Elizabeth Baird's schooner was nearly wrecked in 1815. A lightship was anchored at Waugoshance in 1832. It was replaced with a lighthouse in 1851.[54]

The most dangerous time to sail on the lakes was in the early spring and late fall. Sudden temperature changes could bring down fierce storms, and the icy water limited any chance of survival. Schooners seldom ventured out of port in December, and those that did often paid the ultimate price. The crew of the *Cornealia E. Windiate* took that risk when they signed on for a December run from Milwaukee to Buffalo. The ship's owners felt that the *Windiate* had proven herself a stout bad-weather sailor, and the price they would get in Buffalo for the twenty thousand bushels of wheat in her hold ensured that everyone would be handsomely compensated. The *Windiate,* a topsailed three-master, had been built in Manitowoc only two years before. She was last seen with a full spread of canvas at the mouth of the Milwaukee River. Two days later a violent winter storm clawed its way across the lake, and the *Windiate,* its profitable wheat, and its crew were no more.[55]

The dark side of the colorful tradition of the Christmas tree ships, celebrated each December in the towns that ring Lake Michigan through story, paintings, songs, and plays, is the tragic truth of schoo-

The deck of a typical schooner. Looking aft toward the cabin. Note the snow on the deck and the ice-covered rigging, indicating early- or late-season sailing. Ivan H. Walton Collection, Bentley Historical Library, University of Michigan.

nermen making a desperate gamble they could not long win. Theodore Charrney, the most thorough historian of these ships, dates the emergence of the evergreen runs to the depression that followed the Panic of 1873. The number of sailing ships on Lake Michigan was near its peak, yet freight rates were low. The temptation to extend the season into December and secure a cargo that would find a guaranteed market overcame better judgment. At the same time, substantial cutover lands were emerging along the lake which, aside from a few dairy farms and potato fields, were good for little else than growing trees. Small pine and fir trees sprouted in the cutovers. In December 1876, the aptly named schooner *Reindeer*, with a cargo of trees from Door County, became the first documented Christmas tree ship in Chicago. These ships soon became a feature of the holiday in Chicago, Milwaukee, Detroit, Cleveland, and other leading Great Lakes ports.[56]

The most famous participant in the Christmas tree voyages was Herman Schuenemann. From 1887 to 1918 Schuenemann or his family sold Christmas trees from the deck of a schooner tied up at the Clark Street bridge in the Chicago River. A Wisconsin-born German American, Schuenemann was an experienced lakeman who had the bulk of his wealth tied up in his sailing ship. While he recognized that late-season journeys were a risk, he also tried to minimize his liability. Schuenemann would head north in October, spend several weeks collecting his cargo in northern Wisconsin or the Upper Peninsula of Michigan, and then head back to Chicago in late November. His goal was to make the Chicago River by December 1, the date when marine insurance ran out. The profits from such voyages were considerable and provided the basic means of support for the Schuenemann family. Trees bought for a few cents apiece in the Upper Peninsula could be sold to Chicagoans for seventy-five cents. An old schooner could be bought for $500 and packed with fifteen thousand trees.[57]

Part of the cost, however, was the danger and risk of the voyage. In 1882 the Christmas tree ships arrived in Chicago looking like "floating icebergs." The schooners *F. H. Williams* and *Coaster*, their distress flags frozen into position, had to be rescued by tugs just off the city's shore. The captain of the *Williams* had stayed at the helm through most of the winter storm and had his face badly frostbitten. The men suffered grievously from cold. With the ships weighted down by ice and the rigging all but frozen, the schooners would have likely perished had they been out on the open lake any longer. That was the fate of the *Caledonia*, which sank during a storm on November 27, 1901. Abandoned by the crew in the Manitou Passage, the frozen ship was driven to destruction against Sleeping Bear Point. Three years earlier, August Schuenemann's luck had run out. Like his brother Herman, August was a veteran of the Christmas tree trade. In a leaky, worm-eaten schooner known as the *S. Thal,* a vessel worth less than its $300 purchase price, August Schuenemann and six crew members died when they were caught in a gale off Glencoe and their hulk came apart. Herman's turn came in December 1912 when the *Rouse Simmons,* loaded to the gunwales with Christmas greenery, disappeared into the winter lake. In 1971 a sport diver discovered the ship, almost perfectly intact, in 180 feet of water. He brought up the remains of two Christmas trees.[58]

Epilogue:
Schooner Twilight

In the summer of 1896 a curious ritual was performed in the waters off Chicago. A tugboat let go its hold of an aged schooner. A couple of sailors nailed a flag to the stump of what had once been the schooner's mainmast and then descended to the hold to open the sea cocks. As Lake Michigan flooded into the ship, the men jumped onto the waiting tug.

It had been nearly a decade since the *Clipper City* had performed as a fully rigged sailing schooner. At the end of the 1886 season, she had been turned back by a winter gale from making a final trip to northern Michigan. When the little two-master once more regained the Chicago harbor, her crew was dismayed to find "its side all bulging out and the oakum falling out its widening seems." When she had slid off the stocks in the shipyard of William Wallace Bates in 1853 the *Clipper City* was considered the fastest boat on the lakes, the model for all subsequent clipper schooners. Now she was a useless hulk. But sailing men of the port wanted her to at least have "a gallant death." With her flag flying, the *Clipper City* cheated the scrapyard and slid beneath the waters.[1]

In the 1890s, scores of schooners, many of them once among the finest on the lakes, were abandoned in Lake Michigan harbors. The Chicago harbor master made an annual tour of the river-port, separating the merely dowdy from the obviously derelict. In August 1898, harbor master John Roberts found four ships in the latter category during his inspection. At the Indiana Street bridge he came across the schooner *Annie Thorine,* which, although forty-three years old, had been a good performer until a steamer plowed into her in the river. Not worth repairing, she was left to rot by her owners. A block to the north a second abandoned schooner was found. The *A. J. Mowry* had already been shorn of her masts and was left to rot with a hold half full of unsold Christmas trees. In the north branch, Roberts found the *Charlotte Raab,* mastless, bulwarks worm-eaten, chains flaky with rust. The children of the neighborhood had adopted the hulk as their ship of dreams—playing pirates and imagining romantic adventures in far-away places. At Belmont, tethered to a tree, sat the *John Raber,* a thirty-year veteran of the lumber trade. She had helped to make a fortune for the man whose name she bore. But John Raber lost faith in the schooner when she sprang a leak during a storm off South Chicago. He drowned when he leaped from the ship and tried to swim for shore. Abandoned, the *Raber* rode out the storm, only to be forsaken once more and condemned. All four ships were taken out to deep water and scuttled. As they yielded to the lake's embrace, each in its turn, the shadows lengthened appreciably on the day of the schooner.[2]

Demand for size and speed brought an end to the day of the schooner. During the 1870s, in part due to the national depression, the value of cargoes carried on Great Lakes ships declined. Even after the economy recovered and the volume of shipping reached new heights, the value of the bulk cargoes such as grain, lumber, coal, and iron favored the economies of scale offered by large ships. Some shipbuilders tried to respond by building a new large class of schooners. The *David Dows,* launched in 1881, was the most notable example of this trend. Yet that vessel, with its propensity for accident and cranky handling, demonstrated the difficulty of making sailing vessels larger on the lakes. The 275-foot *Dows* worked better as a barge—with a steam vessel providing the power—than as a sailing ship. Also, as a consort in tow to steam, a schooner could be made to conform to industrial delivery schedules. Wind power was fickle. On one run a ship might make great time, on the next she could be days late. Yielding to such natural cycles was out of tune with the temporal tyranny of the industrial age. After 1885 nearly all schooners launched on the Great Lakes were intended to function as schooner barges.[3]

The twilight of the schooners was accompanied by an extinguishing of the commercial aspirations of numerous small Lake Michigan ports. Towns like Ahnapee and Little Sturgeon, whose shipyards had

The old and the new. The *Bertha Barnes* under full sail as she passes a modern steel laker, ca. 1905. Ivan H. Walton Collection, Bentley Historical Library, University of Michigan.

sent schooners to all the Great Lakes, and mill towns like Manistique and Manistee, which had exported millions of feet of lumber, found their harbor activity reduced to a few fish tugs. In the wake of the age of sail, the ports thriving on Lake Michigan were the mixed industrial cities that merged maritime and rail transportation. Scores of little ports were bypassed by the new direction of the maritime market, only to be rediscovered a half century later when the recreation industry found new value in their failed dreams.

Schooner Barges: History in Tow

The last true schooner built on Lake Michigan was the *Cora A.*, a 149-foot three-master launched at Manitowoc in 1889. A few scows continued to be built. The *Emily Taylor* an Ahnapee, Wisconsin, scow schooner that slipped from her ways in 1893, was one

About 1902, the master and crew of a small lakeshoring schooner display a portion of their cargo of apples from northwestern Michigan. By the beginning of the twentieth century, steam vessels were squeezing the schooners out of what was left of the lumber trade. Schooner captains cruised the lakeshore taking what cargoes they could find. Durable produce such as apples and potatoes, shipped from isolated lake communities, helped keep some schooners active. Photographer unknown. Negative no. DN-00063, Chicago Historical Society.

of the last of her humble breed. More typical of the period, shipbuilder James Davidson of Saginaw, Michigan, produced eighteen schooner barges between 1885 and 1894. As time went on, more and more of the remaining true schooners were adapted to serve as barges. Shorn of their topmasts and cleared of their running gear, they required less crew, and the crew that did serve had less need of the skills of trimming sails, working aloft, and steering that made a man a mariner. Through the use of schooner barges, sailing was deskilled and sailors suffered a loss of status similar to that experienced by industrial workers in steel production and manufacturing.[4]

It was as tow barges that, one by one, most schooners served out their useful lives. For some that end was a long, slow death. In the 1920s, Nora Sanborn, whose Norwegian American family had been steeped in the building and sailing of schooners, took a boat trip on the Sanitary and Ship Canal to Lockport, Illinois. "We were passed by a tugboat towing a barge loaded with crushed rock. Imagine my surprise when I read on the barge the name 'Butcher Boy.' Why that was the once proud three-masted schooner built by my granduncle Captain Elias Sorenson. Now stripped of her masts and sails it had been reduced to this menial service. I felt tears coming into my eyes." Many of the old tall ships met their end in storms after being abandoned by their tow.[5]

In fair weather a tug or steam barge could easily handle several schooner barges in tow, but once a storm hit the burden of the consorts threatened the steamship. Standard procedure was to try to get the entire outfit to safe anchorage, but if the tug was threatened she released the schooner barges to fend for themselves. Poorly maintained and with a small, sometimes unskilled crew, the schooner barge was in grave danger in those circumstances. The end of the *Plymouth,* a veteran of fifty-nine years on the lake, came in the Great Storm of 1913. The old schooner was being pulled by the tug *James H. Martin* to the north end of the lake to take on a cargo of lumber. The tug, however, found it difficult to make headway with the schooner in tow, and released the barge in the lee of Gull Island. The *Plymouth* had an experienced lakeman as master, but the rest of the crew were not real sailors. Among them was Chris Keenan, a deputy U.S. marshal, on board because ownership of the old schooner was subject to litigation. Keenan and the other landsmen aboard were aghast when the *Martin* cut them loose. Captain Axel Larson understood that this was standard practice and dropped anchor, hoping to weather the storm in the lee

213

of the little island. Something went wrong, though, and the *Plymouth* was never seen again. A week after the storm, a bottle with this message was found on a beach near Pentwater, Michigan:

> Dear Wife and Children:
>   We were left up here in Lake Michigan by McKinnon, captain of the *James H. Martin;* tug at anchor. He went away and never said goodbye or anything to us. Lost one man yesterday. We have been out in the storm forty hours. Goodbye dear ones. Might see you in heaven. Pray for me.
>   Chris K.

A second schooner barge, the *Halsted,* was let go by her tow during that same storm. When her anchor dragged the ship came ashore, but a lifesaving crew was at hand, so there was no loss of life.[6]

During that same storm, the fully rigged schooner *J. H. Stevens* was anchored in a slightly more exposed spot near the *Halsted.* Although she was at times completely buried by the driving waves, the *Stevens* safely rode out the gale because, according to local tradition, she was manned by experienced schoonermen. But their ranks were thinning in the period after 1890. With better pay and a more secure future to be had on steam and steel, young men stayed away from the remaining sailing ships. Older men disliked the decline in their status and pay, but as one of their number told the *Chicago Tribune* in 1909, "What's a sailor going to do but sail?" Captain Thomas Murray, a veteran of the lower lakes, claimed that the "last of the old-time sailors" disappeared after 1885. Gone with the schooner sailors was the phenomenon of the independent vessel owner operating his own ship. Large steel ships required large capital investment to build, insure, and operate. After the schoonermen, corporate fleets dominated the lakes. "Dey used to be lots of damn good sailors," Captain Fred Nelson of the schooner *Our Son* complained. "Now its all steamboats an dey take harbor rats aboard and leave de real sailors ashore without a job—wat you tink dis country's coming to?"[7]

The Long Good-Bye

It was particularly demoralizing for the old sailors to see some of the crack ships of the past reduced to mere tow barges. The *Moonlight,* built at the Wolf and Davidson shipyard in Milwaukee in

1874, was renowned for having made, in a single season, twenty-one round trips on the eight-hundred-mile Milwaukee-to-Buffalo run—"a performance that has never been beaten by a sailing craft," one old-timer proudly noted. Yet she ended her days in tow. So did the *Annie M. Peterson*. One of the most lavishly appointed as well as one of the fastest sailing ships, the *Peterson* scudded past all challengers during her career under sail. The *Peterson* and *Moonlight* were two of the ships celebrated in the schooner ballad "Milwaukee's Crack Ships." They both met their end on Lake Superior. The *Moonlight* was parted from its tow, driven aground, and battered apart in 1903. The *Peterson*'s end came with all hands off Grand Marais.[8]

By the early twentieth century, schooners sighted off the Milwaukee or Chicago shore were more likely to be yachts than working vessels. The schooner rig enjoyed great popularity among recreational sailors between 1875 and 1910. The model for these schooners was not the Great Lakes bulk carrier but the smaller and sleeker New England fishing schooner. Several old fishing schooners were brought from the East Coast to Lake Michigan to serve as yachts, although most were built along New England lines by local shipbuilders. In 1911 the racing schooner *Amorita* won the Chicago-to-Mackinac race in a record time that was not bested until 1987. In 1915 one old lumber hooker, the *Carrier*, a three-masted canaller, was saved from a south branch boneyard by the new recreational sailors of the lake. She was patched, painted, and polished to serve as the clubhouse of the Lincoln Park Boat Club, later to merge with the Chicago Yacht Club. The old ship, however impressive it looked with its tall masts towering over the pleasure craft of the club members, was a problem to maintain. Not infrequently, members entertaining guests on the *Carrier*'s resplendent deck would be discreetly called upon to man the pumps due to yet another leak in her aged planks. In 1923 the *Carrier* was replaced with a more durable clubhouse. The yachtsmen intended to donate the *Carrier* to the Waukegan Sea Scouts, but while the ship was being towed up the lake she foundered off Evanston.[9]

Many of the old ships were rewarded with a Viking funeral. Beginning in the 1890s it became a common practice to torch a worm-eaten schooner as part of a holiday spectacle. The vessel would be loaded with flammable material and towed out to a spot off a popular park or beach and set ablaze. The schooner *North Cape* was one of two such victims burned as part of a pageant off Chicago's Lincoln Park in 1896. Toronto's Sunnyside Park, a lakefront amusement park, burned several of the old ships. The *Lyman M. Davis,* the oldest surviving working schooner on any of the Great Lakes, was earmarked for that purpose in 1934 before public protest intervened. Three years earlier the *Julia B. Merrill,* still proudly using her topmasts, was torched off Toronto in honor of the 1931 Canadian National Exhibition.[10]

Those schooners that continued to function as sailing vessels died a slow death to deferred maintenance. When the teenage crew that worked the *City of Grand Haven* in 1925 first saw the ship docked at Muskegon, they thought it was an abandoned derelict. Light shone into the hold through gaps in the planking. After joining the vessel as part of the crew, they found that she had to be pumped out each day. On one occasion she took on four feet of water merely sitting at the wharf. When several of the *City of Grand Haven's* ribs were damaged by a severe blow near the Manitou Islands, all the master could afford by way of repairs was to stiffen the fractured members by slopping on fifteen yards of concrete. Mercifully, that was the schooner's last year in service. In 1928, after a deal to use the old workhorse in a movie fell through, the ship was abandoned to rot in Marinette harbor.[11]

The *Lucia A. Simpson* also worked Lake Michigan under full sail

The last crew of one of the last Lake Michigan schooners, the *City of Grand Haven,* in 1925. Michigan Maritime Museum.

216

The *City of Grand Haven* in a Marinette, Wisconsin, boneyard in August 1937. Built sixty-five years before in Grand Haven, Michigan, as a tow barge, the vessel was later fitted out as a two-masted topsail schooner. Even as a sailing ship the *City of Grand Haven* was rigged with her masts set far apart to allow a large cargo storage space amidships. In her heyday the *Grand Haven* could handle 250,000 board feet of lumber. Her sailing days ended in the early 1930s. From the Great Lakes Marine Collection of the Milwaukee Public Library/Wisconsin Marine Historical Society.

into the 1920s. Built in Manitowoc in 1875, the 127-foot three-master earned her living from cargoes of pulpwood until 1929, when a gale off Algoma partially dismasted her and opened her rotten planks to the lake. Without a tow, the *Simpson* would have likely sunk in the open water. Fortunately, she was brought into Sturgeon Bay. The ship needed repairs that could not be justified on economic grounds. In 1934, Manitowoc officials entertained the idea of restoring her as part of a maritime museum. That idea, however, came a bit too late for the *Simpson,* and a December 1935 fire ravaged the old-timer at dockside.

Even a minimal effort on the part of firefighters could have saved her, but no one bothered. She was considered valueless.[12]

Rise Again: The Rediscovery of the Lake Schooner

In the eyes of the public, nothing enhanced the status of these workhorses of the lakes like losing them. In the 1940s, about a decade after the old schooners had disappeared from the scene, there began a rebirth of interest in Great Lakes maritime history. As part of a general revival of interest in regionalism sparked by the Great Depression, major New York publishers issued books about the Great Lakes ships. The "American Lakes Series" offered popularly written yet well-researched volumes on each of the Great Lakes. A former seaman and full-time college professor, Walter Havighurst, wrote a series of popular maritime and regional histories, the most notable being *The Long Ships Passing: The Story of the Great Lakes* (1942). At the University of Michigan, folklorist Ivan Henry Walton began collecting stories and songs from the schooner era.[13]

Historical societies and museums were another popular response to the reborn interest in sailing ships. The Great Lakes Historical Society, which established a historical museum in Vermilion, Ohio, began to publish a quarterly historical journal, *Inland Seas*, in 1945. Throughout the 1950s maritime museums were founded in lakeshore communities. During the 1960s the growing number of maritime museums had a reciprocal relationship with the popularity of the sport of scuba diving. Maritime museums interested divers in wrecks that were located in adjacent waters, while wreck divers brought to the surface thousands of artifacts from the schooner era.

The most spectacular and tragic example of this interest was the discovery and raising of the *Alvin Clark*. The *Clark*, which sank in a sudden Green Bay squall in 1864, had been lying, hull down, on the floor of the bay for 103 years. Its slumber was disturbed when a sport diver, Frank Hoffmann, discovered the ship while investigating a snagged fishing net. Hoffmann was a genuine enthusiast. He had dived on dozens of Lake Michigan wrecks, and several years earlier he had discovered and tried disastrously to raise the schooner *Jennie Belle*.

218

As soon as he found the *Clark,* Hoffmann knew she was something special. The ship was completely intact—hull, masts, spars, windlass, and hundreds of smaller artifacts. Hoffmann put together a team of fellow enthusiasts, and against great odds, with considerable skill, and after two years and three thousand dives, they brought the *Clark* once more to the surface.[14]

The moment the *Clark* broke water, in front of a crowd of ten thousand cheering spectators in July 1969, she was the finest preserved historic vessel in the United States. The ship's wheel was perfectly intact, anchor chains were attached to the windlass—even the bilge pumps worked! Belowdecks there was a drove of artifacts, including dishes, eating utensils, and ship's stores, even a crock of cheese "still edible." It was a thrilling moment of triumph for Hoffmann and his associates. Although they did not know it, that happy July day was also when things began to go wrong.[15]

The temperature at the bottom of Green Bay is relatively constant, about forty degrees. The cold and the lack of oxygen helped keep the *Clark* intact for more than a century, yet the moment the ship broke the surface it began to deteriorate. Hoffmann and his fellow divers had taken enough schooner artifacts out of the lake to know this. Nonetheless, they had no conservation program planned for the ship. Hoffmann's planning for what would take place next was summed up in the sentiment, "We said to ourselves, now we have her up, now other people are going to take care of her." But he had not worked in association with one of the region's numerous maritime museums or the State Historical Society of Wisconsin. Hoffmann exasperated efforts made to find a permanent home for the ship with the insistence that he be compensated for the considerable sum he had laid out to raise the ship. He made the situation worse with amateurish conservation efforts and by exhibiting the vessel as part of a tourist attraction called "Mystery Ship Seaport." Actually, the ship's setting and an adjacent museum were quite good, but Hoffmann's insistence on referring to the *Clark* as the "mystery ship" confused the public. A classic artifact of American history was marketed as a third-rate curiosity.

Frank Hoffmann sank all of his resources, borrowed from his parents, developed a drinking problem, and angered his wife, friends, and associates, all to try and make a success of his *Alvin Clark* exhibit. The ship's painful deterioration, from pristine artifact to wretched hulk, became a maritime *Picture of Dorian Gray* for its discoverer.

Before a crowd of ten thousand onlookers, the *Alvin Clark* emerges from the waters of Green Bay in July 1969. With no plan for the *Clark*'s preservation, the salvers were unable to prevent the complete ruin of what was the oldest unrestored ship in the United States. From the Great Lakes Marine Collection of the Milwaukee Public Library/Wisconsin Marine Historical Society.

Hoffmann reached rock bottom with the ship in 1985 when, after a day of drinking, he poured five gallons of gasoline on the deck and tried to burn what was left of the ship. After briefly holding off firefighters with a rifle, Hoffmann surrendered. In 1994 the remains of the *Clark* and the Mystery Ship Seaport were demolished to make way for a parking lot.[16]

The *Clark* became a symbol of the danger that unrestrained sport divers posed to underwater historic sites. In 1987, two commercial divers, Taras Lyssenco and Keith Pearson, discovered the wreck of the schooner *Wings of Discovery* in the waters off Chicago. They shared the location of the wreck with other underwater enthusiasts. When they returned to the schooner two weeks later to photograph it, the wreck was completely stripped of all removable artifacts. While the majority of the public might vicariously share sport divers' thrill of shipwreck discovery, the plundering of those vessels for family room decorations has done nothing to advance the general understanding of the history of the Great Lakes. By the 1980s the state governments along the Great Lakes began to wake up to the loss of their underwater historic sites. Michigan led the way with state legislation protecting historic vessels and through the creation of a series of underwater preserves that promote both wreck diving and ship preservation. Indiana and Wisconsin hired underwater archaeologists to inventory and study shipwrecks within their bottomlands. In 1988 the Chicago Maritime Society conducted a study of the newly discovered wreck of the *Wells Burt*. With the cooperation of the Illinois Historic Preservation Agency, a map was made of the site, including all removable artifacts. A plaque was placed on the wreck requesting all divers to respect the integrity of the site. In a dive to monitor the site several weeks later, the society discovered that several deadeyes had been stolen. Within a year the wreck was stripped clean; even the plaque was missing.[17]

Fortunately, the modern fascination with old Lake Michigan sailing vessels has taken a more healthy direction than the plundering of shipwreck sites. Impressive maritime museums thrive in South Haven, Manitowoc, Sturgeon Bay, and at Sleeping Bear Dunes National Lakeshore. All along the shore of Lake Michigan, old lighthouses and lifesaving stations have been opened as historic sites or adaptively reused. The Maritime Heritage Alliance in Traverse City, Michigan, has built reproductions of historic sailing ships, including the fore-and-aft-rigged *Manitou* and a 1770s sailing ship, the *Wel-*

come. In Milwaukee the Wisconsin Lake Schooner Education Association, as part of the Wisconsin Sesquicentennial, built a 137-foot schooner. Inspired by the historic ship *Moonlight* and built between 1995 and 2000, the ship was the result of more than 900,000 hours of volunteer community effort.

These endeavors are proof of the considerable and enduring public interest in the history of the schooner era. Those tall ships were an important part of a unique historical experience shared by all the communities that border Lake Michigan. The schooners bound the towns, great and small, together—regardless of state boundaries. The sailing ships were vehicles for community development and individual economic advancement. They were graceful symbols of the way the lake was at once a threshold to the wider world and the pathway home again. Schooners came to the lake when it was a vast, dangerous bluewater frontier. They carried cargoes of lumber and grain, hopes for a new life, and aspirations of fortune. For the shoreline towns of Michigan and Wisconsin, Illinois and Indiana, they were ships of dreams.

A Last Look at *Our Son*

Our Son was the last of the Lake Michigan schooners. Her name denoted the grief of Captain Harry Kelley, who built her in 1874 after the recent death of his eldest child. The name also reflected the commitment of Kelley and his wife to both commemorate their loss and to work through their grief to build a better future for the rest of their family. For them the ship was both an end and a beginning.[18]

The ship had a long and productive career. So well was she built and maintained that long after most of her contemporaries were rotted hulks, *Our Son* continued to sail the lakes. With all her topsails set she crossed three yards on her foremast and boasted a greater spread of canvas than any other vessel on the lakes. Even after she was reduced to a tow barge, the ship cheated the odds and endured to be sailed again. In 1923 she was bought by W. J. Schlosser of Milwaukee for use by the Central Paper Company, rerigged for sailing, and put in the pulpwood trade. To many she looked like a ghost ship when she spread her wings upon the lake. "Could that really be a three masted schooner," one young sea scout asked in disbelief, "with every piece of canvas set, even the raffee, half-blended into the mist?" For seven years *Our Son* carried on, the last of a proud tradition.[19]

At last, on September 26, 1930, Lake Michigan took the ship to its rest. Seventy-three-year-old Captain Fred Nelson was at the helm when a brief but nasty storm blew across the lake. The stone barge *Salvor* went down off Muskegon with five men lost. *Our Son* was buffeted by waves of more than thirty feet, and her old seams began to come apart. When Captain Nelson went below to check the damage, he found the hold nearly full of water. He and his crew of six likely would have perished had it not been for the presence of the steel freighter *Nelson*. *Our Son*'s sails were cut away, and the waterlogged ship was abandoned. Fred Nelson genuinely loved the old sailing ship, and he knew what her loss meant. Even after the crew was rescued, he was loath to leave the stricken vessel. Finally, one of his men reached down and pulled him off the schooner. For forty-five minutes the freighter stood by, and the men gathered at the rail to watch *Our Son*'s death throes as the rolling seas of Lake Michigan first broached, then swarmed over her. *Our Son*'s final voyage was to join the *Rouse Simmons*, the *Wells Burt*, and the *Griffon* at the frigid bottom and in the treasured history of Lake Michigan.[20]

Notes

Introduction

1. Norberg, "Schooner's Last Trip."
2. Brehm, "Reconfiguring a Literature of Place"; Martin, "Sailing the Freshwater Seas"; D. J. Cooper, *Fire, Storm, and Ice;* Warner and Warner, "Lives and Times," 5–16.
3. Bogue, *Around the Shores of Lake Michigan,* 3.
4. See Webb, *The Great Plains;* Hunter, *Steamboats on the Western Rivers;* and Wade, *Urban Frontier.* For size of Great Lakes sailing fleet see Mills, *Our Inland Seas,* 112–13, 182–84.
5. Cather, *The Professor's House,* 30; Worster, *Rivers of Empire.*

Chapter 1

1. Chapelle, *American Sailing Ships,* 219.
2. Ericson, "Evolution of Great Lakes Ships," 91–96.
3. Ibid., 97–101; Martin, "Sailing the Freshwater Seas," 32.
4. Quaife, *Lake Michigan,* 100–107; Innis, *Fur Trade in Canada,* 220–26.
5. Innis, *Fur Trade in Canada,* 220–26.
6. Quaife, "Royal Navy of the Upper Lakes," 49–64; Quaife, *Lake Michigan,* 99–110.
7. Chapelle, *American Sailing Ships,* 219–49.
8. Ibid., 268–69.
9. Barkhausen, *Focusing on the Centerboard,* 5–22; Gabriel Franchere to William Brewster, September 27, 1837, Gabriel Franchere Letters, 1835–38, Baylis Library, Sault Ste. Marie, Michigan.
10. Neuschel, "Bird's Eye View of Ahnapee," 97.
11. Martin, "Sailing the Freshwater Seas," 36; Gabriel Franchere to Ramsay Crooks, January 10, 1836, Franchere Letters; Martin, "Not for Shallow Water Only"; Charrney, "The Christmas Tree Ship," pt. 1, p. 223.

12. Martin, "Sailing the Freshwater Seas," 35; Strough, "Crews on Early Great Lakes Vessels," 259–60.

13. Creighton, *Empire of the St. Lawrence,* 343, 358–59; Careless, *The Union of the Canadas,* 132–39.

14. Bancroft, "Memoir of Capt. Samuel Ward," 337–38.

15. *Democratic Press* (Chicago), July 19, 1856; Angle, "The Seaport of Chicago"; Dornfeld, "Chicago's Age of Sail."

16. *Chicago Daily Press,* July 15, 1857; Angle, "Direct to Europe," 197–200; *Chicago Times,* August 3, 1862; Norberg, "First European Ship," 75–77.

17. Mills, *Our Inland Seas,* 184–85; Hirthe and Hirthe, *Schooner Days in Door County,* 20–21; Harold, *Shipbuilding at Manistee,* 16–19; Palmer, "The Grand Haven Rig," 154–56; "Great Lakes Perspective— The Schooners," 154.

18. Mills, *Our Inland Seas,* 185; Clary, *Ladies of the Lakes,* 89–94.

19. Stephenson. *Recollections of a Long Life,* 165–68; Morris, *Schooners and Schooner Barges,* 1–5; Burke, *I Lived at Peshtigo Harbor,* 19–20; Harold, *Shipbuilding at Manistee,* 7–10; Laurent, "Trade, Transport, and Technology," 16; Barkhausen, *Great Lakes Sailing Ships,* 2.

20. Palmer, "The Grand Haven Rig," 154–57; Martin, "Sailing the Freshwater Seas," 40.

21. Francaviglia, *From Sail to Steam,* 269; *Chicago Times,* August 3, 1862.

Chapter 2

1. Dornfeld, "Chicago's Age of Sail," 156.

2. Ibid.; Keating, *Narrative of an Expedition,* 166–67.

3. Bruce, *History of Milwaukee,* 271; Cropley, *Kenosha,* 4–5; F. S. Stone, *Racine: Belle City of the Lakes,* 273; Seibold, *Coast Guard City,* 27–29; *Pioneer Reminiscence,* 14–15; Hanna, *Sand, Sawdust, and Saw Logs,* 4–5.

4. Log of the schooner *Gazelle,* 1838, Justice Bailey, master. State Historical Society of Wisconsin, Madison.

5. Log of the schooner *Mary Elizabeth, Hero,* Henry B. Ketcham, captain, ca. 1844–46, State Historical Society of Wisconsin, Area Research Center, University of Wisconsin, Green Bay. Original log is in the possession of James Borski, Menominee, Michigan.

6. Baird, "Windjammer to Chicago," 343–46; Baird, "Reminiscences of Early Days on Mackinac Island."

7. Journal of Jacob B. Varnum of Petersburg, Virginia, manuscript in the Chicago Historical Society, Chicago, Illinois, p. 41; M. P. Lee, "To Michigan by Water—1844."

8. Mansfield, *History of the Great Lakes,* 1:264; Quaife, "The Schooner *Hercules.*"

9. Larson, *Those Army Engineers,* 13–35.

10. Ibid., 17; Keating, *Narrative of an Expedition,* 166; Koss, *Milwaukee,* 72.

11. McLear, "Rise of the Port of Chicago," 20; Falge et al., *History of Manitowoc County,* 132; Heath, *Early Memories of Saugatuck,* 59.

12. Larson, *Those Army Engineers,* 29–33; Diary of Captain Morris Sleight, June 30, 1834, typescript "Excerpts from Capt. Sleight's Letters and Diaries," Manuscripts Division, Chicago Historical Society, Chicago, Illinois. E. O. Gale in his *Reminiscences of Early Chicago* (25) describes the *Illinois,* a ship he sailed on from Buffalo to Chicago early in 1834, as a brig. Yet Gale also refers to "birch-bark Mackinaw boats" used as lighters. Morris Sleight's description of the ship as a schooner is more trustworthy, as he was a veteran vessel captain.

13. Garraghan, "Early Catholicity in Chicago," 160; Hatcher, "Sails," 347–50.

14. Statistics on harbors, Chicago Harbor, 1854–55, in George W. Wilbur Papers, Beinecke Rare Book Library, Yale University, New Haven, Connecticut.

15. Larson, *Those Army Engineers,* 42–43.

16. Havighurst, *Long Ships Passing,* 128–29.

17. Report of the Milwaukee Harbor Commission, 1842, quoted in Bruce, *History of Milwaukee,* 277–88; Stephenson, *Recollections of a Long Life,* 92–94; Milwaukee Board of Trade, *Annual Report, 1855,* 7.

18. Bruce, *History of Milwaukee,* 275–76.

19. Ibid.; Western Historical Company, *History of Racine and Kenosha Counties,* 340–42.

20. Hyde, *Northern Lights,* 16–17.

21. Durrie, "Green Bay for Two Hundred Years," 8; Bancroft, "Memoir of Capt. Samuel Ward," 338–39; Plumb, "Lake Michigan Shipping," 68.

22. Plumb, "Lake Michigan Shipping," 68; Durrie, "Green Bay for Two Hundred Years," 8.

23. Larson, *Those Army Engineers,* 80–94; Cropley, *Kenosha,* 26.

24. Gagnon, *Neshotah,* 46–47; *Sheboygan (Wis.) Mercury,* July 21, 1849, February 2, 1850, quoted in Buchen, *Historic Sheboygan County,* 199–200; Montalto, *Port Washington,* 6; Falge et al., *History of Manitowoc County,* 34; Heath, *Early Memories of Saugatuck,* 56–63.

25. McLear, "Rise of the Port of Chicago," 86–90; *Chicago Daily American,* September 8, 1841; Milwaukee Board of Trade, *Annual Report, 1855,* 4.

26. McLear, "Rivalry between Chicago and Wisconsin Ports," 225–31.

27. F. S. Stone, *Racine and Racine County,* 275.

28. Cronon, *Nature's Metropolis,* 111–14.

29. F. S. Stone, *Racine and Racine County,* 275–79; McLear, "Rivalry between Chicago and Wisconsin Ports," 232–33; Buchen, *Historic Sheboygan County,* 197–207.

30. Atwood, "Commerce of the Great Lakes," 39–40; Hirthe and Hirthe, *Schooner Days in Door County,* 21; Log of the schooner *Wells Burt,* Manitowoc Maritime Museum, Manitowoc, Wisconsin; T. Kelley, "Reminiscences of Things Maritime," 133–38.

31. *Chicago Inter-Ocean,* November 3, 4, 6, 13, 1882.

32. Plumb, "Lake Michigan Navigation," 231; T. Kelley, "Reminiscences of Things Maritime," 135; Dickson, "*David Dows* Revisited."

33. Hotchkiss, *Lumber and Forest Industry,* 661–68.

34. Krog, "Marinette," 140–44, 306–8; Hanna, *Sand, Sawdust, and Saw Logs,* 14–17; Cronon, *Nature's Metropolis,* 160.

35. Kilar, *Michigan's Lumbertowns,* 49, 144–47.

36. Theodore S. Charrney was the most through and knowledgeable historian of the *Rouse Simmons*. His most notable publications on this subject are "The *Rouse Simmons* and the Port of Chicago" and *Chicago's Christmas Tree Ship.* Mr. Charrney also wrote a much larger history of the *Rouse Simmons* in which he placed the ship in the context of the lumber trade and tradition of Christmas tree ships. This unpublished manuscript, an 850–page typescript, was the result of eleven years of painstaking research through the newspapers and shipping records of Lake Michigan's nineteenth-century communities. The manuscript "The Christmas Tree Ship: The Saga of the *Rouse Simmons*" is part of the collection of the Chicago Maritime Society. In everything I write about the *Rouse Simmons* I am merely following gratefully in Theodore Charrney's wake.

37. Cronon, *Nature's Metropolis,* 172–73; Gjerset, *Norwegian Sailors on the Great Lakes,* 15; Parton, "Chicago," 331.

38. Rae, "Great Lakes Commodity Trade," 53–54; Eyler, *Muskegon County,* 25–72; Current, *History of Wisconsin,* 2:468–69; Nesbit, *History of Wisconsin,* 3:186–87.

39. Stephenson, *Recollections of a Long Life,* 74; Cronon, *Nature's Metropolis,* 162–63.

40. Cronon, *Nature's Metropolis,* 162–63; Rood, "The Christmas Tree Ship," 92–95.

41. Charrney, *Chicago's Christmas Tree Ship,* n.p.

42. Norberg, "Biography of the Schooner *C. H. Hackley*"; Rae, "Great Lakes Commodity Trade," 110; Tunell, "Transportation on the Great Lakes," 100–101.

43. Mansfield, *History of the Great Lakes,* 2:518.

44. Atwood, "Commerce of the Great Lakes," 60; Krog, "Marinette," 138; Dornfeld, "Chicago's Age of Sail," 162.

45. Neuschel, "Bird's Eye View of Ahnapee."

Chapter 3

1. Callaway, "A Sailor's Narrative," 73.

2. Hennipen, *A Description of Louisiana,* 95–108.

3. Although Jacob Varnum recorded the vessel master's name as Packer, it is possible that he was referring to John Packett, who served as a lieutenant in command of the *Ariel* under Oliver Hazard Perry during the Lake Erie campaign. Skaggs and Altoff, *A Signal Victory,* 98.

4. Journal of Jacob Varnum, October 16, 1815.

5. Brehm, "Reconfiguring a Landscape of Place," 128–29; J. F. Cooper, *The Pathfinder,* 114–15; Herman Melville, *Moby Dick,* quoted in Havighurst, *Great Lakes Reader,* 289–91.

6. "Sailor's Customs," Box 5, Ivan Henry Walton Collection, Bentley Historical Library, Ann Arbor, Michigan.

7. Kenlon, *Fourteen Years a Sailor,* 191–94.

8. Leonard Noyes to Brother, August 15, 1841, June 25, August 31, 1842, Leonard Withington Noyes Papers, Peabody Essex Museum and Library, Salem, Massachusetts.

9. T. Kelley, "Reminiscences of Things Maritime," 136–37; Martin, "Sailing the Freshwater Seas," 78.

10. Blegen, *Norwegian Migration to America*, 3–8; Gjerset, *Norwegian Sailors on the Great Lakes*, 18, 74–77. An interesting examination of this question using the patient records at the Milwaukee Marine Hospital is John Odin Jensen's "Hospitals and Mariners: A Study in Great Lakes Maritime History." Jensen confirms the strong predilection of Scandinavians for service on sailing ships as opposed to steam, but his sample indicates that only 12 percent of lake schoonermen were Scandinavian.

11. Miller, *Emigrants and Exiles*, 291–315; Zipperer, "A Life on the Lakes," 73; U.S. Bureau of the Census, Ninth Census, Manuscript Population Returns for Chicago, 1870; U.S. Bureau of the Census, Twelfth Census, Manuscript Population Returns for Chicago, 1900.

12. M. P. Lee, "To Michigan by Water—1844," 123; Martineau, *Society in America*, 10.

13. Martineau, *Society in America*, 10; Quaife, "The Schooner *Hercules*," 76; Stephenson, *Recollections of a Long Life*, 95; Jensen, "Hospitals and Mariners," 56; U.S. Census, Manuscript Population Returns, 1870 and 1900.

14. T. Kelley, "Reminiscences of Things Maritime," 136.

15. "The Shanty-Boys Song," Walton Collection; Stephenson, *Recollections of a Long Life*, 94–97; *Milwaukee Sentinel*, November 21, 1877, quoted in Martin, "Sailing the Freshwater Seas," 140; *Pioneer Reminiscences*, 2.

16. Lane, *Built on the Banks of the Kalamazoo*, 5; Timothy Kelley Diary, March 1871, Wisconsin Maritime Museum, Manitowoc; Waite and Anderson, *Old Settlers*, 34–35.

17. Quaife, *Lake Michigan*, 103–4; Journal of Jacob Varnum, October 16, 1815; *Chicago Tribune*, September 27, 1860; Ehle, *Cleveland's Harbor*, 9–10; Peskin, *North into Freedom*, 49–50, 56.

18. Charrney, "The Christmas Tree Ship," pt. 1, pp. 339–40; *Chicago Inter-Ocean*, April 28, 29, 30, 1883.

19. Kenlon, *Fourteen Years a Sailor*, 188–92.

20. *Chicago Inter-Ocean*, October 15, 1875, May 26, 1882, July 25, 1882; Brehm, *Women's Great Lakes Reader*, 251–55.

21. Charrney, "The Christmas Tree Ship," pt. 1, pp. 341–42; *Chicago Times*, June 2, 1878.

22. *Chicago Inter-Ocean*, July 6, 1884; Kelley Diary, June 5, 1872; Heath,

Early Memories of Saugatuck, 133; *Chicago Tribune,* September 27, 1860; Kristiansen, *Diary,* 20; Reber, *History of St. Joseph,* 1927), 71; *Chicago Inter-Ocean,* April 28, 1883.

23. Norberg, "Early Days on the Great Lakes," 157; Murray, "Some Recollections," 28; Martin, "A Star to Steer By," 45.

24. T. Kelley, "Reminiscences of Things Maritime," 141–42; Strough, "Crews on Early Great Lakes Vessels," 259; Martin, "Sailing the Freshwater Seas," 87, 92–95; Martin, "A Star to Steer By," 45.

25. Norberg, "Early Days on the Great Lakes," 158.

26. "Shanties," Box 6, Walton Collection; Campbell, *Work and the Waterways.*

27. Norberg, "Early Days on the Great Lakes," 160.

28. *Chicago Tribune,* August 3, 1860; H. Kelley, "Lakes, Lore, and Lingo," 87.

29. *Chicago Tribune,* April 28, August 11, April 3, 1860; Log of the *Wells Burt,* May 8, 1880.

30. Boardman, "Water Front and Shipping," 62; *Milwaukee Sentinel,* May 23, 1878; Pott, "Hauling Wind and Heaving Short," 30–31.

31. Martin, "A Star to Steer By," 45; Gibbs, "Extracts from the Log Schooner *Augusta.*"

32. Stephenson, *Recollection of a Long Life,* 105; *Detroit Free Press,* October 2, 1885, found in "Sailor Life," Walton Collection; T. Kelley, "Reminiscences of Things Maritime," 136.

33. "The Bigler," Box 6, Walton Collection; Norberg, "Early Days on the Great Lakes," 157.

34. Norberg, "Early Days on the Great Lakes," 157.

35. Martin, "Sailing the Freshwater Seas," 85–86; *Chicago Tribune,* April 9, October 23, 1860.

36. Norberg, "Early Days on the Great Lakes," 156–57; Callaway, "A Sailor's Narrative," 75–76; Log of the schooner *Lottie Wolf,* July 1, 1881, Timothy Kelley Collection, Wisconsin Maritime Museum, Manitowoc.

37. Strough, "Crews on Early Great Lakes Vessels," 260; Norberg, "Early Days on the Great Lakes," 157.

38. Martin, "A Star to Steer By," 44; T. Kelley, "Reminiscences of Things Maritime," 136; Norberg, "Early Days on the Great Lakes," 157.

39. Strough, "Crews on Early Great Lakes Vessels," 260; "A Sailor's Fare," *Inland Marine,* April 4, 1884, quoted in Martin, "Sailing the Freshwater Seas," 61.

40. *Detroit Free Press,* October 2, 1885, quoted in "Schooner Sailors," Box 5, Walton Collection; Payroll Records, 1898, Sparrow-Kroll Lumber Company, Kenton, Michigan, Bentley Historical Library, Ann Arbor, Michigan; Engberg, "Labor in the Lake States Lumber Industry," 300–301; Callaway, "A Sailor's Narrative," 75; Warner and Warner, "Lives and Times," 8–9; Martin, "Sailing the Freshwater Seas," 145–46.

41. *Chicago Tribune,* April 2, 1860; *Buffalo Express,* April 20, 24, 1874, September 11, 1873, quoted in "Schooner Sailors," Box 5, Walton Collection;

42. *Chicago Tribune,* September 4–5, 26, 1860; Hoagland, *Wage Bargaining on the Lakes,* 10.

43. Schneirov, "Chicago's Great Upheaval of 1877"; Hoagland, *Wage Bargaining on the Lakes,* 13.

44. Hoagland, *Wage Bargaining on the Lakes,* 14–15.

45. Ibid., 17–29; Kristiansen, *Diary,* 82.

46. *Chicago Tribune,* May 2, 1902.

47. "Schooner Sailors," Box 5, Walton Collection.

48. Ibid.; Norberg, "Early Days on the Great Lakes," 157.

49. T. Kelley, "Reminiscences of Things Maritime," 133; Gjerset, *Norwegian Sailors on the Great Lakes,* 18–21, 58; Palmer, "One Inch from Success," 236.

50. Dutton, "Recollections of A. P. Dutton," 279.

51. Havighurst, *Long Ships Passing,* 83; *Chicago Tribune,* August 21, 1883.

52. Palmer, "One Inch from Success," 238; Charrney, "The Christmas Tree Ship," pt. 1, pp. 143–45.

53. George Nelson Smith Diary, September 3, 1849, Bentley Historical Library, Ann Arbor, Michigan; Bancroft, "Memoir of Capt. Samuel Ward," 346–47.

54. Leonard Noyes to Brother, June 21, 1848, and September 9, 1849, Noyes Papers.

55. Callaway, "A Sailor's Narrative," 75–76.

56. Dutton, "Recollections of A. P. Dutton," 279; Buchen, *Historic Sheboygan County,* 205–6.

57. Bancroft, "Memoir of Capt. Samuel Ward," 339–40; Gjerset, *Norwegian Sailors on the Great Lakes,* 15; Martin, "Long in the Trade," 67; Charrney, "The Christmas Tree Ship," pt. 1, p. 230.

58. Martin, "Sailing the Freshwater Seas," 119; Zipperer, "A Life on the Lakes," 77–78; H. Kelley, "Lakes, Lore, and Lingo," 87.

59. Kelley Diary, November 6, 1870; H. Kelley, "Lakes, Lore, and Lingo," 87; Charrney, "The Christmas Tree Ship," pt. 1, pp. 127–28.

60. Charrney, "The Christmas Tree Ship," pt. 1, pp. 127–28, 33.

61. "Sailor's Customs," Box 6, Walton Collection.

62. Ibid.

63. "Sailor's Superstitions," Box 6, Walton Collection; *Chicago Inter-Ocean,* April 27, 1883.

64. "Sailor's Customs," Box 6, Walton Collection; *Detroit News,* November 23, 1930.

65. "Sailor's Customs," Box 6, Walton Collection.

66. Kelley Diary, November 17–18, 1872; John Treiber to Mary Treiber, October 17, 1872, quoted in Warner and Warner, "Lives and Times," 9, 12; Leonard Noyes to brother, May 19, 1845, Noyes Papers; H. Kelley, "Lakes, Lore, and Lingo," 85.

67. Warner and Warner, "Lives and Times," 9; "Schooner Sailors," Box 5, Walton Collection.

Chapter 4

1. Larson, *Those Army Engineers,* 105; Parton, "Chicago," 330.

2. Staudenraus, "Empire City of the West."

3. Dreiser, "Smallest and Busiest River."

4. Norris, *The Pit,* 55–56; Pierce, *History of Chicago,* 2:322; Piehl, "Shall We Gather at the River," 200.

5. "Chicago in 1856," 606–13.

6. Ibid.; Wright, *Autobiography,* 63.

7. *Chicago Tribune,* November 4, 1863.

8. Piehl, "Shall We Gather at the River," 201–2.

9. Ibid.

10. *Chicago Tribune,* November 4, 1863; Dunne, *Mr. Dooley and the Chicago Irish,* 176–77.

11. Dunne, *Mr. Dooley and the Chicago Irish,* 176–77; *Chicago Daily News,* December 1, 1893.

12. Charrney, "The Christmas Tree Ship," pt. 1, pp. 304–13; Charrney,

"The Port of Chicago"; *Chicago Tribune,* April 28, 1895; Dunne, *Mr. Dooley and the Chicago Irish,* 181.

13. *Chicago Daily Democrat,* September 25, 1855; Charrney, "The Christmas Tree Ship," pt. 1, pp. 324–26.

14. *Chicago Inter-Ocean,* April 27, 1883; Andreas, *History of Chicago,* 3:294–95.

15. *Chicago Tribune,* October 17, 1861, July 2, 1877.

16. Kristiansen, *Diary,* 8–9.

17. *Chicago Record-Herald,* March 28, April 20, September 19, 1904; *Chicago Tribune,* August 14, 1898; Charrney, "The Christmas Tree Ship," pt. 1, p. 303.

18. Pierce, *History of Chicago,* 2:322–23; Flower, "Chicago's Great River-Harbor," 484–86; Larson, *Those Army Engineers,* 205.

19. *London Times,* October 21, 1887; Cronon, *Nature's Metropolis,* 175; M. E. Stone, "Chicago before the Fire," 675–76; Chicago River Improvement Association, *Chicago! Where Railroad Traffic and Lake Transportation Meet,* 19.

20. Cronon, *Nature's Metropolis,* 169–70; Chicago River Improvement Association, *The Story of a River,* n.p.

21. Schneirov, "Chicago's Great Upheaval of 1877"; Charrney, "Chicago Harbor a Century Ago," 15; Shelton, "Buffalo Grain Shovellers' Strike," 211–12.

22. Norberg, "Early Days on the Great Lakes," 162; Wendt and Kogan, *Bosses in Lusty Chicago,* 26–27.

23. *Chicago Tribune,* August 11, 1862, July 15–16, 30, 1864.

24. *Constitution and By-Laws of the Chicago Lumber Vessels Unloaders' Union,* 1–21.

25. Schneirov, "Chicago's Great Upheaval," 4–16; *Chicago Tribune,* July 26, 27, 28, August 1, 1877.

26. *Chicago Inter-Ocean,* April 1, 4–6, 1878.

27. G. A. Lee, "Chicago Grain Elevator System"; *Chicago Tribune,* March 9, 1861.

28. Charrney, "Chicago Harbor a Century Ago," 12; Parton, "Chicago," 331.

29. *Chicago Tribune,* August 11, 1860, August 24, 1862.

30. Flower, "Chicago's Great River-Harbor," 483–92; Friends of the Chicago River, *Chicago River Trail,* n.p.; *Chicago Tribune,* August 11, 1860, August 25, 1862.

31. Joyaux, "A Frenchman's Visit to Chicago," 45–49.

32. Sinclair, *The Jungle*, 97; Bigot, "Forgotten Chicago," 148; Wilkie, *Walks About Chicago*, 14.

33. *Chicago Tribune*, October 25, 1860; Flower, "Chicago's Great River-Harbor," 484; Dunne, *Mr. Dooley and the Chicago Irish*, 475–77.

34. Flower, "Chicago's Great River-Harbor," 484; *Chicago Tribune*, May 26, 1862, March 7, 1863; Cain, *Sanitation Strategy*, 61–64.

35. *Chicago Tribune*, May 25, August 25, December 29, 1862, May 20, 1863.

36. Cain, *Sanitation Strategy*, 64–65; Dublin, Lotka, and Spiegelman, *Length of Life*, 159.

37. Karamanski, *Deep Woods Frontier*, 111–15; Kilar, *Michigan's Lumbertowns*, 102–4.

38. Asbury, *Gem of the Prairie*, 96.

39. Ibid., 52.

40. Ibid., 51–53, 71–74.

41. Ibid., 57–58; Wolper, *Chicago Dock and Canal Trust*, 12–13.

42. Duis, *The Saloon*, 236–37; *Chicago Tribune*, September 29, 1862; *Chicago Times*, August 7, 1865.

43. Asbury, *Gem of the Prairie*, 116–17.

44. Ibid., 171–76; *Chicago Tribune*, March 26, 1860.

45. *Chicago Tribune*, April 28, 1895, July 2, 1860, November 22, 1876.

46. Ibid., April 28, 1895.

47. *Chicago Times*, June 11, 1883.

48. *Chicago Inter-Ocean*, November 22, 1876.

49. Charrney, "The Potato Ships," 47–49; Harrison, "A Kentucky Colony," 170–71.

50. *Chicago Evening Post*, November 5, 1900; Charrney, "The Potato Ships," 48–49.

51. *Chicago Tribune*, October 15, November 2, March 16, 1860.

52. Pierce, *History of Chicago*, 2:450, n. 74.

53. *Chicago Tribune*, February 26, 1861; Pierce, *History of Chicago*, 2:368–69.

54. *Chicago Inter-Ocean*, May 8, 1883; Hirthe and Hirthe, *Schooner Days in Door County*, 99, 127; Charrney, "The Christmas Tree Ship," pt. 1, pp. 344–45.

55. *Chicago Tribune,* July 7, 1877.

56. Flower, "Chicago's Great River-Harbor," 484; Larson, *Those Army Engineers,* 197.

57. Larson, *Those Army Engineers,* 196–98.

58. Ibid.

59. Ibid.; Flower, "Chicago's Great River-Harbor," 490–91.

60. Flower, "Chicago's Great River-Harbor," 490–91; Clary, *Ladies of the Lakes,* 134; Larson, *Those Army Engineers,* 197; Bukowski, *Navy Pier,* 11.

61. Wolper, *Chicago Dock and Canal Trust,* 20–23; Ericsson and Myers, *Sixty Years a Builder,* 265.

62. Bukowski, *Navy Pier,* 14–15.

63. Ibid.; Board of Harbor Commissioners, *Port of Milwaukee,* 12–13.

64. Larson, *Those Army Engineers,* 199–202.

65. *Grand Haven Times,* November 1851, quoted in Seibold, *Coast Guard City,* 44.

Chapter 5

1. Kristiansen, *Diary,* frontispiece; Edward Carus quoted in "Weather Lore," Box 5, Walton Collection.

2. Ratigan, *Great Lakes Shipwrecks and Survivals,* 71; Francis Comte de Castlenau quoted in Weeks, *Sleeping Bear,* 125–26.

3. For a examples of the new military history see Royster, *A Revolutionary People at War;* Keegan, *The Face of Battle;* Linderman, *Embattled Courage;* McPherson, *For Cause and Comrades.*

4. Quimby, *Indian Culture and European Trade Goods,* 54–62.

5. *Milwaukee Sentinel,* May 23–24, 1883; *Wells Burt* record, Herman G. Runge Collection, Milwaukee Public Library, Milwaukee, Wisconsin; McManamon, "The Sinking of the *Wells Burt.*"

6. McManamon, "The Sinking of the *Wells Burt*"; *Milwaukee Sentinel,* May 29, 1883.

7. *Chicago Inter-Ocean,* May 24–25, June 2, 1883.

8. *Chicago Times,* June 2, 7, 1883; Martin, "Sailing the Freshwater Seas," 36.

9. Hirthe and Hirthe, *Schooner Days in Door County,* 15–21.

10. George Cuthbertson, in his wonderful 1931 book *Freshwater: A History and Narrative of the Great Lakes,* states categorically that the "only vessel which had leeboards fitted was the three-masted topsail schooner *Lizzie A. Low* of Port Huron, Michigan" (236). More recently, Henry Barkhausen has identified at least two other schooners fitted with leeboards. In 1873 the *Toronto Globe* reported that the 223-foot *James Couch* and the schooner *Comet* both used leeboards, although the article noted that the *Comet,* docked in Chicago, was having a centerboard installed at a cost of $5,000. Barkhausen, *Focusing on the Centerboard,* 15, 21–22.

11. Valli, "William Wallace Bates."

12. Ibid.

13. Barkhausen, *Focusing on the Centerboard,* 14; Valli, "William Wallace Bates," 34–36.

14. D. J. Cooper and Jensen, *Davidson's Goliaths;* D. J. Cooper and Rogers, *Report on Phase I Marine Magnetometer Survey;* D. J. Cooper, ed., *By Fire, Storm, and Ice;* Labadie, *Submerged Cultural Resources Study;* Lyssenco et al., *The "Wells Burt" Project.*

15. D. J. Cooper, "The *Fleetwing:* A Preliminary Report."

16. Cuthbertson, *Freshwater,* 234–36; *Chicago Tribune,* December 3, 1874, July 3, 1877.

17. McManamon, "Sinking of the *Wells Burt,*" 180–81; Inches, *Great Lakes Shipbuilding Era,* n.p.; Havighurst, *Long Ships Passing,* 88–89.

18. Kenlon, *Fourteen Years a Sailor,* 188–95.

19. Inches, *Great Lakes Shipbuilding Era,* n.p.; Charrney, "The Christmas Tree Ship," pt. 1, p. 41; Harold, *Shipbuilding at Manistee,* 1; Hirthe and Hirthe, *Schooner Days in Door County,* 49–61.

20. *Chicago Times,* June 7, 1883.

21. *Chicago Inter-Ocean,* March 4, 1878; *Chicago Times,* June 7, 1883.

22. *Chicago Inter-Ocean,* March 4, 1878; Swayze, "Great Spring Gale of 1894," 102; Hirthe and Hirthe, *Schooner Days in Door County,* 49–60.

23. Mansfield, *History of the Great Lakes,* 1:393; Martin, "Sailing the Freshwater Seas," 166–68.

24. Norberg, "Schooner's Last Trip," 12.

25. Swayze, "Great Spring Gale of 1894," 106; Martin, "A Star to Steer By," 44.

26. Krog, "Marinette," 141–42.

27. Hyde, *Northern Lights*, 18–28.

28. Kristiansen, *Diary*, 82.

29. Hyde, *Northern Lights*, 53–54.

30. *Chicago Tribune*, May 24–25, 1883.

31. Woodford, *Charting the Inland Seas*, 13–14, 20–21, 37–41.

32. W. H. Hearding, Address to the Houghton County Historical Society, n.d., Hearding Journal and Papers, Bentley Historical Library, University of Michigan, Ann Arbor; Kenlon, *Fourteen Years a Sailor*, 187.

33. Wakefield and Wakefield, *Sail and Rail*, 73; Plumb, *History of the Navigation of the Great Lakes*, 65–66.

34. Hyde, *Northern Lights*, 34–35.

35. *Evanston Index*, November 30, 1895.

36. Ibid.

37. *Chicago Tribune*, May 19, 1894.

38. Ibid.

39. Swayze, "Great Spring Gale of 1894," 103–4.

40. *Chicago Tribune*, May 2, 1860; Mansfield, *History of the Great Lakes*, 1:767.

41. Barry, *Wrecks and Rescues*, 17; Callaway, "A Sailor's Narrative," 78–80.

42. Plumb, "Lake Michigan Shipping," 69; "Bad Day at Grand Haven."

43. *Chicago Inter-Ocean*, May 24–25, 1891; Charrney, "The Christmas Tree Ship," pt. 1, pp.386–97.

44. *Chicago Tribune*, June 4, 7, 1853.

45. Mansfield, *History of the Great Lakes*, 1:614–15.

46. Ibid., 763–75.

47. *Chicago Tribune*, September 8, 10, 11, 12, 1860; *Frank Leslie's Illustrated Newspaper*, September 22, 1860; Boyer, *True Tales of the Great Lakes*, 177–208.

48. Boyer, *True Tales of the Great Lakes*, 177–208.

49. The official numbered of dead was 297, but this was an estimate because there was no accurate record of who was on the ship. There is a similar lack of agreement on the number of the survivors, from a low of 100 to a high of 155. See Boyer, *True Tales of the Great Lakes*, 203.

50. *Chicago Tribune*, September 10–12, 1860; Ratigan, *Great Lakes Shipwrecks and Survivals*, 48–49.

51. Boyer, *True Tales of the Great Lakes,* 208.

52. Bogue, *Around the Shores of Lake Michigan,* 222–23; Hyde, *Northern Lights,* 147–48; Hirthe and Hirthe, *Schooner Days in Door County,* 33; Larson, *Those Army Engineers,* 181–82.

53. Weeks, *Sleeping Bear,* 126–31; Log of the schooner *Wells Burt,* November 20, 1880.

54. Hyde, *Northern Lights,* 96–109.

55. Ratigan, *Great Lakes Shipwrecks and Survivals,* 37–38.

56. Charrney, "The Christmas Tree Ship," pt. 2, pp. 2–3.

57. Ibid.

58. Ibid.; *Chicago Inter-Ocean,* December 8, 1882; *Detroit Free Press,* November 27, 1901; *Chicago Tribune,* December 5–7, 1912; Rood, "The Christmas Tree Ship," 95.

Epilogue

1. *Chicago Tribune,* August 14, 1898.

2. Ibid.

3. Barry, *Ships of the Great Lakes,* 136–42; D. J. Cooper and Jensen, *Davidson's Goliaths,* 14–15, 28–29.

4. D. J. Cooper and Jensen, *Davidson's Goliaths,* 14–15, 28–29; Neuschel, "Bird's Eye View of Ahnapee," 98; Martin, "Sailing the Freshwater Seas," 162–64.

5. Gjerset, *Norwegian Sailors on the Great Lakes,* 98.

6. Boyer, *True Tales of the Great Lakes,* 214–24.

7. Hirthe and Hirthe, *Schooner Days in Door County,* 27; *Chicago Tribune,* May 2, 1909; Murray, "Some Recollections," *Inland Seas,* 29; "Schooner Sailors," Box 7, Walton Collection.

8. Shipley and Addis, *Schooners,* 59; Barry, *Wrecks and Rescues,* 21–22.

9. Van Mell and Van Mell, *The First Hundred Years;* Deane Tank, personal communication, October 12, 1997.

10. Snider, *Tales from the Great Lakes,* 106, 183; Van Mell and Van Mell, *First Hundred Years,* 62; Gjerset, *Norwegian Sailors on the Great Lakes,* 98.

11. Martin, "A Star to Steer By," 44–47.

12. Clary, *Ladies of the Lakes,* 96–98; *Lucia A. Simpson* file, Great Lakes Marine Historical Collection, Milwaukee Public Library.

13. Landon, *Lake Huron;* Quaife, *Lake Michigan;* Nute, *Lake Superior;* Hatcher, *Lake Erie;* Pound, *Lake Ontario;* Havighurst, *Long Ships Passing.*

14. McCutcheon, *"Alvin Clark:* An Unfinished Voyage"; Spectre, *"Alvin Clark:* The Challenge of the Challenge"; *Alvin Clark* file, Great Lakes Marine Historical Collection, Milwaukee Public Library.

15. Spectre, *"Alvin Clark:* The Challenge of the Challenge."

16. Ibid.

17. *Chicago Tribune,* December 8, 1988.

18. "Schooners," Box 7, Walton Collection.

19. Norberg, "Lake Michigan, 1925," 266.

20. *"Our Son,"* Box 7, Walton Collection.

Works Cited

Books, Articles, Theses, and Dissertations

Andreas, Alfred T. *History of Chicago*. Vols. 2–3. Chicago: A. T. Andreas, 1886.

Angle, Paul M. "Direct to Europe." *Chicago History* 5, no. 7 (1959): 197–200.

———. "The Seaport of Chicago." *Chicago History* 1, no. 4 (1946): 89–91.

Asbury, Herbert. *Gem of the Prairie: An Informal History of the Chicago Underworld*. New York: Knopf, 1940.

Atwood, Jane Kellogg. "Development of the Commerce of the Great Lakes." Master's thesis, University of Chicago, 1915.

"Bad Day at Grand Haven: Wreck of the *Jesse Martin*." *Inland Seas* 48, no. 1 (1992): 36–40.

Baird, Elizabeth Therese. "Reminiscences of Early Days on Mackinac Island." *Wisconsin Historical Collections* 14 (1898): 17–64.

———. "Windjammer to Chicago." In *The Great Lakes Reader*, ed. Walter Havighurst, 343–46. New York: Collier, 1966.

Bancroft, William L. "Memoir of Capt. Samuel Ward, with a Sketch of the Early Commerce of the Upper Lakes." *Michigan Pioneer and Historical Collections* 21 (1892): 336–67.

Barkhausen, Henry N. *Focusing on the Centerboard*. Manitowoc, Wis.: Manitowoc Maritime Museum, 1990.

———. *Great Lakes Sailing Ships*. Milwaukee: Kalmbach Publishing, 1947.

Barry, James P. *Ships of the Great Lakes: Three Hundred Years of Navigation*. Berkeley, Calif.: Howell-North Books, 1973.

———. *Wrecks and Rescues of the Great Lakes: A Photographic History*. Burbank, Calif.: Howell Books, 1981.

Bigot, Madame Charles. "Forgotten Chicago." In *Chicago's Yesterdays: A Sheaf of Reminiscences*, ed. Caroline Kirkland, 143–61. Chicago: Daughaday & Co., 1919.

Blegen, Theodore C. *Norwegian Migration to America: The American*

Transition. Northfield, Minn.: Norwegian American Historical Association, 1940.

Boardman, M. A. "Water Front and Shipping in the Fifties." *Early Milwaukee: Eyewitness Accounts of Life in Milwaukee, Wisconsin, 1830–1890, Written by the Settlers and Residents*, 62–69. Madison: Roger Hunt, 1977.

Board of Harbor Commissioners. *Port of Milwaukee: The Most Progressive Port on the Great Lakes*. Milwaukee: City of Milwaukee, 1949.

Bogue, Margaret Beattie. *Around the Shores of Lake Michigan: A Guide to Historic Sites*. Madison: University of Wisconsin Press, 1985.

Boyer, Dwight. *True Tales of the Great Lakes*. New York: Dodd, Mead, 1971.

Brehm, Victoria. "Reconfiguring a Literature of Place: The Economics of Great Lakes Maritime Literature." Ph.D. diss., University of Iowa, 1992.

———, ed. *The Women's Great Lakes Reader*. Duluth, Minn.: Holy Cow Press, 1998.

Bruce, William George. *History of Milwaukee, City and County*. Chicago: S. J. Clarke, 1922.

Buchen, Gustave William. *Historic Sheboygan County*. Sheboygan, Wis.: privately printed, 1944.

Bukowski, Douglas. *Navy Pier: A Chicago Landmark*. Chicago: Ivan Dee, 1996.

Burke, F. C. *I Lived at Peshtigo Harbor: The History of an Early Saw-Mill Village*. Peshtigo, Wis.: Peshtigo Times, 1971.

Cain, Louis P. *Sanitation Strategy for a Lakefront Metropolis: The Case of Chicago*. DeKalb: Northern Illinois University Press, 1978.

Callaway, William. "A Sailor's Narrative." *Early Milwaukee: Eyewitness Accounts of Life in Milwaukee, Wisconsin, 1830–1890, Written by the Settlers and Residents*, 70–87. Madison: Roger Hunt, 1977.

Campbell, Melinda. *Work and the Waterways: An Aural History of Midwestern Workers*. Audiotape. Executive producer: Theodore J. Karamanski. Producers: Melinda Campbell, and Norman Schroder. Chicago: Loyola University and Chicago Maritime Society, 1987.

Careless, J. M. S. *The Union of the Canadas*. Toronto: McClelland and Stewart, 1967.

Cather, Willa. *The Professor's House*. New York: Vintage Books, 1973.

Ceasar, Peter. *Lake Michigan Wreck*. Vols. 1–9. Green Bay, Wis., and Kalamazoo, Mich.: Great Lakes Marine Research, 1987–98.

Chapelle, Howard I. *The History of American Sailing Ships.* New York: Norton, 1955.

Charrney, Theodore S. "Chicago Harbor a Century Ago." *Sea History* 47 (Summer 1988): 12–15

———. *Chicago's Christmas Tree Ship.* Chicago: privately printed, 1962.

———. "The Christmas Tree Ship: The Saga of the *Rouse Simmons.*" Unpublished manuscript. Chicago Maritime Society, Chicago, Illinois.

———. "The Port of Chicago." Paper presented to the Illinois State History Symposium, Springfield, Illinois, December 1987. On file at Chicago Maritime Society, Chicago, Illinois.

———. "The Potato Ships of Lake Michigan." *Inland Seas* 44, no. 1 (1988): 46–50.

———. "The *Rouse Simmons* and the Port of Chicago." *Inland Seas* 43, no. 4 (1987): 242–46.

"Chicago in 1856." *Putnam's Monthly Magazine,* June 1856, 606–13.

Chicago River Improvement Association. *Chicago! Where Railroad Traffic and Lake Transportation Meet.* Chicago: Chicago River Improvement Association, 1896.

———. *The Story of a River.* Chicago: Henry W. Ternau, 1898.

Clary, James. *Ladies of the Lakes.* Lansing: Michigan Department of Natural Resources, 1981.

Constitution and By-Laws of the Chicago Lumber Vessels Unloaders' Union. Chicago: Lightner & Schmalbach, n.d.

Cooper, David J. "The *Fleetwing:* A Preliminary Report." *Anchor News* 20, no. 3 (1989): 44–51.

———, ed. *By Fire, Storm, and Ice: Underwater Archeological Investigations in the Apostle Islands.* Madison: State Historical Society of Wisconsin, 1991.

Cooper, David J., and John O. Jensen. *Davidson's Goliaths: Underwater Archeological Investigations of the Steamer "Frank O'Conner" and the Schooner-Barge "Pretoria."* Madison: State Historical Society of Wisconsin, 1995.

Cooper, David J., and Bradley A. Rogers. *Report on Phase I Marine Magnetometer Survey in Death's Door Passage, Door County, Wisconsin, 1989.* Madison: State Historical Society of Wisconsin, 1990.

Cooper, James Fenimore. *The Pathfinder, or The Inland Sea.* New York: Penguin, 1989.

243

Creighton, Donald. *The Empire of the St. Lawrence.* Toronto: Macmillan, 1956.

Creviere, Paul John, Jr. *Wild Gales and Tattered Sails: The Shipwrecks of Northwest Lake Michigan.* N.p.: privately published, 1997.

Cronon, William. *Nature's Metropolis: Chicago and the Great West.* New York: Norton, 1991.

Cropley, Carrie. *Kenosha: From Pioneer Village to Modern City, 1835–1935.* Kenosha, Wis.: Kenosha County Historical Society, 1958.

Current, Richard N. *The History of Wisconsin.* Vol. 2, *The Civil War Era, 1848–1873.* Madison: State Historical Society of Wisconsin, 1976.

Cuthbertson, George A. *Freshwater: A History and Narrative of the Great Lakes.* New York: Macmillan, 1931.

Dickson, Kenneth. "The *David Dows* Revisited." *Telescope,* September/October 1985, 128–31.

Donahue, James L. *Schooners in Peril: True and Exciting Stories about Tall Ships on the Great Lakes.* Holt, Mich.: Thunder Bay Press, 1995.

Dornfeld, A. A. "Chicago's Age of Sail." *Chicago History* 2, no. 3 (1973): 156–65.

Dreiser, Theodore. "The Smallest and Busiest River in the World." *Metropolitan,* October 1898, 355–63.

Dublin, Louis I., Alfred J. Lotka, and Mortimer Spiegelman. *Length of Life.* New York: Ronald Press, 1949.

Duis, Perry. *The Saloon: Public Drinking in Chicago and Boston, 1880–1920.* Chicago: University of Illinois Press, 1983.

Dunne, Peter Finley. *Mr. Dooley and the Chicago Irish: An Anthology.* Ed. Charles Fanning. New York: Arno Press, 1976.

Durrie, Daniel. "Green Bay for Two Hundred Years, 1639–1839." Paper presented before the State Historical Society of Wisconsin, Madison. December 26, 1872.

Dutton, A. P. "Recollections of A. P. Dutton." In *Racine: Belle City of the Lakes,* ed. Fanny Stone, 275–82. Chicago: S. J. Clarke, 1916.

Ehle, Jay C. *Cleveland's Harbor: The Cleveland–Cuyahoga County Port Authority.* Kent, Ohio: Kent State University Press, 1996.

Engberg, George Barker. "Labor in the Lake States Lumber Industry, 1830–1930." Ph.D. diss., University of Minnesota, 1949.

Ericson, Bernard E. "The Evolution of Great Lakes Ships, Part 1—Sail." *Inland Seas* 25, no. 2 (1969): 91–104.

Ericsson, Henry, and Lewis E. Myers. *Sixty Years a Builder: The Autobiography of Henry Ericsson.* Chicago: Kroch & Son, 1942.

Eyler, Jonathan. *Muskegon County: Harbor of Promise.* Northridge, Calif.: Windsor Publications, 1986.

Falge, Louis, et al. *History of Manitowoc County, Wisconsin.* Vol. 1. Chicago: Goodspeed Historical Association, 1912.

Flower, Elliott. "Chicago's Great River-Harbor." *Century Magazine,* February 1902, 483–92.

Francaviglia, Richard V. *From Sail to Steam: Four Centuries of Texas Maritime History, 1500–1900.* Austin: University of Texas Press, 1998.

Friends of the Chicago River. *Chicago River Trail: North Branch Section from the Waterfall to Goose Island.* Chicago: Open Lands Project, 1986.

Gagnon, Evan. *Neshotah: The Story of Two Rivers, Wisconsin.* Stevens Point, Wis.: Worzalla, 1969.

Gale, E. O. *Reminiscences of Early Chicago and Vicinity.* Chicago: Fleming H. Revell Company, 1902.

Garraghan, Gilbert J. "Early Catholicity in Chicago, 1673–1843, Part II." *Illinois Catholic Historical Review* 1, no. 2 (1918): 147–72.

Gibbs, S. G. "Extracts from the Log of the Schooner *Augusta,* April to November, Captain S. G. Gibbs, Master Sailing, Season of 1856." *Inland Seas* 45, no. 2 (1989): 117–32.

Gjerset, Knut. *Norwegian Sailors on the Great Lakes.* Northfield, Minn.: Norwegian-American Historical Association, 1928.

"Great Lakes Perspective—The Schooners." *Inland Seas* 39, no. 3 (1983): 154.

Haeger, John D. "Capital Mobilization and the Urban Center: The Wisconsin Lakeports." *Mid-America: An Historical Review* 60, no. 2 (1976): 75–94.

———. "A Time of Considerable Change: Green Bay, 1815–1834." *Wisconsin Magazine of History* 54, no. 4 (1971): 285–98.

Hanna, Frances Caswell. *Sand, Sawdust, and Saw Logs: Lumber Days in Ludington.* Ludington, Mich.: privately printed, 1955.

Harold, Steve. *Shipbuilding at Manistee.* Manistee, Mich.: Steve Harold, 1979.

Harrison, Carter. "A Kentucky Colony." In *Chicago's Yesterdays: A Sheaf of Reminiscences,* ed. Caroline Kirkland, 162–78. Chicago: Daughaday & Co., 1919.

Hatcher, Harlan. *Lake Erie*. New York: Bobbs-Merrill, 1945.

———. "Sails." In *The Great Lakes Reader*, ed. Walter Havighurst, 347–56. New York: Collier-Macmillan, 1966.

Havighurst, Walter. *The Long Ships Passing: The Story of the Great Lakes*. New York: Macmillan, 1942.

———, ed. *The Great Lakes Reader*. New York: Collier-Macmillan, 1966.

Heath, May Francis. *Early Memories of Saugatuck, Michigan, 1830–1930*. Grand Rapids, Mich.: Eerdmans, 1930.

Hennipen, Louis. *A Description of Louisiana*. New York: John G. Shea, 1880.

Hirthe, Walter, and Mary K. Hirthe. *Schooner Days in Door County*. Minneapolis: Voyageur Press, 1986.

Hoagland, Henry Elmer. *Wage Bargaining on the Vessels of the Great Lakes*. Urbana: University of Illinois, 1917.

Hotchkiss, George W. *History of the Lumber and Forest Industry of the Northwest*. Chicago: George W. Hotchkiss, 1898.

Hunter, Louis C. *Steamboats on the Western Rivers: An Economic and Technological History*. Cambridge: Harvard University Press, 1949.

Hyde, Charles K. *The Northern Lights: Lighthouses of the Upper Great Lakes*. Lansing, Mich.: Two Peninsula Press, 1986.

Inches, H. C. *The Great Lakes Shipbuilding Era*. Cleveland: privately printed, 1962.

Innis, Harold A. *The Fur Trade in Canada*. Toronto: University of Toronto Press, 1956.

Jennings, Patrick R. "A Distant Mirror: British Naval Operations on the Upper Great Lakes during the American Revolution." Paper presented to the Fourteenth Naval History Symposium, Annapolis, Maryland, September 1999.

Jensen, John Odin. "Hospitals and Mariners: A Study in Great Lakes Maritime History." *American Neptune* 57, no. 1 (1997): 47–63.

Joyaux, Georges J. "A Frenchman's Visit to Chicago in 1886." *Journal of the Illinois State Historical Society* 47, no. 1 (1954): 45–56.

Karamanski, Theodore J. *Deep Woods Frontier: A History of Logging in Northern Michigan*. Detroit: Wayne State University Press, 1989.

Keating, William H. *Narrative of an Expedition to the Source of St. Peter's River*. Philadelphia, 1824.

Keegan, John. *The Face of Battle*. New York: Viking Press, 1976.

246

Kelley, Harry. "Lakes, Lore, and Lingo: Captain Timothy J. Kelley." *Anchor News* 12, no. 4 (1981): 85–88.

Kelley, Timothy. "Reminiscences of Things Maritime," In *History of Manitowoc County, Wisconsin,* ed. Louis Falge et al., 131–38. Vol. 1. Chicago: Goodspeed Historical Association, 1912.

Kenlon, John. *Fourteen Years a Sailor.* New York: George H. Doran, 1923.

Kilar, Jeremy W. *Michigan's Lumbertowns: Lumbermen and Laborers in Saginaw, Bay City, and Muskegon, 1870–1905.* Detroit: Wayne State University Press, 1990.

Koss, Rud A. *Milwaukee.* Milwaukee: Milwaukee Herald, 1871.

Kristiansen, Soren. *Diary of Soren Kristiansen: Lake Michigan Schooner Captain, 1891–1893.* Iron Mountain, Mich.: Mid-Peninsula Library Cooperative, 1981.

Krog, Carl E. "Marinette: Biography of a Nineteenth-Century Lumbering Town, 1850–1910." Ph.D. diss., University of Wisconsin, Madison, 1971.

Labadie, C. Patrick. *Submerged Cultural Resources Study, Pictured Rocks National Lakeshore.* Omaha: National Park Service, 1991.

Landon, Fred. *Lake Huron.* New York: Bobbs-Merrill, 1944.

Lane, Kit. *Built on the Banks of the Kalamazoo.* Douglas, Mich.: Pavilion Press, 1993.

Larson, John W. *Those Army Engineers: A History of the Chicago District of the U.S. Army Corps of Engineers.* Chicago: Chicago District, U.S. Army Corps of Engineers, 1979.

Laurent, Jerome K. "Trade, Transport, and Technology: The American Great Lakes, 1866–1910." *Journal of Transport History* 4 (March 1983): 1–24.

Lee, Guy A. "The Historical Significance of the Chicago Grain Elevator System." *Agricultural History* 2, no. 1 (1937): 20–21.

Lee, Mary Per. "To Michigan by Water—1844." In *The Women's Great Lakes Reader,* ed. Victoria Brehm, 121–25. Duluth, Minn.: Holy Cow Press, 1998.

Linderman, Gerald. *Embattled Courage: The Experience of Combat in the American Civil War.* New York: Free Press, 1987.

Lyssenco, Taras, Kurt Anderson, David J. Keene, Valerie Olson, and Keith Pearson. *The "Wells Burt" Project.* Chicago: Chicago Maritime Society, 1989.

Mansfield, J. B. *History of the Great Lakes*. Vols. 1 and 2. Chicago: J. H. Beers, 1899.

Martin, Jay. "Long in the Trade: The Career of the Lumber Schooner *City of Grand Haven*." *Anchor News* 21, no. 4 (1990): 64–71.

———. "Not for Shallow Water Only: Scow Construction along the Maumee River, 1825–1859." *Marine History Lines: Journal of the Western Lake Erie Historical Society* 10, no. 1 (1991), 2–6.

———. "Sailing the Freshwater Seas: A Social History of Life aboard the Commercial Sailing Vessels of the United States and Canada on the Great Lakes." Ph.D. diss., Bowling Green State University, 1995.

———. "A Star to Steer By: The Last Season of the *City of Grand Haven*." *Michigan History* 74, no. 4 (1990): 43–47.

Martineau, Harriet. *Society in America*. London: Saunders and Otlety, 1837.

McCutcheon, C. T., Jr. "*Alvin Clark:* An Unfinished Voyage." *Wooden Boat* 52 (May/June 1983): 53–57.

McLear, Patrick E. "The Rise of the Port of Chicago to 1848." Master's thesis, University of Missouri, Kansas City, 1967.

———. "Rivalry between Chicago and Wisconsin Lake Ports for Control of the Grain Trade." *Inland Seas* 24, no. 3 (1968): 225–33.

McManamon, John, S.J. "The Sinking of the *Wells Burt*." *Inland Seas* 46, no. 3 (1990): 174–82.

McPherson, James. *For Cause and Comrades: Why Men Fought in the Civil War*. New York: Oxford University Press, 1997.

Miller, Kirby A. *Emigrants and Exiles: Ireland and the Irish Exodus to North America*. New York: Oxford, 1985.

Mills, James Cook. *Our Inland Seas: Their Shipping and Commerce for Three Centuries*. Chicago: McClurg & Co., 1910.

Milwaukee Board of Trade. *Annual Report of Commerce, Manufactures, and Improvements for the Year 1855*. Milwaukee: Daily Wisconsin Press, 1855.

Montalto, Suzanne M. *Port Washington, 1835 to 1985*. Port Washington, Wis.: Port Publications, 1985.

Morris, Paul C. *Schooners and Schooner Barges*. Orleans, Mass.: Lower Cape Publishing, 1984.

Murray, Thomas E. "Some Recollections." *Inland Seas* 2, no. 4 (1946): 28–33.

Nesbit, Robert C. *The History of Wisconsin*. Vol. 3, *Urbanization and In-*

dustrialization, 1873–1893. Madison: State Historical Society of Wisconsin, 1985.

Neuschel, Fred. "Bird's Eye View of Ahnapee." *Anchor News* 23, no. 5 (1992): 92–100.

Norberg, Carl A. "Biography of the Schooner *C. H. Hackley,* Lumber Hooker . . . Trader . . . Pirate Vessel." *Inland Seas* 37, no. 4 (1981): 244–51.

———. "Early Days on the Great Lakes . . . Nels Palmer Recollects." *Inland Seas* 39, no. 3 (1983): 156–62.

———. "First European Ship Direct to Chicago." *Inland Seas* 42, no. 2 (1986): 74–77.

———. "Lake Michigan, 1925: Sailing with the Last of the Windjammers." *Inland Seas* 35 (1979): 258–68.

———. "Schooner's Last Trip Began from Douglas." *Inland Seas* 45, no. 1 (1989): 10–12.

Norris, Frank. *The Pit: A Story of Chicago.* 1902. New York: Bantam Books, 1994.

Nute, Grace Lee. *Lake Superior.* New York: Bobbs-Merrill, 1944.

Palmer, Richard F. "The Grand Haven Rig." *Inland Seas* 43, no. 3 (1987): 154–58.

———. "One Inch from Success: Captain Pickering and the *Columbia.*" *Inland Seas* 39, no. 4 (1983): 235–38.

Parton, James. "Chicago." *Atlantic Monthly,* March 1867, 330–33.

Peskin, Allan, ed. *North into Freedom: The Autobiography of John Malvin, Free Negro, 1795–1880.* Cleveland: Western Reserve University Press, 1966.

Piehl, Frank J. "Shall We Gather at the River." *Chicago History* 2, no. 4 (1973): 196–205.

Pierce, Bessie Louise. *A History of Chicago.* Vol. 2, *From Town to City, 1848–1871.* New York: Knopf, 1940.

Pioneer Reminiscence of an Old Settler by One of the Boys. Manistee, Mich.: Manistee County Historical Society, 1960.

Plumb, Ralph G. *History of the Navigation of the Great Lakes.* Washington, D.C.: Government Printing Office, 1911.

———. "Lake Michigan Navigation in the 1850s." *Inland Seas* 7, no. 4 (1951): 229–36.

———. "Lake Michigan Shipping, 1830–1850." *Inland Seas* 5, no. 2 (1949): 67–75.

Pott, Kenneth. "Hauling Wind and Heaving Short: Language of the Lakemen." *Anchor News* 25, no. 2 (1994): 28–33.

Pound, Arthur. *Lake Ontario.* New York: Bobbs-Merrill, 1945.

Quaife, Milo M. *Lake Michigan.* New York: Bobbs-Merrill, 1944.

———. "The Royal Navy of the Upper Lakes." *Burton Historical Collection Leaflet* 2, no. 5 (1924): 49–64.

———. "The Story of the Schooner *Hercules.*" *Inland Seas* 6, no. 2 (1950): 74–79.

Quimby, George Irving. *Indian Culture and European Trade Goods: The Archaeology of the Historic Period in the Western Great Lakes Region.* Madison: University of Wisconsin Press, 1966.

Rae, James David. "The Great Lakes Commodity Trade, 1850–1900." Ph.D. diss., Purdue University, 1967.

Ratigan, William. *Great Lakes Shipwrecks and Survivals.* New York: Galahad Books, 1960.

Reber, L. Benj. *History of St. Joseph.* St. Joseph, Mich.: St. Joseph Chamber of Commerce, 1927.

Rood, David. "The Christmas Tree Ship." In *A Most Superior Land: Life in the Upper Peninsula of Michigan,* ed. Russell McKee, 92–95. Lansing: Michigan Department of Natural Resources, 1983.

Royster, Charles. *A Revolutionary People at War: The Continental Army and the American Character, 1775–1783.* New York: Vintage, 1979.

Schneirov, Richard. "Chicago's Great Upheaval of 1877." *Chicago History* 9, no. 1 (1980): 3–17.

Seibold, David H. *Coast Guard City, U.S.A.: A History of the Port of Grand Haven.* Ann Arbor: Historical Society of Michigan, 1990.

Shelton, Brenda K. "The Buffalo Grain Shovellers' Strike of 1899." *Labor History* 9, no. 2 (1968): 210–38.

Shipley, Robert, and Fred Addis. *Schooners.* St. Catherines, Ontario: Vanwell, 1991.

Sinclair, Upton. *The Jungle.* New York: Signet Classics, 1960.

Skaggs, David Curtis, and Gerard T. Altoff. *A Signal Victory: The Lake Erie Campaign, 1812–1813.* Annapolis: Naval Institute Press, 1997.

Snider, C. H. J. *Tales from the Great Lakes: Based on C. H. J. Sinder's "Schooner Days."* Toronto: Dunduran Press, 1995.

Spectre, Peter H. "The *Alvin Clark:* The Challenge of the Challenge." *Wooden Boat* 52 (May/June 1983): 59–65.

Staudenraus, P. J., ed. "The Empire City of the West—A View of Chicago in 1864." *Journal of the Illinois State Historical Society* 56, no. 2 (1963): 340–49.

Stephenson, Isaac. *Recollections of a Long Life, 1829–1915*. Chicago: privately printed, 1915.

Stone, Fanny S. *Racine and Racine County, Wisconsin*. Chicago: S. J. Clarke, 1916.

———. *Racine: Belle City of the Lakes*. Chicago: S. J. Clarke, 1916.

Stone, Melville E. "Chicago before the Fire, after the Fire, and To-day." *Scribner's Magazine*, June 1895, 663–79.

Strough, Arthur B. "Crews on Early Great Lakes Vessels." *Inland Seas* 49, no. 4 (1993): 259–62.

Swayze, David. "The Great Spring Gale of 1894." *Inland Seas* 48, no. 2 (1992): 99–112.

Tunell, George G. "Transportation on the Great Lakes of North America." Ph.D. diss., University of Chicago, 1898.

Valli, Isacco A. "William Wallace Bates: The Practical Shipbuilder." *Anchor News* 13, no. 2 (1982): 28–37.

Van Mell, Richard, and Wendy Van Mell. *The First Hundred Years, 1875–1975*. Chicago: Chicago Yacht Club, 1975.

Wade, Richard C. *The Urban Frontier: The Rise of Western Cities, 1790–1830*. Cambridge: Harvard University Press, 1959.

Waite, S. E., and W. S. Anderson. *Old Settlers: A Historical and Chronological Record of the Grand Traverse Region*. Traverse City, Mich.: S. E. Waite, 1918.

Wakefield, Lawrence, and Lucille Wakefield. *Sail and Rail: A Narrative History of Transportation in the Traverse City Region*. Traverse City, Mich.: privately printed, 1980.

Warner, Edward S., and Colleen Oihus Warner. "Lives and Times in the Great Lakes Commercial Trade under Sail." *Hayes Historical Journal: A Journal of the Gilded Age* 11, no. 1 (1991): 5–21.

Webb, Walter Prescott. *The Great Plains*. Boston: Ginn & Co., 1931.

Weeks, George. *Sleeping Bear: Yesterday and Today*. Frankfort, Mich.: A & M Publishing, 1990.

Wendt, Lloyd, and Herman Kogan. *Bosses in Lusty Chicago: The Story of Bathhouse John and Hinky Dink*. Bloomington: Indiana University Press, 1971.

Western Historical Company. *The History of Racine and Kenosha Counties, Wisconsin.* Chicago: Western Historical Company, 1879.

Wilkie, Franc. *Walks About Chicago, 1871–1881.* Chicago: Belford, Clarke, 1882.

Wolper, Greg. *The Chicago Dock and Canal Trust, 1857–1987.* Chicago: privately printed, 1987.

Woodford, Arthur M. *Charting the Inland Seas: A History of the U.S. Lake Survey.* Detroit: U.S. Army Corps of Engineers, Detroit District, 1991.

Worster, Donald. *Rivers of Empire: Water, Aridity, and the Growth of the American West.* New York: Oxford University Press, 1985.

Wright, Frank Lloyd. *Frank Lloyd Wright: An Autobiography.* New York: Duell, Sloan and Pearce, 1943.

Zipperer, Sandra J. "A Life on the Lakes: Sailing with Timothy Kelley, 1870–1873." *Anchor News* 25, no. 4 (1994): 72–81.

Newspapers

Chicago Daily Democrat, 1855

Chicago Daily News, 1893

Chicago Daily Press, 1857

Chicago Evening Post, 1900

Chicago Inter-Ocean, 1875–91

Chicago Record-Herald, 1904

Chicago Times, 1862–83

Chicago Tribune, 1853–1988

Daily Chicago American, 1841

Democratic Press (Chicago), 1856

Detroit Free Press, 1901

Detroit News, 1930

Evanston Index, 1895

Frank Leslie's Illustrated Newspaper, 1860

London Times, 1887

Milwaukee Sentinel, 1878–83

Sheboygan (Wis.) Mercury, 1849–50

Manuscripts and Archival Material

Alvin Clark. File. Great Lakes Marine Historical Collection. Milwaukee Public Library, Milwaukee, Wisconsin.

Franchere, Gabriel. Letters, 1835–38. Baylis Library, Sault Ste. Marie, Michigan.

Gazelle. Log of the schooner, 1838, Justice Bailey, master. State Historical Society of Wisconsin, Madison.

Graham, J. D. Papers. Peabody Essex Museum Library, Salem, Massachusetts.

Hearding, W. H. Journal and Papers. Bentley Historical Library, University of Michigan, Ann Arbor.

Kelley, Timothy. Diary. Wisconsin Maritime Museum, Manitowoc.

Lottie Wolf. Log of the schooner. Timothy Kelley Collection. Wisconsin Maritime Museum, Manitowoc.

Lucia A. Simpson. File. Great Lakes Marine Historical Collection. Milwaukee Public Library, Milwaukee, Wisconsin.

Mary Elizabeth, Hero. Log of the schooner, ca. 1844–46, Henry B. Ketcham, captain. State Historical Society of Wisconsin, Area Research Center, University of Wisconsin, Green Bay. Original log is in the possession of James Borski, Menominee, Michigan.

Noyes, Leonard Withington. Papers. Peabody Essex Museum and Library, Salem, Massachusetts.

Sleight, Captain Morris. "Excerpts from Capt. Sleight's Letters and Diaries." Manuscripts Division, Chicago Historical Society, Chicago, Illinois.

Smith, George Nelson. Diary. Bentley Historical Library, University of Michigan, Ann Arbor.

Sparrow-Kroll Lumber Company. Payroll Records 1898. Kenton, Michigan, Bentley Historical Library, Ann Arbor, Michigan.

U.S. Bureau of the Census. Seventh Census, Manuscript Population Returns for Chicago, 1850.

———. Eighth Census, Manuscript Population Returns for Chicago, 1860.

———. Ninth Census, Manuscript Population Returns for Chicago, 1870.

———. Tenth Census, Manuscript Population Returns for Chicago, 1880.

———. Twelfth Census, Manuscript Population Returns for Chicago, 1900.

Varnum, Jacob B., of Petersburg, Virginia. Journal. Manuscript in the Chicago Historical Society, Chicago, Illinois.

Walton, Ivan Henry. Collection. Bentley Historical Library, University of Michigan, Ann Arbor.

Wells Burt. Log of the schooner. Timothy Kelley Collection. Wisconsin Maritime Museum, Manitowoc.

Wells Burt. Record. Herman G. Runge Collection. Milwaukee Public Library, Milwaukee, Wisconsin.

Wilbur, George W. Papers. Beinecke Rare Book Library, Yale University, New Haven, Connecticut.

Index

A. B. Ward, tug, 137
Ackerman, Alfred, 121
Adams, brig, 28
Addie, schooner, 198
African Americans, 49, 86–87,
    147–48
Ahnapee, schooner, 75
Ahnapee, Wis. *See* Algoma, Wis.
A. J. Mowry, schooner, 210
Algoma, Wis., 75, 210, 211, 217
Allan, McClelland and Company, 69
Alpena, steamer, 205
Alvin Clark, brigantine, 218–21
A. M. Beers, schooner, 163
American Federation of Labor, 148
American Fur Company, 29, 31
Amorita, schooner, 215
Anderson, John, 114
Annie M. Peterson, schooner, 63,
    113, 215
Annie Sherwood, schooner, 120
Annie Thorine, schooner, 210
Annie Vaught, schooner, 108
Archange, schooner, 27
Articles of Agreement, 104–5
Askin, John, 27
Atlanta, schooner, 183
Augusta, schooner, 201–4
Austerlitz, schooner, 52

Bailey, Fred A., 160
Bailey, Justice, 47
Bailey Brothers shipyard, 37
Baileys Harbor, Wis., 47, 193
Baird, Elizabeth Therese, 48–49, 206
Baltimore clipper, 28–29
Baraga, Mich., 183
barks. *See* brigantines
Bates, William Wallace, 29, 180–82,
    185, 209

Beaver Island, 190
Bergh, Andrew, 200–201
Black Hawk War, 54
Blantom, P. J., 121
Bohemians, 148–49
Bolivar, schooner, 30
Boston, Mass., 28
Brandt, Henry, 163
brigantines, 26, 30
Bristol, R. C., 179–80
Buffalo, N.Y., 22, 38, 45, 53, 54, 59,
    63–64, 79, 84, 87, 99, 108–10,
    120, 124, 179, 185
Buie, Daniel, 80
Bundy, Henry, 164–65
Burger, Henry, 182
Burnham, Daniel, 169–70
Burton, William, 114
Busse, Fred, 168–69
Butcher Boy, schooner, 213

Caledonia, schooner, 208
Callaway, William, 77–78, 107, 117–
    18, 198
Calumet, Ill., 54, 170
Calumet River, 170
Canada, schooner, 62
Carland, Frank, 75
Carrier, schooner, 215
Carus, Edward, 173
Castlenau, Francis Comte de, 174
Caswell, Burr, 45
Cather, Willa, 23
Cedar River, Mich., 72
Centerville, Mich., 197
Central Paper Company, 222
C. G. Breed, schooner, 113
Challenge, schooner, 28, 180, 185
Chambers, Frank, 89
chanteys, 93

Charles K. Nims, schooner, 37
Charlotte Raab, schooner, 210
Charrney, Theodore, 12–13, 69, 87,
    120, 136, 163, 185, 207, 228n. 36
Chesapeake Bay, 28
Chicago, Ill., 20, 28, 30, 31, 43–44,
    56, 83, 84, 87, 99, 103–4, 108,
    109, 110, 117, 127–28, 176, 182,
    186, 193–95, 209, 215; decline of
    port, 166–71; grain trade, 59–65,
    150–52; harbor opened, 51–54;
    lumber trade, 65–66, 68–73,
    143–46; transatlantic trade, 34;
    vice districts, 156–60; volume of
    shipping, 17, 69, 127, 168; wrecks
    and rescues, 194–204
Chicago Board of Trade, 34, 58
Chicago Board of Trade, schooner,
    63
Chicago Dock and Canal Trust, 169
Chicago Lumber Vessel Unloaders'
    Union, 148
Chicago Maritime Society, 221
Chicago Packet, schooner, 45
Chicago River, 17, 45, 48, 51, 97,
    105–6, 159, 190, 209–10; bridges,
    129–36; Bubbly Creek, 152–53;
    decline of river-harbor, 166–71;
    harbor, 128–29, 140–42; north
    branch, 152; pollution, 151–55;
    sandbar cleared, 51–53, 58; steve-
    dores, 146–51; tunnels, 141; wa-
    terfront, 159–60
Chicago Sanitary and Ship Canal,
    155, 167, 169, 213
Chicago Seamen's Union, 148–50
Chicago Yacht Club, 215
Christmas tree ships, 162–63, 170,
    206–8
City of Duluth, steamer, 201
City of Grand Haven, schooner, 92,
    102, 120, 189, 216, 217
Civil War, 22, 26, 35, 74, 152, 154,
    190, 192, 196
Cleveland, Ohio, 54, 108–10, 186,
    204, 207

Clipper City, 29, 209
Coaster, schooner, 208
Colfax, Harriet, 190
Colonel Cook, schooner, 204
Columbia, schooner, 115
Comet, schooner, 237
Congress. *See* U.S. Congress
Cooper, Davis, 182
Cooper, James Fenimore, 79
Cora A., schooner, 211
Cornealia E. Windiate, schooner, 206
Cortez, schooner, 113
Cortland, bark, 119
Costhwaite, schooner, 140
Cram, Thomas Jefferson, 54, 56
Cregier, DeWitt, 166

Danes, 82
David Dows, brigantine, 37–38, 63–
    64, 210
Davidson, James, 213
Davis, Jefferson, 58
Dean Richmond, 34
Death's Door, 47, 182, 204–5
Des Plaines River, 155
Detroit, Mich., 28, 108, 143, 176, 184,
    186, 204, 207
Dibble, John, 199
Dick Somers, schooner, 185
Door Peninsula, 92, 204, 207
Dreiser, Theodore, 128
Duluth, Minn., 129
Dunham, James S., 137, 176–77
Dunne, Peter Finley, 135–36, 153
DuSable, Jean-Baptiste Point, 86
Dutch, 86
Dutton, A. P., 114

Eagle, schooner, 45
Eastland, steamer, 170
Elizabeth A. Nicholson, schooner,
    194–95
Ellen, schooner, 121
Ellen Williams, 93, 96–97, 103–4,
    113
E. M. Portch, schooner, 159

Emily Taylor, schooner, 211–12
Epoufette, Mich., 72
Erie, Penn., 30–31
Erie Canal, 22, 32–34, 54, 57, 119
Escanaba, Mich., 74–75, 83, 85, 89,
   155–56, 190, 197
Evanston, Ill., 193–95, 203–4
Experiment, schooner, 91

Falcon, Peter, 177
F. B. Gardner, schooner, 179
Felicity, sloop, 27–28, 86
Ferry, William M., 45
Fessenden, cutter, 88
Fever River, 57
F. H. Williams, schooner, 208
Fillmore, Millard, 189
Finn, Mickey, 158
Fleetwing, schooner, 182
Ford River, Mich., 62
Fort Dearborn, 28, 45, 48, 51, 53, 164
Fort Howard, 57
Fountain, Thomas, 176–77
Fowle, J., 51
Fox River, 57–58, 70
Franchere, Gabriel, 29
Frankfort, Mich., 193, 198
Fred Bill, schooner, 99
French, 86

Gallinipper, schooner, 71
Garden, Mich., 72
Gassliaf, schooner, 113
Gazelle, schooner, 47
Geo. R. Roberts, schooner, 201
George Dunbar, barge, 89
George Nestor, schooner, 183–84
Germans, 82–83
Gilbert Hubbard & Company, 163–64
Glad Tidings, schooner, 165
grain trade, 59–65
Grand Haven, Mich., 40, 45, 49, 75,
   81, 116, 117, 178, 193, 199, 200,
   217
Grand Haven rig, 40, 187, 217
Grand Marais, Mich., 215

Grand River, 27
Grand Traverse Bay, 86, 99
Grapeshot, schooner, 99
Great Lakes Historical Society, 218
Great Strike of 1877, 109, 148–49
Green Bay, 27, 28, 75, 165, 179, 205,
   218–19
Green Bay, Wis., 43–44, 57–58, 60,
   70, 97, 127, 205
Griffiths, John Willis, 181
Griffon, 25, 27, 78, 176
Grosse Point, 176
Gull Island, 213
Gunderson, S.T., 114

Hackley, Charles, 67–69, 116
Hackley-Hume Lumber Company,
   72–73, 121, 199
Halstead, schooner, 214
Harrison, Carter, Jr., 135
Harrison, Carter, Sr., 166
Harvest Home, schooner, 88
Harvey Bissell, schooner, 88
Havighurst, Walter, 184, 218
Hearding, W. H., 193
Helfenstein, 63
Hennepin, Louis, 78
Herald, schooner, 121
Hercules, schooner, 50, 83
Hero, schooner, 47–48
High Island, 201
H. Merrill, schooner, 199
Hoffman, Frank, 218–21
Holland, Mich., 193
Houghton, William, 125
H. P. Murray, schooner, 103
Hungarians, 86
Huntley, A. L., 116

Illinois, 23, 24, 221
Illinois, schooner, 53, 114
Illinois and Michigan Canal, 53, 57–
   58, 65–66, 117, 143, 154
Illinois Central Railroad, 53–54
Illinois Historic Preservation Agency,
   221

Indiana, 23, 24, 221
Indians. *See* Native Americans
Invincible, schooner, 36
Irene, schooner, 75
Irish, 82–83, 135–36, 147–48, 150, 153, 158, 202

Jack Thompson, schooner, 197
James Crouch, schooner, 37, 237
James H. Martin, tug, 213–24
J. Emory Owen, steamer, 194–95
Jenney, William Le Baron, 150
Jennie Belle, schooner, 218
Jesse Martin, schooner, 199
J. H. Stevens, schooner, 214
J. Loomis McLaren, schooner, 188–89
John Raber, schooner, 210
Johnson, Andrew B., 114
Joy Morton & Company, 170
Julia B. Merrill, schooner, 216
Juneau, Solomon, 45
Jungle, The, 152–53
J. Young Scammon, brig, 205

Kalamazoo River, 27
Keating, William H., 51
Keenan, Chris, 213–24
Kelley, Harry, 222
Kelley, Timothy, 63, 81, 83, 90, 92, 99, 103, 105–6, 120–21, 123–25, 205
Kenlon, John, 80, 88, 184, 192
Kenosha, Wis., 54, 56, 58, 85, 89, 121, 193
Kewanee, Wis., 54, 165
Kinzie, John, 48
Knight, A. G., 45
Knights of Labor, 109–11
Kristiansen, Soren, 111, 140, 173, 190

Lady Elgin, steamer, 201–4
Lake Carriers Association, 110–11
Lake Erie, 27, 29, 47, 65, 69, 78, 204
Lake Forest, schooner, 36, 62

Lake Huron, 27, 29, 206
Lake Michigan: charted, 192–93; grain trade, 59–65; lifesaving stations, 193–95; lumber trade, 65–74; schooner barges on, 38–40, 211–14; shipwrecks, 197–207, 218–19; size of schooners on, 36–37; storms, 174
Lake Ontario, 32, 79, 183
Lake Superior, 27, 29, 183–84
Lamplighter, schooner, 189
Larson, Axel, 213–14
La Salle, René-Robert Cavelier de, 25, 60
Latrobe, Charles, 50
Lawson, Lawrence O., 194
L. B. Crocker, schooner, 97–98
Lee, Mary Per, 49
Lee, Seth, 121
Leelanau Peninsula, 205
Leonard, Joseph H., 164
Little Sturgeon, Wis., 178–79, 210–11
Liverpool, U. K., 34
Lizzie A. Low, schooner, 237
Lockport, Ill., 213
longshoremen, 109–11, 147–50
Lottie Wolf, schooner, 105–6
Lucia A. Simpson, 185, 216–18
Ludington, Mich., 45, 67
Lyman M. Davis, 216
Lyssenco, Taras, 221

Mackinac, Mich., 27, 28, 47–49, 78, 87, 129, 215
Madeira Pet, 34
Madeline, schooner, 86
Malott, Darius Nelson, 202–4
Malvin, John, 86
Manistee, Mich., 40, 65, 69, 85–86, 193, 211
Manistique, Mich., 65, 104, 146, 211
Manitou, schooner, 221
Manitou Passage, 192, 205–6, 208, 216
Manitowoc, Wis., 29, 51–52, 54, 59,

81, 114, 116, 125, 180–82, 184, 198, 201, 206, 217, 221
Maria, schooner, 89
Mariner, schooner, 118
Marinette, Wis., 38–40, 65, 67, 155, 205, 216, 217
Marinette Barge Company, 38–40
Maritime Heritage Alliance, 221
Marquette, Mich., 204
Marshall, William, 167
Martin, Jay, 12, 81–82
Mary A. Gregory, schooner, 17, 187
Mary D. Ayer, schooner, 201
Mary Elizabeth, schooner, 47
Mary Ellen Cook, schooner, 185, 191–92
Mary G. Boneystiel, schooner, 45
Mary Margaret, schooner, 200–201
Mary Stockton, schooner, 181
McCormick Reaper plant, 148
McKinley, Peter, 190
Meade, George G., 192
Mears, Charles, 67, 71, 147–48
Mechanic, schooner, 113
Melville, Herman, 79
Menominee, Mich., 65, 67, 155, 205
Menominee River, 67
Meridian, schooner, 147
Merrill, schooner, 116
Metropolitan Sanitary District, 155
Michigan, 22, 24, 30, 54, 85, 163, 221
Michigan, schooner, 194–95
Michigan City, Ind., 50, 190
Miller Brothers shipyard, 163
Milwaukee, Wis., 23, 27, 31, 43, 45, 51, 59, 65. 69, 75, 83, 84, 85–86, 97, 99, 102, 105, 109, 114, 117, 124, 137, 143, 155, 167, 184, 186, 193, 195, 198, 202, 207, 230; grain trade, 58–65; harbor improvements, 54–56, 170; Milwaukee schooners, 214–15, 222
Milwaukee River, 55, 206
Mississippi River, 24, 57, 70
M. J. Cummings, schooner, 198
Moby Dick, 79

Mojave, schooner, 204
Monteith, 63
Montreal, Quebec, 32
Moonlight, schooner, 36, 214–15, 222
Morning Star, schooner, 119
Morning Star, steamer, 119
Mosher, Albert, 137
Muskegon, Mich., 44, 65, 67–70, 72–73, 120, 127, 156, 193, 199, 216, 223
Muskegon River, 69–70, 86
Murray, Thomas, 91–214
Myrtle, schooner, 195–97, 199

Nahma, Mich., 72
Native Americans, 27, 28
Naubinway, Mich., 48
Navy Pier, 169
Nelson, Arthur N., 119–20
Nelson, Fred, 214, 223
Nelson, steamer, 223
Newell, Daniel, 60
New York, N.Y., 57, 77
Niagara Falls, 31
Norris, Frank, 129
Norris, James, 40
North Chicago Rolling Mill, 170
North Manitou Island, 205
North Pier Terminal, 169
Northwest Company, 27
North Yuba, schooner, 201
Norwegians, 24, 40, 42, 82–83, 106, 119, 213
Noyes, Leonard Withington, 80–81, 117, 124

O'Brien, Mike, 157
Oconto, Wis., 146
Ogden, William B., 157
Ohio River, 24, 31
Old Mission Point, 86
Onoko, steamer, 201
Ostrich, schooner, 201
Oswego, N.Y., 22–23, 84, 108

Our Son, schooner, 185, 187, 214, 222–23
Outward Bound, schooner, 119

Packer, Lieutenant, 78–79, 86, 229n. 3
Palmer, Nels, 91–98, 103–4, 106, 147
Panic of 1837, 54
Panic of 1873, 119, 207
Parton, James, 69, 127
Pathfinder, The, 79
Pearson, Keith, 221
Pensaukee, bark, 63, 179
Pensaukee, Wis., 178
Pentwater, Mich., 193, 214
Pere Marquette River, 45, 67
Perry, Oliver Hazard, 78
Peshtigo, Wis., 38, 65, 178, 205
Petrel, 77
Pickering, Augustus, 114, 115–16
Pit, The, 129
Plumerville, Mich., 59
Plum Island, 92, 193
Plymouth, schooner, 213–14
Point Au Sable, 193
Point Betsey, 193
Polish, 148
Pontiac's Rebellion, 28
Porcupine, schooner, 78, 86
Porter, schooner, 63
Port Washington, Wis., 59, 62
potato ships, 162–63
Pride, schooner, 90
Professor's House, The, 23
Protection, tug, 195
Put-in-Bay, 29

Racine, Wis., 45, 54–56, 58, 59, 60–62, 65, 67, 114, 115, 127, 193, 198
Rapid, schooner, 105
Rawley Point, 198
Reed, Harry, 120
Reindeer, schooner, 207
Resumption, schooner, 80, 184
Robertson, Samuel, 27
Rothwell, William C., 116, 121

Rouse Simmons, schooner, 69–70, 72–73, 116, 117, 120, 174, 208, 223
Royal Navy, 28

Saginaw, Mich., 184, 213
Sailor lore, 122–23
Salvor, steamer, 223
Sandburg, Carl, 127
Saugatuck, Mich., 59, 90
Scandinavians, 34, 40, 82, 230
Schank, John, 28
schooners: canallers, 31–32, 182–83, 187; captains, 111–20; coal trade, 64–65; construction, 178–82; cooks, 86–89; crews, 82–86, 91–104, 187–88; defined, 25; grain trade, 59–64; lakeshoring, 47–50, 187; lumber trade, 65–73; maintenance, 185–87; numbers, 22; women on, 87–91. *See* scow schooners
Schuenemann, Herman, 72, 208
Scott, brig, 34
scow schooners, 30–31, 182–83
Seamen's Mutual Benevolent Society, 109–11, 164
Sea Witch, clipper ship, 181
Sheboygan, Wis., 59–60, 62, 65, 90, 119, 129, 140, 193
Sherwin, Luke, 83
shipbuilding, 163–64, 178–82
Silver Cloud, schooner, 90
Simmons, Jeannie, 88
Sinclair, Upton, 152
Skillagalee, 206
Sleeping Bear Dunes, 83, 119, 193, 205, 208, 221
Sleipner, schooner-brig, 34, 42
Smith, George Nelson, 116
Smith, William, 196
Smiths Falls, Ont., 99
Solomon Juneau, brig, 86
Sorenson, Elias, 213
South Chicago, Ill., 37, 167, 170
South Haven, Mich., 59. 92, 221

South Manitou Island, 96, 193, 205–6

Southport, Wis., *See* Kenosha

Spear, Thomas, 179

Stafford, Anne, 157

State Historical Society of Wisconsin, 182, 219

St. Catherine, Ont., 40

St. Clair, schooner, 32, 57

Stephen Bates, schooner, 181

Stephenson, Isaac, 38, 55, 83, 102–3

S. Thal, schooner, 208

St. Joseph, Mich., 34, 44, 51, 56, 59, 65, 75, 179–80, 193

St. Joseph, schooner, 45, 49, 81, 83, 179

St. Lawrence River, 31–32

St. Mary, schooner, 86, 92

Straits of Mackinac, 63

Strough, Arthur B., 92, 106

Sturgeon Bay, Wis., 193, 205, 217, 221

Swanson, Alver, 104, 113

Swedes, 40, 82, 86, 106

Swift, George B., 158

Tempest, schooner, 119

Thomas Hume, schooner, 199–201

Thompson, Mich., 72

Toledo, Ohio, 37

Toledo, schooner, 198

Tonawanda, N.Y., 137

Torch Lake, Mich., 72

Toronto, Ont., 215–16

Tracy, sloop, 28, 45

Traverse City, Mich., 221–12

Treiber, John, 123–25

tugboats, 136–40

Two Brothers, schooner, 92

Two Rivers, Wis., 47, 59, 180, 193, 198

Tyson & Robinson, 40

U.S. Army Corps of Engineers, 51–54, 56, 67, 141, 167–68, 189, 192

U.S. Congress, 50–51, 55–56, 67, 168, 189, 193

U.S. Department of the Treasury, 189–90

U.S. Lake Survey, 192–93

U.S. Lighthouse Service, 189–96

U.S. Marine Hospital Service, 164

Van Buren, schooner, 45

Van Riper, Elizabeth Whitney, 190

Van Valkenberg, schooner, 122

Varnum, Jacob B., 49, 78–79

Virginia-built boat. *See* Baltimore clipper

voyageurs, 27

Walbridge, brig, 105

Walk-in-the-Water, steamer, 22

Walton, Ivan Henry, 218

Wanderer, schooner, 183

Ward, Samuel, 32, 57, 116–17

War of 1812, 28

Washington Island, 204

Watchful, schooner, 189

Watts Sherman, schooner, 185–86

Waugoshance Shoal, 206

Waukegan, Ill., 27, 167

Welcome, brig, 221–22

Welland Canal, 22, 31–34, 115, 124, 183

Wells Burt, schooner, 63, 102, 176–77, 183, 185, 190, 201, 205, 221, 223

Wentworth, John, 157

W. H. Gilcher, steamer, 201

Whirlwind, schooner, 197

White Mary, schooner, 120

William Aldrich, schooner, 185, 186

William Sanderson, schooner, 183

Williams, Edward, 191

Wilson, Jack, 202–4

Wings of Discovery, schooner, 221

Winnetka, Ill., 203

Wisconsin, 23, 24, 30, 54, 60, 163, 221, 222

Wisconsin, 58

Wisconsin Lake Schooner Education
    Association, 222
Wisconsin River, 57, 70
Wolf and Davidson shipyard, 214–25
Wolf River, 70, 75
women, 87–91, 157–58
Wooldridge, Clifton, 158

Worster, Donald, 23
Wright, Frank Lloyd, 131

X-10-U-8, schooner, 30

Yerkes, Charles, 167

Titles in the Great Lakes Books Series

Freshwater Fury: Yarns and Reminiscences of the Greatest Storm in Inland Navigation, by Frank Barcus, 1986 (reprint)

Call It North Country: The Story of Upper Michigan, by John Bartlow Martin, 1986 (reprint)

The Land of the Crooked Tree, by U. P. Hedrick, 1986 (reprint)

Michigan Place Names, by Walter Romig, 1986 (reprint)

Luke Karamazov, by Conrad Hilberry, 1987

The Late, Great Lakes: An Environmental History, by William Ashworth, 1987 (reprint)

Great Pages of Michigan History from the Detroit Free Press, 1987

Waiting for the Morning Train: An American Boyhood, by Bruce Catton, 1987 (reprint)

Michigan Voices: Our State's History in the Words of the People Who Lived It, compiled and edited by Joe Grimm, 1987

Danny and the Boys, Being Some Legends of Hungry Hollow, by Robert Traver, 1987 (reprint)

Hanging On, or How to Get through a Depression and Enjoy Life, by Edmund G. Love, 1987 (reprint)

The Situation in Flushing, by Edmund G. Love, 1987 (reprint)

A Small Bequest, by Edmund G. Love, 1987 (reprint)

The Saginaw Paul Bunyan, by James Stevens, 1987 (reprint)

The Ambassador Bridge: A Monument to Progress, by Philip P. Mason, 1988

Let the Drum Beat: A History of the Detroit Light Guard, by Stanley D. Solvick, 1988

An Afternoon in Waterloo Park, by Gerald Dumas, 1988 (reprint)

Contemporary Michigan Poetry: Poems from the Third Coast, edited by Michael Delp, Conrad Hilberry and Herbert Scott, 1988

Over the Graves of Horses, by Michael Delp, 1988

Wolf in Sheep's Clothing: The Search for a Child Killer, by Tommy McIntyre, 1988

Copper-Toed Boots, by Marguerite de Angeli, 1989 (reprint)

Detroit Images: Photographs of the Renaissance City, edited by John J. Bukowczyk and Douglas Aikenhead, with Peter Slavcheff, 1989

Hangdog Reef: Poems Sailing the Great Lakes, by Stephen Tudor, 1989

Detroit: City of Race and Class Violence, revised edition, by B. J. Widick, 1989

Deep Woods Frontier: A History of Logging in Northern Michigan, by Theodore J. Karamanski, 1989

Orvie, The Dictator of Dearborn, by David L. Good, 1989

Seasons of Grace: A History of the Catholic Archdiocese of Detroit, by Leslie Woodcock Tentler, 1990

The Pottery of John Foster: Form and Meaning, by Gordon and Elizabeth Orear, 1990

The Diary of Bishop Frederic Baraga: First Bishop of Marquette, Michigan, edited by Regis M. Walling and Rev. N. Daniel Rupp, 1990

Walnut Pickles and Watermelon Cake: A Century of Michigan Cooking, by Larry B. Massie and Priscilla Massie, 1990

The Making of Michigan, 1820–1860: A Pioneer Anthology, edited by Justin L. Kestenbaum, 1990

America's Favorite Homes: A Guide to Popular Early Twentieth-Century Homes, by Robert Schweitzer and Michael W. R. Davis, 1990

Beyond the Model T: The Other Ventures of Henry Ford, by Ford R. Bryan, 1990

Life after the Line, by Josie Kearns, 1990

Michigan Lumbertowns: Lumbermen and Laborers in Saginaw, Bay City, and Muskegon, 1870–1905, by Jeremy W. Kilar, 1990

Detroit Kids Catalog: The Hometown Tourist, by Ellyce Field, 1990

Waiting for the News, by Leo Litwak, 1990 (reprint)

Detroit Perspectives, edited by Wilma Wood Henrickson, 1991

Life on the Great Lakes: A Wheelsman's Story, by Fred W. Dutton, edited by William Donohue Ellis, 1991

Copper Country Journal: The Diary of Schoolmaster Henry Hobart, 1863–1864, by Henry Hobart, edited by Philip P. Mason, 1991

John Jacob Astor: Business and Finance in the Early Republic, by John Denis Haeger, 1991

Survival and Regeneration: Detroit's American Indian Community, by Edmund J. Danziger, Jr., 1991

Steamboats and Sailors of the Great Lakes, by Mark L. Thompson, 1991

Cobb Would Have Caught It: The Golden Age of Baseball in Detroit, by Richard Bak, 1991

Michigan in Literature, by Clarence Andrews, 1992

Under the Influence of Water: Poems, Essays, and Stories, by Michael Delp, 1992

The Country Kitchen, by Della T. Lutes, 1992 (reprint)

The Making of a Mining District: Keweenaw Native Copper 1500–1870, by David J. Krause, 1992

Kids Catalog of Michigan Adventures, by Ellyce Field, 1993

Henry's Lieutenants, by Ford R. Bryan, 1993

Historic Highway Bridges of Michigan, by Charles K. Hyde, 1993

Lake Erie and Lake St. Clair Handbook, by Stanley J. Bolsenga and Charles E. Herndendorf, 1993

Queen of the Lakes, by Mark Thompson, 1994

Iron Fleet: The Great Lakes in World War II, by George J. Joachim, 1994

Turkey Stearnes and the Detroit Stars: The Negro Leagues in Detroit, 1919–1933, by Richard Bak, 1994

Pontiac and the Indian Uprising, by Howard H. Peckham, 1994 (reprint)

Charting the Inland Seas: A History of the U.S. Lake Survey, by Arthur M. Woodford, 1994 (reprint)

Ojibwa Narratives of Charles and Charlotte Kawbawgam and Jacques LePique, 1893–1895. Recorded with Notes by Homer H. Kidder, edited by Arthur P. Bourgeois, 1994, co-published with the Marquette County Historical Society

Strangers and Sojourners: A History of Michigan's Keweenaw Peninsula, by Arthur W. Thurner, 1994

Win Some, Lose Some: G. Mennen Williams and the New Democrats, by Helen Washburn Berthelot, 1995

Sarkis, by Gordon and Elizabeth Orear, 1995

The Northern Lights: Lighthouses of the Upper Great Lakes, by Charles K. Hyde, 1995 (reprint)

Kids Catalog of Michigan Adventures, second edition, by Ellyce Field, 1995

Rumrunning and the Roaring Twenties: Prohibition on the Michigan-Ontario Waterway, by Philip P. Mason, 1995

In the Wilderness with the Red Indians, by E. R. Baierlein, translated by Anita Z. Boldt, edited by Harold W. Moll, 1996

Elmwood Endures: History of a Detroit Cemetery, by Michael Franck, 1996

Master of Precision: Henry M. Leland, by Mrs. Wilfred C. Leland with Minnie Dubbs Millbrook, 1996 (reprint)

Haul-Out: New and Selected Poems, by Stephen Tudor, 1996

Kids Catalog of Michigan Adventures, third edition, by Ellyce Field, 1997

Beyond the Model T: The Other Ventures of Henry Ford, revised edition, by Ford R. Bryan, 1997

Young Henry Ford: A Picture History of the First Forty Years, by Sidney Olson, 1997 (reprint)

The Coast of Nowhere: Meditations on Rivers, Lakes and Streams, by Michael Delp, 1997

From Saginaw Valley to Tin Pan Alley: Saginaw's Contribution to American Popular Music, 1890–1955, by R. Grant Smith, 1998

The Long Winter Ends, by Newton G. Thomas, 1998 (reprint)

Bridging the River of Hatred: The Pioneering Efforts of Detroit Police Commissioner George Edwards, by Mary M. Stolberg, 1998

Toast of the Town: The Life and Times of Sunnie Wilson, by Sunnie Wilson with John Cohassey, 1998

These Men Have Seen Hard Service: The First Michigan Sharpshooters in the Civil War, by Raymond J. Herek, 1998

A Place for Summer: One Hundred Years at Michigan and Trumbull, by Richard Bak, 1998

Early Midwestern Travel Narratives: An Annotated Bibliography, 1634–1850, by Robert R. Hubach, 1998 (reprint)

All-American Anarchist: Joseph A. Labadie and the Labor Movement, by Carlotta R. Anderson, 1998

Michigan in the Novel, 1816–1996: An Annotated Bibliography, by Robert Beasecker, 1998

"Time by Moments Steals Away": The 1848 Journal of Ruth Douglass, by Robert L. Root, Jr., 1998

The Detroit Tigers: A Pictorial Celebration of the Greatest Players and Moments in Tigers' History, updated edition, by William M. Anderson, 1999

Father Abraham's Children: Michigan Episodes in the Civil War, by Frank B. Woodford, 1999 (reprint)

Letter from Washington, 1863–1865, by Lois Bryan Adams, edited and with an introduction by Evelyn Leasher, 1999

Wonderful Power: The Story of Ancient Copper Working in the Lake Superior Basin, by Susan R. Martin, 1999

A Sailor's Logbook: A Season aboard Great Lakes Freighters, by Mark L. Thompson, 1999

Huron: The Seasons of a Great Lake, by Napier Shelton, 1999

Tin Stackers: The History of the Pittsburgh Steamship Company, by Al Miller, 1999

Art in Detroit Public Places, revised edition, text by Dennis Nawrocki, photographs by David Clements, 1999

Brewed in Detroit: Breweries and Beers Since 1830, by Peter H. Blum, 1999

Detroit Kids Catalog: A Family Guide for the 21st Century, by Ellyce Field, 2000

"Expanding the Frontiers of Civil Rights": Michigan, 1948–1968, by Sidney Fine, 2000

Graveyard of the Lakes, by Mark L. Thompson, 2000

Enterprising Images: The Goodridge Brothers, African American Photographers, 1847–1922, by John Vincent Jezierski, 2000

New Poems from the Third Coast: Contemporary Michigan Poetry, edited by Michael Delp, Conrad Hilberry, and Josie Kearns, 2000

Arab Detroit: From Margin to Mainstream, edited by Nabeel Abraham and Andrew Shryock, 2000

The Sandstone Architecture of the Lake Superior Region, by Kathryn Bishop Eckert, 2000

Looking Beyond Race: The Life of Otis Milton Smith, by Otis Milton Smith and Mary M. Stolberg, 2000

Mail by the Pail, by Colin Bergel, illustrated by Mark Koenig, 2000

Great Lakes Journey: A New Look at America's Freshwater Coast, by William Ashworth, 2000

A Life in the Balance: The Memoirs of Stanley J. Winkelman, by Stanley J. Winkelman, 2000

Schooner Passage: Sailing Ships and the Lake Michigan Frontier, by Theodore J. Karamanski, 2000